Australian Fiction

Twayne's World Authors Series

TWAS 735

Australian Fiction

By Joseph and Johanna Jones

Twayne Publishers • Boston

Australian Fiction

Joseph and Johanna Jones

Copyright © 1983 by G. K. Hall & Company
All Rights Reserved
Published by Twayne Publishers
A Division of G. K. Hall & Company
70 Lincoln Street
Boston, Massachusetts 02111

Book Production by Marne B. Sultz

Book Design by Barbara Anderson

Printed on permanent/durable acid-free
paper and bound in the United States of
America.

Library of Congress Cataloging in Publication Data

Jones, Joseph Jay, 1908–
    Australian fiction.

    (Twayne's world authors series ; TWAS 735)
    Bibliography: p. 139
    Includes index.
    1. Australian fiction—History and criticism.
I. Jones, Johanna. II. Title. III. Series.
PQ9612.2.J66 1983   823'.009'994   83-12691
ISBN 0-8057-6472-0

To the memory of
C. Hartley Grattan (1902–1980), author, scholar, lecturer, collector,
citizen of the world, which remains indebted to him for much of what
it knows about Australia.

Contents

About the Authors
Preface
Chronology

      Chapter One
      Settlers, Convicts, and Early Narrative   1

      Chapter Two
      Pre-Federation Fiction   8

      Chapter Three
      From Federation into the 1930s   25

      Chapter Four
      Through World War II   44

      Chapter Five
      Postwar: Exile and Hope   63

      Chapter Six
      Postwar: The Moderns   87

Notes and References   129
Selected Bibliography   139
Index   170

About the Authors

Joseph and Johanna Jones, both native Nebraskans, arrived in Austin, Texas, in 1935 as newlyweds. Dr. Jones at that time joined the English staff at the University of Texas where he is now Professor Emeritus. Mrs. Jones was a student at the university and later taught in the Austin schools in addition to writing book reviews. In 1953 a Fulbright assignment took the family, now numbering five, to New Zealand. Subsequently, they went to South Africa (1960–61) and Hong Kong (1965–66) where Professor Jones lectured.

He has contributed to various journals and edited *American Literary Manuscripts* (1960), *Image of Australia* (1962), and *WLWE Newsletter* (1962–70), together with upwards of fifty volumes for Twayne's World Authors Series, concerning authors from Australia, Canada, Africa, New Zealand, and the West Indies. His books include *The Cradle of Erewhon: Samuel Butler in New Zealand* (1959), *Terranglia: The Case for English as World-Literature* (1965), a small volume of poems entitled *Handful of Hong Kong* (1966), several similar volumes of "seventeener" (free-style haiku) poems of various dates, *Radical Cousins: Nineteenth Century American & Australian Writers* (1976), and *Life on Waller Creek* (1982), a historical and personal account of Austin and the University of Texas.

The Joneses have worked together in various library collections in England, Australia, and elsewhere for some fifteen years on what they call "World English." This volume on Australian fiction and two companion volumes on Canadian and New Zealand fiction (the latter in press) are among the fruits of this collaboration. Professor Jones, in retirement, has turned gradually toward nonacademic writing. Both continue to enjoy traveling, especially by ship, and hope to make several more voyages on whatever type of seagoing craft remains available.

Preface

Australians, given to speaking of their literary heritage in terms of tradition and legend, are encouraged to continue doing so by the expectations of faraway audiences in our own time no less than a hundred years ago. For example, parallel to the American Wild West there is—or once upon a time there was—the Australian Outback or The Bush (the latter a more mythological, poetic, and pervasive concept), where possibly dark but nevertheless mighty deeds were done. When examining the occurrence of the word *Outback* itself in the titles of Australian fiction, one encounters it first in A. B. ("Banjo") Paterson's *An Outback Marriage* (1906) but not again until the time of World War II and after, when it surfaces in such titles as *Outback Occupations* (1943), *Outback Emergency* (1962), *Outback Heiress* (1963), and, inevitably, *The Outback Doctor* (1967). These are all titles in popular fiction, and their dates have something to tell us about group images and archetypes. We hope that this book on Australian fiction will help extend the reader's consciousness of Australian experience at least a little.

Among the more positive developments following World War II has been a most remarkable growth of a "Third World of English"—writing, that is, outside the British Isles and the United States, literally in all parts of the globe. The Southwest Pacific has shared abundantly in this upsurge, as the fiction of both Australia and New Zealand shows, together with strong beginnings in the island communities of the region: Fiji, Tonga, Samoa, Papua-New Guinea. In keeping with these developments, we have endeavored to emphasize in this volume the more recent authors of Australian fiction without neglecting their predecessors: this is a survey of the whole field, necessarily brief as it must be. No history of Australia per se is included, but principal historical events are noted in the Chronology, parallel with literary landmarks, and the reader is referred in the Bibliography to a number of works on political and social history, much of which is reflected in works of fiction.

Each of three parts—colonial Australia, the earlier twentieth century, and contemporaries—contains two chapters. Within chapters, a topical arrangement invites exploration of such matters as convict life, expatriation, aboriginal life, and counterculture writings. Short fiction is treated in two sections, the second appearing just before the third part begins. Following the still general classification of science fiction (somewhat like crime and detective fiction) as a special branch outside ordinary literary history and criticism, we do not treat it here, but a compilation of Australian science fiction titles is included in the Bibliography. At the same time we think it possible that in another ten to twenty years, science fiction will have made its way out of the limbo it now occupies.

Limbo is a term that might, in fact, be used to describe the situation of most Australian writers in places where they ought to be better known. Nearly any author working outside the chief publishing centers of Britain and North America still has difficulty in being recognized and read. Despite statistical studies and protests from scholars in both Australia and New Zealand, the mother country, so called, has long since abandoned whatever cultural obligations she may once have felt. Recalling Fielding's passage in *Tom Jones* in which the parson defines religion (". . . not only religion but the Christian religion . . . the Protestant religion . . . the Church of England"), our experience in Britain strongly suggests that in most public libraries there, the librarian would be obliged to say, willy-nilly, "When we say fiction we mean modern fiction, and not only modern fiction but modern fiction in English, and not only modern fiction in English but that published in the British Isles." Surely literary publications of merit, broadly regarded as being in English *the* world language, should be receiving at least a little more attention.

The Bibliography contains references to a working collection of books on Australian literary history and criticism as well as to a number of good recent story anthologies. The list of authors provides information about a novelist's chief publications but does not attempt complete coverage, which is available elsewhere.

We are grateful to the staffs of several libraries within which our work has been done: the University of Texas in Austin, and in London, the Commonwealth Institute, Royal Commonwealth Society, Australia House, and University of London. Special thanks are owing, as well, to John Sherrill for help in preparing the manuscript for publication.

Joseph and Johanna Jones

Chronology

This chronology includes only landmark dates in Australian political and social history, together with approximately fifty titles of novels or books of stories and some important scholarly works and periodicals. It is intended to indicate, for the most part, the *first appearances* of authors whose works represent shifts in literary direction or are otherwise historically significant; thus, it is not in any sense a listing of all the "most important" works of Australian fiction. For more detailed information on authors and titles, the reader should consult the Bibliography.

1606–1697   Various Dutch sea-captain explorers, including Hartog and Tasman, make sporadic contacts in the western and northern coastal regions of Australia and along southern Tasmania; partial charts of the coastlines of "Terra Australis Incognita" become available.

1768   Bougainville sights the Great Barrier Reef.

1770   Captain James Cook sails along eastern coast of Australia, then called New Holland, and names the territory New South Wales (N.S.W.).

1779   Sir Joseph Banks recommends Botany Bay as site for a penal colony.

1786   Decision taken to follow Banks's recommendation.

1788   Arrival of First Fleet and establishment of penal settlement at Sydney, January 26, now celebrated annually as Australia Day.

1791   Whaling and sealing operations begin, to be followed shortly by foreign trading operations.

1793   Arrival of first free immigrants (eleven in number); first church opened.

1795   First printing press (Sydney).

1796   Discovery of coal at Newcastle (N.S.W.).

1797   Introduction of Merino sheep (first shipment of wool to England, 1803).

1803   Beginnings of settlement in Tasmania (then called Van Diemen's Land); *Sydney Gazette* commences publication.

1808   Governor Bligh deposed by "Rum Corps" and civilian backers.

1813   Crossing of Blue Mountains to interior of N.S.W.

1819   Barron Field's *First Fruits of Australian Poetry.*

1823   Initial settlement in what is now Queensland; first gold discovery (in N.S.W. near Bathurst).

1825   Beginnings of decentralization of government with proclamation of Van Diemen's Land as separate colony.

1827   Earliest official claim of British sovereignty over all Australia.

1829   First settlement in Western Australia (Swan River, now Perth).

1830–1831   Savery's *Quintus Servinton* (serialized).

1831   First assisted immigration; *Sydney* [Morning] *Herald* begins.

1835   Settlement at Melbourne.

1836   Settlement at Adelaide.

1839   Discovery of Port Darwin.

1840   Abolition of transportation of convicts to N.S.W.

1843   First representative constitution, N.S.W.; financial panic; Rowcroft's *Tales of the Colonies.*

1844–1845   Tucker's *Ralph Rashleigh* (serialized).

1845   Vidal's *Tales for the Bush.*

1846   Initiation of meat preserving.

1847   Iron smelting undertaken in N.S.W.; Harris's *Settlers and Convicts.*

1849   Heavy emigration to California goldfields; transportation of ticket-of-leave men to N.S.W. renewed.

1851   Gold discovered in N.S.W. and Victoria, with beginning of periodic rushes; Victoria separated from N.S.W. as a new colony.

1852   University of Sydney founded; transportation of convicts to eastern colonies finally abolished.

1854 Spence's *Clara Morison.*

1855 First railway opened for traffic; Van Diemen's Land becomes officially Tasmania; Lang's *The Convict's Wife.*

1856 Responsible government initiated in N.S.W., Victoria, South Australia, Tasmania.

1858 Sydney, Melbourne, Adelaide in telegraphic communication.

1859 Queensland proclaimed a separate colony (formed from part of N.S.W.); Kingsley's *Geoffrey Hamlyn,* Leakey's *The Broad Arrow.*

1860 Center of continent first reached (by Stuart).

1861 Anti-Chinese riots on N.S.W. gold fields, with beginning of efforts to restrict Oriental immigration (white Australia policy); beginning of American Civil War.

1862 Continent first crossed.

1864 First sugar made from Queensland cane.

1867 Victoria imposes first protective tariff; last shipload of convicts sent from Britain (to Western Australia).

1870 Imperial troops withdrawn.

1870–1871 Clarke's *His Natural Life* (serialized).

1872 Cable connection with Europe established.

1873 Mail service to San Francisco established; Trollope's *Harry Heathcote.*

1876 Australia and New Zealand connected by cable.

1877 Western Australia connected by telegraph with South Australia and other eastern colonies.

1879 First artesian bore driven; O'Reilly's *Moondyne.*

1880 First Australian telephone exchange, Melbourne; Sydney *Bulletin* founded.

1882 *Bulletin* editors Archibald and Haynes jailed for failure to pay costs of libel suit.

1882–1883 Boldrewood's *Robbery under Arms* (serialized).

1883 Discovery of silver at Broken Hill.

1887 Operatic debut in Brussels of soprano Nellie Melba.

1888 Centennial celebrations at Sydney.

1889   Heidelberg School of Australian painters exhibit (Melbourne).

1890   Western Australia granted responsible government (last colony to win this form); extensive maritime strike.

1891   Labor elects thirty-five members of the lower house, N.S.W.

1893   Gold discovered at Kalgoorlie.

1894   Women given vote in South Australia; Becke's *By Reef and Palm,* Lawson's *Short Stories in Prose & Verse,* "Warung's" *Tales of the Early Days.*

1896   Melbourne Cup horse race filmed.

1901   Proclamation of commonwealth; first federal Parliament opened; Australian population 3.77 million; Franklin's *My Brilliant Career.*

1902   Women given vote in federal elections; Baynton's *Bush Studies.*

1903   Furphy's *Such Is Life.*

1905   First Australian film, *The Story of the Kelly Gang.*

1908   U.S. Great White Fleet visits Australia; Gunn's *We of the Never-Never.*

1911   Earliest federal census; Northern Territory taken over by commonwealth; compulsory military training begins; Stone's *Jonah.*

1913   Capital named Canberra.

1914   Outbreak of World War I.

1915   First steel produced by Broken Hill Proprietary (Newcastle); Gallipoli campaign; Prichard's *The Pioneers.*

1917   Richardson's *Australia Felix.*

1918   End of World War I; Australian population reaches 5 million; first wireless message received from England; Lindsay's *The Magic Pudding.*

1919   Peace conference; Hay's *The Escape of the Notorious Sir William Heans.*

1925   Widows' pensions and forty-four-hour week established, N.S.W.

1927 Seat of federal government transferred to Canberra.

1928 Flying-doctor service begun.

1929 Barnard Eldershaw's *A House Is Built;* Richardson's *Mahoney* trilogy completed.

1930 Depression, with export prices half 1928 level; Palmer's *The Passage.*

1931 England-Australia airmail (on regular basis, 1934); Davison's *Man-Shy.*

1932 Sydney Harbour Bridge opened.

1933 Dark's *Prelude to Christopher.*

1934 Stead's *Seven Poor Men of Sydney.*

1935 Herbert's *Capricornia;* Tennant's *Tiburon.*

1938 Ingamells' *Conditional Culture,* with beginnings of Jindyworobak movement.

1939 Outbreak of World War II; *Southerly* established; White's *Happy Valley.*

1940 *Meanjin* established.

1941 *Angry Penguins* established.

1942 Fall of Singapore; Langley's *The Pea Pickers.*

1944 Ern Malley hoax.

1945 End of World War II; Casey's *Downhill Is Easier.*

1946 Boyd's *Lucinda Brayford.*

1947 Post-World War II immigrants begin arriving.

1949 Union of Papau and New Guinea; Menzies becomes prime minister.

1950 Colombo Plan; Hardy's *Power without Glory.*

1952 Soprano Joan Sutherland's debut at Covent Garden.

1953 Korean War armistice.

1954 SEATO founded; Petrov affair.

1956 Olympic Games at Melbourne; Stow's *A Haunted Land.*

1960 Australian population reaches 10 million; first Adelaide Festival of the Arts; Harrower's *The Catherine Wheel.*

1961 Green's *History of Australian Literature;* Porter's *The Tilted Cross.*

1964 Keneally's *The Place at Whitton*.

1965 Johnson's *Wild Cat Falling*.

1966 Menzies retires; Mathers's *Trap*.

1968 Ireland's *The Chantic Bird*.

1969 Moorhouse's *Futility and Other Animals*.

1970 Cook bicentennial.

1971 Eri's *The Crocodile*.

1972 *Tabloid Story* founded.

1973 Papua-New Guinea attains self-government; Sydney Opera House opened; Patrick White awarded Nobel Prize.

1974 Darwin hurricane, severe floods elsewhere; Public Lending Right granted authors and publishers by Australian government.

1975 Whitlam government dismissed by governor general.

1978 Rise in unemployment; death of R. Menzies.

1979 Austere measures against welfare-state benefits; continued acceptance of Vietnam refugees.

1980 Fraser government returned; royal visit; Olympic boycott fails; increasing inflation.

1981 Aboriginals given large freehold territory (central Australia) in first land rights agreement; sales tax on books established; diamond discovery in N.W. Australia.

1982 Continuing drought (since 1979, most severe on record) in S.E. Australia.

Chapter One
Settlers, Convicts, and Early Narrative

In the spring of 1788, the First Fleet of eleven nondescript vessels set sail for New Holland, carrying just under fifteen hundred convicts and their military guards to exactly where, and what, they weren't at all certain. Not many years before this event, it could be said, the English novel had embarked on a voyage equally unforeseeable. To be sure, it had not committed any crimes but was thought nevertheless to be socially reprehensible. It would remain under suspicion for another half century or more, by which time it would long since have justified itself before all but the most puritanical of juries. Instead of a few names to show—Richardson, Fielding, Burney, Smollett, Radcliffe, Sterne (you could count very nearly all the English novelists on the fingers of your two hands in 1788, which was the way most people at that time still did count, and they were unable to read or write at all)—by the time of Victoria's accession in 1837 Britain had welcomed such figures as Sir Walter Scott, Jane Austen, and Charles Dickens. Even in America, there were storytellers like Irving and Cooper, though few enough as yet in Australia for reasons that will become clear.

Who, after all, cared very much about society's misfits once they had been transported to the other side of the earth? Even when, after the better part of a generation, immigration and settlement appeared possible, and at length desirable, the home audience wanted and needed factual descriptions, not fanciful pictures, of the places they thought of going to: Canada, the new United States, or reluctantly enough because of the distance, expense, and irreversibility of such a commitment, Australia. Recalling the dismal pictures of prerevolutionary America suggested in Goldsmith's "The Deserted Village"—

> . . . To distant climes, a dreary scene,
> Where half the convex world intrudes between,
> Through torrid tracts with fainting steps they go, . . .

> Those blazing suns that dart a downward ray,
> And fiercely shed intolerable day;
> Those matted woods where birds forget to sing,
> But silent bats in drowsy clusters cling,
> Those poisonous fields with rank luxuriance crowned,
> Where the dark scorpion gathers death around;
> Where at each step the stranger fears to wake
> The rattling terrors of the vengeful snake;
> Where crouching tigers wait their hapless prey,
> And savage men, more murderous still than they;
> While oft in whirls the mad tornado flies,
> Mingling the ravaged landscape with the skies.[1]

—could Australia as an alternative appear much more attractive?

To leap ahead for just a moment, we can observe that even a hundred years later than the Age of Scott, following in the wake of a quickening of talent in the 1890s and for a brief time afterward, Australian fiction was not in a very flourishing state. The critic-historian Geoffrey Serle, referring to the paucity of serious writing up to and onward through World War I and into the 1920s (after which there occurred a sudden renascence) reports:

> Critics would have to agree that relatively half a dozen times as many good novels were written between 1925 and 1940 as between 1900 and 1925. (My own rough count of worthwhile novels in the two periods is fifty-six to thirteen.)[2]

Today there is no lack of similar quickening on an ever-enlarging scale. Australian writers of fiction range all the way from a "battler" like Kosti Simons, 28-year-old author of *Not with a Kiss* (1962) who "had the courage to publish and distribute it himself, even to selling copies in person from a booth in a Sydney arcade"[3] on up to the winner of a Nobel Prize.

For the better part of a century, in consequence, what we find in the earliest stirrings of Australian fiction, or British fiction in Australia, carries the stamp of utility along with any artfulness with which it may be presented. And British fiction at home, in the latter eighteenth and earlier nineteenth centuries, as we have seen, was a slender reed in itself. *Any* novel lay under suspicion of being frivolous or else positively corruptive of morals; if fiction indeed was any good at all (as many still doubted), what was it good *for*? Fictionalized descriptions of a new country could plead utility for themselves (perhaps more convincingly than could delineations of society in the motherland), purporting to answer the natural question, "What's it like out (or over, or down) there?"

Biologically, anthropologically, climatically, the new land of "New Holland" or "New South Wales" was as un-European as any that might be imagined. Into this environment came the First Fleet, which—in functional knowledge of how to cope with what it might find—was as innocent as Adam in Eden, whatever else its shortcomings might have been. But an Australian society at length developed out of the mere fact of European habitation in significant numbers, no matter the original purpose. For a long time it remained economically precarious and stratified along sharp lines between convicts, free settlers, and ex-convicts or "emancipists," along with a special class of military and civil officers and men, many with families, who arrived and departed with some regularity, whereas most of the others stayed. Fiction in its earliest forms shows these divisions, as revealed for example in the title of Alexander Harris's *Settlers and Convicts* (1847). Let us here reverse the order of the title (which in Harris's mind would have seemed only natural and proper) and take early convict fiction first.

Convict Fiction before Marcus Clarke

Appropriately, the first convict novel (as well as the first novel of any category) to appear in Australia was by a convict, a journalist named Henry Savery transported in 1825 for forgery to Van Diemen's Land (after 1855, officially Tasmania). His book, *Quintus Servinton,* subtitled "A tale, founded upon incidents of real occurrence," appeared at Hobart during 1830–31, in three volumes. The first two-thirds or more takes place in England, from where Quintus, also convicted of forgery and having a death sentence commuted to transportation (rather a common occurrence), is sent to New South Wales. There he undergoes numerous privations and personal slights that at one point drive him to attempt suicide.

It was not long after convicts began arriving that the bushranger made his appearance—the escaped convict who, as his name suggests, took to the bush and survived as best he could. Sometimes he associated himself with aboriginals; at other times he might be captured by them and either killed or enslaved. With so limited a society to prey upon, the earliest bushrangers were not very effective as criminals and certainly not very romantic figures; glorification was to be a later development. Revenge against their captors was often bloody, however, and some of the escape narratives contain episodes as lurid as anything from North American records of Indian captivity or flight from black slavery.

Ralph Rashleigh (1844–45) was likewise the production of a convict, James Tucker, transported in 1827 for blackmail. The hero, to begin with, is much less a man put-upon than Savery imagined his hero to be: he is a thief and a trickster, sent out for life. Rashleigh's sufferings in prison or as an assigned laborer intermingle with episodic escapes during which he consorts with bushrangers (fugitives like himself) and aborigines. At length he is pardoned for heroism in rescuing a white woman from the aborigines (a theme that, interestingly enough, appears in a recent novel by Patrick White, *A Fringe of Leaves,* 1976) and becomes thereafter "respected as a man of singular integrity."

Bushrangers and their victims occupy the full stage in Charles Rowcroft's *The Bushranger of Van Diemen's Land* (1846). In this thriller a ship is pirated by escaped convicts who take the captain's daughter as hostage. The leader of the band is the convict Mark Brandon, capable but quite unscrupulous, who must be hunted down in Cooperesque pursuit before the heroine (Helen) can be delivered from him (and by that time, from a tribe of aborigines as well). Whatever the characterization may have lacked, the story line—and to a degree the setting—did hold interest. "It is worthwhile remarking," says Cecil Hadgraft, "the readability of some of these early novels, which with all their faults contrast with the doughy competence of many Australian novels a century later."[4] Novels written by convicts themselves include one published in the United States in 1879, *Moondyne,* by John Boyle O'Reilly. Its author, a political prisoner sent to West Australia in 1868 (the last year any convicts arrived from Britain anywhere in Australia) escaped from the timberworkings in southwestern Australia below Perth and, with the help of an American whaler and other ships, made his way to Boston, where he became a well-known poet, editor, and pro-Irish partisan.

Up to this point we have seen that males not only wrote the fiction but were the chief actors in it; that the function of women characters, more often than not, was to be captured and, after suitable hardships, successfully rescued. In the work of John Lang, the first native-born Australian novelist, the woman—suffering though she still may be—

takes a somewhat more active role. In *The Convict's Wife* (alternatively titled *Assigned to His Wife; or, the Adventures of George Flowers, the Celebrated Detective Officer*) of 1855, the heroine Emily follows her husband, Captain Harcourt, a convicted forger, to Australia. The captain, she learns, has deserted his assigned master, but through the good offices of Flowers, an ex-convict turned detective, he is reassigned to his wife. Incorrigible, Harcourt is finally killed in a fight with Flowers' forces, and we learn at the close that Flowers is Emily's long-lost half brother.

The woman as convict herself (equal opportunity apparently—but not actually—having been achieved) appears in the final story of the group, *The Broad Arrow: Being Passages from the History of Maida Gwynnham, a Lifer* (1859), by the woman as novelist herself, Caroline W. Leakey. Maida, having been seduced by a charmer named Norwell (like Harcourt, a captain), is doubly betrayed in that she murders her baby and is involved in a forgery as well as associated with the machinations of Norwell. She is transported to Tasmania, where at length Norwell also appears, but he is able to see Maida only in her coffin. This experience is too much, even for so hardened a villain (now repentant, it must be added), and he sinks into madness. As in all these and countless other cautionary tales (and coeval ballads and melodramas), crime rewards the author by allowing him or her to point the moral that it never pays. At the same time, as Brian Elliott reminds us,

> Caroline Leakey made a stoic heroine of Maida Gwynnham; in spite of her lapse she retains a proud spirit, a spiritual virginity to the end. Like Clarissa Harlowe, she dies in the grand manner, literally of tuberculosis but spiritually of sheer pride and injured innocence; her death is a purification.[5]

This, however, is as far as the author could go, and that is far short of what was needful. Caroline Leakey's work exemplifies, John Barnes concludes,

> . . . a recurring feature of Australian fiction, particularly fiction written by women during the nineteenth century: the defeat of intelligence by a sentimental notion of fiction. She is an intelligent and thoughtful interpreter of colonial society, but when she consciously sets about writing fiction—creating characters and developing situations—she falsifies, and shamelessly plays upon the emotions of her readers.[6]

Settlers' Novels to 1860

Less sensational than the convict novels with which it was contemporary, fiction treating early Australian settlement undertook to be useful as well as entertaining. This was a more difficult task, inasmuch as willing suspension of disbelief was easily granted stories about convicts, of whom nearly anything could be believed and whose repetitious lives in confinement were a natural foil to the liberated sensations of escape into bushranging or piracy. The "system" was quickly understandable, or at least thought to be so. These stories had also the advantages of immediacy and decisiveness: something could be done quickly and finally. Daily life in the settlements, on the other hand, did not proceed at nearly so brisk a rate, partly because it was presumed to be lived for the future as well as for the present. It is hardly surprising, then, to find some of the early chroniclers of pioneering being attracted to sensationalism as a means of gingering up their narratives.

Charles Rowcroft was one such divided author, whose bushranger story we have already encountered. His *Tales of the Colonies* (1843) uses a splenetic but finally loyal-to-Van-Diemen's-Land character nicknamed Crab to supply the driving force in what might otherwise have been only an immigration tract. "The statistical parts of the book are excrescences," says H. M. Green,

but they help to give the story its queer, attractive, miscellaneous flavour, and the very lack of arrangement in the miscellany makes it resemble a cross-section of life, though it is life as viewed by a humorist who has no use for the intensities. It is, as Rowcroft intended it to be, a happy life, though it contains plenty of effort and hardship and some disasters, and it would be hard to imagine a stronger enticement to the type of possible immigrant at which it was aimed.[7]

Mary Theresa (Johnson) Vidal, a clergyman's wife who lived in Australia from 1840 to 1845, published three novels after her return to England: *Tales for the Bush* (1845), *Cabramatta* (1849), and *Bengala* (1860). The first two are of the "beware of sin" variety, providing admonitory examples which must be known about to be avoided. The third is somewhat more socially descriptive, having been based on the relationships among the quasi gentry in the district served by her husband. No very vigorous claim has been made for the merits of her work.

The writer who offers the most typical promotion-type novels is Alexander Harris, author of *Settlers and Convicts* (1847) and *The Emigrant Family* (1849), both accessible in modern reprints. In the first of these, he brings a young man to New South Wales at about age twenty and keeps him there some fifteen years (1825–40) during which time he is able to establish himself as a comfortable, even rather well-to-do pastoralist with a growing family. More of lasting interest, the novel reports in considerable detail the routine life of the period as well as the various types of people encountered. *The Emigrant Family* is a more conscious example of guidebook fiction, though not without the machinery of a conventional novel. Of its comparative merits, Hadgraft writes:

There is in this novel, as in some others, not only a tolerant condescension towards things Australian, but at the same time an attempt to be impartial: both the unattractive and the crude aspects of the people are noted. There is an unconscious surprise that the good is so good. Miss Smart, for example, the reader is made to feel, can hardly be considered a lady, but Reuben Kable is shown as acceptable—tall, lean, nonchalant, knowledgeable. And the Australian vocabulary is occasionally recorded in the use of such words as *ghibber* and *gunyah* and *bogie*.[8]

Harris's works have been valued by social historians for fidelity to everyday life, but they are clearly not books to be read for depth of characterization or subtlety of plot. *The Emigrant Family,* says W. S. Ramson,

. . . is individual, owing little to earlier novels and too little known itself to have influenced later. Its peculiar strength derives from the way in which Harris's "Australian experience" informed his vision of colonial society and gave it a universal application; humble as the novel is in origin, and imperfect in execution, this vision remains of no little interest.[9]

One wishing to follow the course of the establishment and early history of Australia through fiction has a good many novels to choose from in addition to the ones mentioned in this chapter. A few such are Louis Becke's *A First Fleet Family* (1896), Eleanor Dark's *The Timeless Land* (1941), and succeeding volumes, Hal Porter's *The Tilted Cross* (1961), Thomas Keneally's *Bring Larks and Heroes* (1967), and Patrick White's *A Fringe of Leaves* (1976). The possibilities for both realism and romance generated by Botany Bay have lasted for two centuries and in all likelihood have not yet been exhausted.

Chapter Two
Pre-Federation Fiction

Do not go to the ordinary novel for your ideas on the subject of Australia. Even *David Copperfield* is misleading. Now-a-days Mr. Micawber would be more likely to get into the Insolvency Court than the Commission of Peace.

—Edward Kinglake
(*Useful Hints to Those Intending to Settle in Australia*, 1891)

Early Australian fiction relates closely to the literary modes and expectations of the British eighteenth century: what induced men and women in that age to write? For one thing, close association with one another, of the kind that invited recording of opinion and emotional response to events and people. For another, an audience that natural growth, along with mercantile prosperity, had enlarged and broadened. Few may have cared very deeply about society's misfits after they had been safely transported to the other side of the earth, but there was still a lingering curiosity to be satisfied. This could be built upon, as writers all the way back to Daniel Defoe and John Gay realized; the affairs of criminals command a perennial fascination.

Probably the one most powerful stimulus to something more than piecemeal reporting, however, was the discovery of gold both in Victoria and New South Wales. After 1850, it was only a question of time, and a brief time at that, before Australia would become a separate nation. By the 1890s, the sentiment for independence was common in literary as well as political works. "There is, in truth," said an anonymous writer in *The Australasian Critic* of November 1, 1890,

. . . so wide and healthful an eclecticism of style among our rising writers that it seems useless to search for any common feature which may be taken as promise of a future national school. But in regard to subject matter, however wide their range may be, and however various their methods of treatment, they all are marked by a restless, and sometimes unnecessary, patriotism.[1]

Toward Professionalism:
Early Anglo-Australian Novelists

In the middle and later years of the nineteenth century, the pioneer-turned-writer persisted, but the demand for Australian fiction was already coming to be supplied (and in part created as well) by men who made their living by the pen and were identifiable first of all as writers. All of them were English, at least to begin with, and two of them—Henry Kingsley and Anthony Trollope, highly esteemed novelists in Britain—were brief visitors only. Marcus Clarke and Rolf Boldrewood (T. A. Browne), on the other hand, were migrants arriving in childhood or early young manhood and remaining to establish literary careers. The first of this group, Henry Kingsley, is known to Australians for his novel *Geoffrey Hamlyn* (1859). Kingsley spent five years in Australia during the 1850s but chose to set his novel earlier, in the 1830s, for socially strategic purposes. Other English novelists, using the Australian setting, like Charles Reade whose *It Is Never Too Late to Mend* (1856), were able—if they worked at it—to derive their facts from a growing mass of travel literature, sharply augmented by the gold rushes of the 1850s. Reade wrote to William Howitt, speaking of preparing to write *It Is Never Too Late to Mend,* "To avoid describing Hyde Park and calling it Australia, I read some thirty books about that country; but yours was infinitely the best."[2] Charles Dickens, not unsimilarly, having originally formed an opinion of Australia as no more than a prison, changed his ideas through contacts with Samuel Sidney (an English writer on Australia) and Caroline Chisholm. Thus, in sending the Micawbers of *David Copperfield* (1850) to Australia, he was consigning them to a "lesser world," not the ends of the earth.

The Recollections of Geoffrey Hamlyn, which takes its title from the narrator, not from a hero, transplants (*transports* is a forbidden term in this particular context!) an entire set of upper-class English families—the Buckleys, Brentwoods, and Thorntons—to Victoria and establishes them in squatterdom[3] without very much exposition. (Kingsley explains that his interests are social rather than environmental, but the background does make some demands, which are met.) Class distinctions are obvious, and noblesse oblige ensures both that English social institutions are maintained, even in the bush, and that the challenge of the bushrangers is sternly faced, captives (women and others) being released and order restored. Kingsley's craftsmanship is more than adequate to the production of a still-readable novel; and it is instructive to observe in it the aristocratic ideals that for one reason or another—chiefly the gold rushes, which Kingsley observed while resident in Australia but chose not to write about—did not thrive on Australian soil.

Violence, which the gold rushes undoubtedly helped produce (though the mining camps themselves were generally not socially anarchic), figures in the work of Kingsley and of the next two writers, Marcus Clarke and Rolf Boldrewood. Clarke arrived in Melbourne at age seventeen and became a journalist there, showing abundant and versatile talent as well as great promise, but died at thirty-five. [*For the Term of*] *His Natural Life* (serialized 1870–71, published 1874, republished many times later—bibliographically complicated by changes in title and ending) is the convict novel par excellence. It recounts the sufferings of Richard Devine, who is mistakenly convicted of a crime (murder or robbery—the versions differ) and who as Rufus Dawes is transported for life in 1827, undergoing all the worst indignities and brutalities of convict life. Romance is present as well, however, and in the end (the first ending, that is) Dawes/Devine is vindicated. But Clarke seems to have wondered whether genuine rescue from so thoroughgoing a hell is really possible, and the second reading is tragic. Tragic also is the career of the Reverend James North, prison chaplain, whose ambivalent feelings and escapes into alcoholism are revealed through a diary. Dawes's persecutor, Lieutenant Frere, is the embodiment of everything monstrous in the convict system, believable chiefly in the sense that Victorian villains were at least *meant* to be believed in. The total monstrousness of the system itself is described in these terms as Dawes arrives in Van Diemen's Land:

We have already a notion of what life on a convict ship means; and we have seen through what a furnace Rufus Dawes had passed before he set foot on the barren shore of Hell's Gates. But to appreciate in its intensity the agony he had suffered since that time, we must multiply the infamy of the 'tween decks of the *Malabar* an hundred fold. In that prison was at least some ray of light. All were not abominable; all were not utterly lost to shame and manhood. Stifling though the prison, infamous the companionship, terrible the memory of past happiness—there was yet ignorance of the future, there was yet hope. But at Macquarie Harbour was poured out the very dregs of this cup of desolation. The worst had come, and the worst must for ever remain. The pit of torment was so deep that one could not even see Heaven. There was no hope there so long as life remained. Death alone kept the keys of that island prison.

Is it possible to imagine, even for a moment, what an innocent man, gifted with ambition, endowed with power to love and to respect, must have suffered during one week of such punishment? We ordinary men, leading ordinary lives—walking, riding, laughing, marrying and giving in marriage—can form no notion of such misery as this. Some dim ideas we may have about the sweetness of liberty and the loathing that evil company inspires; but that is all. We know that were we chained and degraded, fed like dogs, employed as beasts of burden, driven to our daily toil with threats and blows, and herded with wretches among whom all that savours of decency and manliness is held in an open scorn, we should die, perhaps, or go mad. But we do not know, and can never know, how unutterably loathsome life must become when shared with such beings as those who dragged the tree trunks to the banks of the Gordon, and toiled, blaspheming, in their irons, on the dismal sandpit of Sarah Island. No human creature could describe to what depth of personal abasement and self-loathing one week of such a life would plunge him. Even if he had the power to write, he dared not.[4]

Clarke wrote stories, narrative sketches, criticism, and indeed ranged through all the literary genres, but his reputation rests mainly on his one prodigious novel which has been read as a primary indictment of British official cruelty for over a hundred years.

Anthony Trollope, whose travel works make lively reading along with his novels, visited Australia at the time Clarke's novel was appearing in the *Australian Journal*. The fact that he had arranged a formal contract with his publishers to write on Australia and New Zealand is a measure of the interest being taken by then in "Our Antipodes," as these colonies were sometimes called; and the books he produced no doubt helped increase this interest, for he liked much of what he saw. A son, Frederick, had gone out to New South Wales in 1863, forming another link, and Trollope made a second visit in 1875. *Harry Heathcote of Gangoil: A Tale of Bush Life,* first published in the London *Graphic* (1873) as a Christmas story, is a novelette in which a station hand dismissed by the young squatter Harry Heathcote plots with an ex-convict neighbor to burn Harry's property. This they attempt on Christmas Day (a very hot, dry time of year in the southern hemisphere) but are unsuccessful: a free-selector (homesteader) neighbor, Giles Medlicot, helps Harry put out the fire and at the ensuing Christmas dinner is rewarded by being accepted as

suitor by Harry's sister-in-law, Kate. In summary, says Coral
Lansbury,

It was a slight story, carried by little more than the pace of its narrative.
The characters were pasteboard, the incidents stereotypes of Australian fiction. But as a Christmas ornament it served well enough and was less contrived and mawkish than the contemporary blight of Christmas novelettes.[5]

John Caldigate (1879) is a fortune-from-Australian-gold story embroi-
dered with complications resulting from an Australian mistress who
shows up in England to cast a shadow over John's marriage there.

The egalitarian nature of Australian society affronted Trollope personally,
[says Dr. Lansbury] but he saw its advantages for black sheep of good families who would soon take on the uniform grey of an Australian flock. Despite the experiences of his own son [who lost money both for his father and
himself as a grazier], Trollope believed that it was a country where a man
could restore his fortune and return eventually to England.[6]

Last in the quartet of Anglo-Australians is Rolf Boldrewood, whose
transit to Australia occurred when he was so very young that he has
a claim to have been the most nearly native of the group. He can be
said, also, to have lived his novels more completely than they, having
been a squatter, goldfields official, and police inspector. He began
publishing at about age fifty, and during the final forty years of a very
long life, he remained a prolific writer with his best work appearing
in the 1880s and 1890s: *Robbery under Arms* (serialized 1882–83, published in book form 1888) and *The Miner's Right* (1890).

Robbery under Arms, exactly contemporary with *Huckleberry Finn,*
missed being an Australian counterpart to Mark Twain's masterpiece
by not too wide a margin. It begins in an engaging colloquial style,
first person, and contains adventures enough: midnight chases
through bush and mountains on horseback, cattle stealing, coach rob-
bing (including seizures of gold), race meetings, even a short spell of
obtaining gold the hard way by mining it, and so forth. Unfortu-
nately, however, Boldrewood's energy or his perception flagged, and
the narrator, Dick Marston, is inconsistent enough in style to mar
the total effect. Two examples, one from the opening chapter and another from Chapter 50, near the end, will show the difference:

It's more than hard to die in this settled, infernal, fixed sort of way, like a bullock in the killing-yard, all ready to be "pithed." I used to pity them when I was a boy, walking round the yard, pushing their noses through the rails, trying for a likely place to jump, stamping and pawing and roaring and knocking their heads against the heavy close rails, with misery and rage in their eyes till their time was up. Nobody told *them* beforehand, though.[7]

> It all passed like a dream. The court was crowded till there wasn't standing room, every one wanting to get a look at Dick Marston, the famous bush-ranger. The evidence didn't take so very long. I was proved to have been seen with the rest the day the escort was robbed; the time the four troopers were shot. I was suspected of being concerned in Hagan's party's death, and half-a-dozen other things. Last of all, when Sub-Inspector Goring was killed, and a trooper, besides two others badly wounded.[8]

It could be said, on the other hand, that no such inconsistency interrupts the career and deportment of Captain Starlight, gentleman bushranger and the ideal outlaw which some Australians still mistakenly appear to believe Ned Kelly was. Foreseeing that capture and trial inevitably must tarnish so bright an image, Boldrewood had the sound judgment to let him die with his boots on, mourned by his mates if not by all his victims. Dick Marston, the survivor of two brothers gradually drawn into Starlight's golden web, provides the requisite amount of penitence and the resolution to serve out his sentence (commuted from hanging) and then go straight—straight into the arms of Gracie, the sweetheart who has dutifully waited for him.

At one point in *Robbery under Arms,* Dick Marston, recounting some feat of extraordinary horsemanship, is made to exclaim, "My word, Australia is a horsey country and no mistake!" This amounts to a tacit admission that the early-modern Australian novel, and indeed some representatives of the near-contemporary as well, did rely pretty heavily upon the convention that later, in film, was to be the stock-in-trade of the American western. This, and some other developing stereotypes, did not go unnoticed, as we can see from a quatrain contributed to A. G. Stephens's magazine the *Bookfellow* at the turn of the century by a versifier signing himself "R. H. C.":

> Whaler,[9] damper, swag and nosebag, johnny-cakes and
> billy-tea,
> Murrumburrah, Meremendicookwoke, Yoularbudgeree,

Cattle-duffers, bold bushrangers, diggers, drovers, bush
race-courses,
And on all the other pages, horses, horses, horses horses. [10]

The Miner's Right, told also in the first person (by a young Englishman, Hereward Pole), takes the narrator to the goldfields to win his
fortune and thus qualify for the hand of Ruth, daughter of Squire
Allerton of Allerton Court, "a grand old Elizabethan pile" in southeastern England. There are exciting episodes, as in *Robbery under
Arms:* a court trial, false accusations to impede the path of true love,
and of special interest, a great deal about the day-to-day practicalities
of gold mining. Hereward does well, and all ends well, as one comes
to expect long before the end.

Whatever the nineteenth-century Australian novel may have
lacked, it was not variety of style. Consider, for example, these two
passages from *The Miner's Right:*

"That's Harry Pole, of No. 4. Liberator, and the best claim on Green-
stone atop of it," said an old Yatala shepherd, charmed to have the opportunity of explanation. "Richest claim on the lead, but disputed. Got
£20,000 in the bank, and two thousand ounces in that bloomin' escort.
Very awkward, ain't it?"

"What's he want to go to town for?" queried a cynical listener. "What
'ud you or I, mate, want to go to town for, supposin't we washed up once
a fortnight to that tune? Wants to have his 'air cut Paris-fashion, or to see
the theayter, or leave his card on the Governor-General, may be." [11]

The sun-god of the south, celestial, effulgent, rose on the most entranc-
ing day that had dawned since first the summer breeze whispered to the
ocean 'neath the lone headlands or by the silver sands of Rose Bay; surely on
that charmed strand the fays of the southern main first danced to the mystic
morn. Clear and bright as the "gold bar of heaven" I watched God's glorious
messenger of light and warmth majestically uprise through an azure cloud-
less sky. [12]

"What's he want to go to England for?" a cynical critic might well
have queried. "Wants to have his prose style cut London-fashion,
may be."

Summing up, Alan Brissenden credits Boldrewood with being

. . . a sympathetic recorder of the pastoral society of the 1850s and 1860s,
especially of Western Victoria, and books like *The Miner's Right* [1890] and

Nevermore [1892] are rich in detail of mining life. His romantic novels are examples of current fashion, not noticeably good, and occasionally as in *War to the Knife* [1899] downright bad. He is best when he writes of historical events and from his own experience, worst when he writes of what he knows only in his imagination. He was primarily a journalist who aimed to please the public because he needed to make money; in this he succeeded, moderately before Macmillan published *Robbery under Arms,* and then beyond all his hopes and expectations.[13]

The *Bulletin* Welcomes New Talents

Australian prose style, however much it may have been permitted to luxuriate throughout most of the nineteenth century, was given close attention during the early 1890s and afterward by the editors of the Sydney *Bulletin.* This enormously influential weekly, started in 1880, maintained a policy toward the stories it accepted and wished to receive that required very strict brevity. Although this may have been at times detrimental to story structure, it had the good effect of obliging writers to watch story length very carefully, inviting them to look closely at sentences as well. Particularly after the critic A. G. Stephens joined its staff in 1894 to remain for twelve years, the *Bulletin* became a literary magnet of very strong drawing power, publishing work of virtually all the important writers in Australia and discovering a number of others. Of these, three rose to prominence in the nineties through its specific agency: Price Warung, Henry Lawson, and Banjo (A. B.) Paterson.

So pervasive did the *Bulletin's* influence become that it seems almost, at times, to have been the sole generating force in Australian literature, especially in style, during the closing years of the nineteenth century. But powerful as it unquestionably was, it scarcely created talent; it gave what was already there, waiting, an outlet, concentrating it and providing it with editorial discipline at the same time. Once we have said this, however, we should look for exceptions, for non-*Bulletin* writers of the period; and such may be found. Michael Wilding, a close student of Marcus Clarke, tells us that a reading of Clarke's stories, as apart from *His Natural Life,* leads us to the realization that "Lawson was not starting with a complete *tabula rasa:* Clarke, and others, had been opening up this territory [i.e., of "realistic, up-country, outback bush stories"]; indeed they had consciously seen it as 'Australian' territory. . . . Clarke was one of the pioneers."[14] This can be seen, similarly, in a book of sketches pub-

lished in 1882, shortly after the *Bulletin* was founded and some years
before it had begun to marshal its force of writers: A. J. Boyd's *Old
Colonials* (1882) by a Queenslander who was a teacher and editor and
whose sketches appeared in various Queensland papers. This excerpt
from "The Independent Schoolmaster," one of several dozen "types,"
gives us several of the ingredients that went into the *Bulletin*-esque
story sketch—colloquialism shading into dialect at times, bush in its
background, brevity, and humor:

Ah! they think a schoolmaster has fine easy times. Open at 9 and close at
4! Yes, that is the way these poor ignorant folk look at it. Only five hours'
light work, and then it's over. Light work! Why, compared with teaching,
ploughing and splitting are enjoyments. Oh! the dull routine of the work in
a little country school like this. Compelled to go over and over the same
ground again and again. Abused, slandered, charged with incompetency by
men whose total learning barely enables them to make out the brand on a
cow! I often feel quite disheartened, and inclined to give up the contest; but
when I look at the poor children, and reflect on the possibility—nay, very
great probability—of their growing up in the debasing ignorance which is
the lot of their parents, I rescind my resolution to retire from the field, and
work on day after day, content if I find the smallest spark of interest awak-
ened in the slumbering minds of my charges. To give you an instance of the
sort of persecution I endure:—A labourer one day walked into the school-
room, and informed me that he had come to know "whoy his Bill warn't
larnin' nothink." Now, the said Bill had come to the school six months previously to the father's visit. His stay had been limited to four days, and
latterly he had attended irregularly for a week. Under these circumstances,
it was not very probable that Master William should have made rapid ad-
vances in learning. I tried to explain this to the father.

"Doant ee tell I! I has larnin' enuff to teach this skule myself. Aint my
lad been 'ere? Why carn't he read es buke? You bearn't no gade. You a
skulemaister! Whoy you carn't teach my Bill a little bit, and I'se gwine to
take 'un hoam!" What could I do? Reasoning was no use, so Bill departed.
He will most probably grow up a vicious, ignorant lout, and, like his father, will boast of his "larnin" and of the days when he went to school, and
the master was too stupid to teach him anything.

The mothers are often as bad. [15]

Price Warung (pseudonym of William Astley) is, after Marcus
Clarke, a second notable practitioner of convict fiction, but in short
form as prescribed by *Bulletin* editors. A mixture of fact, reported
from extensive researches into records (even more meticulous than

Clarke's, which was conscientiously done), together with fiction still hovering close above the documents, Warung's *Tales of the Early Days* (1894) and succeeding volumes did not exclude very much (obscenity excepted) that characterized the convict system—by the 1880s, of course, long abandoned. (In passing it may be somewhat ironic to note that in 1882 two of the *Bulletin*'s editors served a term in jail for publishing an overly frank account of behavior by "larrikins," or young hoodlums, at a Sydney pleasure resort: an instance of an undiscriminating, mindless sort of censorship from which Australia is still not altogether free, although the court itself had been sympathetic and the sentence was over payment of costs.)

Barry Andrews describes Astley's stories as uneven—some not carefully enough written, some acceptable as "rattling good yarns," some having merit as literature—and attaches special importance to Astley as a cultural phenomenon of the 1890s:

> For the historian, Astley's fiction is important evidence of how some Australians saw their past at a significant stage of the nation's development: he helped to perpetuate and publicize the legend about the convicts which is only now being brought into perspective. The convict legend was an integral part of the group myth about Australians and their destiny promoted by the *Bulletin*. And because the *Bulletin* is commonly regarded as the most significant literary journal in this country, Astley's position in the history of Australian literature seems assured. [16]

Henry Lawson, whose melancholy face with its sweeping mustaches now graces the Australian ten-dollar bill (a considerably larger sum than Henry usually had in his pocket), was the *Bulletin*'s chief ornament; and it is gratifying to learn that its editors were early aware of the fact. Later, chronic alcoholism rendered him far less ornamental—indeed, at times, an acute embarrassment—but the great apostle of mateship still kept a few of his mates to the anticlimactic end. A very early *Bulletin* story, "The Drover's Wife" (still not as widely known outside Australia as it ought to be), contains many of what came to be recognized as Lawson's hallmarks: lean, hard-stabbing descriptive patches within an equally frugal narrative; dialogue as phonetically correct as the methods of the day allowed (also, Lawson was hard of hearing); quick bursts of action; a starved-down background—the bush at its grimmest, let us say—all suffused with a singular compassion that rises very naturally and quietly out of the

circumstances related. This is a great deal to claim for an author, but
not too much for the best of Lawson. Here are the opening sentences:

> The two-roomed house is built of round timber, slabs, and stringy-bark,
> and floored with split slabs. A big bark kitchen standing at one end is larger
> than the house itself, veranda included.
> Bush all round—bush with no horizon, for the country is flat. No ranges
> in the distance. The bush consists of stunted, rotten native apple-trees. No
> undergrowth. Nothing to relieve the eye save the darker green of a few she-
> oaks which are sighing above the narrow, almost waterless creek. Nineteen
> miles to the nearest sign of civilization—a shanty on the main road.
> The drover, an ex-squatter, is away with sheep. His wife and children are
> left here alone.
> Four ragged, dried-up-looking children are playing about the house. Sud-
> denly one of them yells: "Snake! Mother, here's a snake!"

T. Inglis Moore sees this story as offering "an authentic illustration"

> . . . of human ecology, since it shows the organism functioning in its en-
> vironment, the bush woman living out a life determined almost wholly by
> the bush, adapting herself to the demands of the land, and following the
> rhythms of nature prevailing in the Australian outback.[17]

The extended narrative, for personal and perhaps stylistic reasons
as well, was not congenial to Lawson or to his chief employer, the
Bulletin; he never produced a novel. Nevertheless, there are groups of
stories such as the Joe Wilson series, and characters such as Mitchell,
which suggest linkages and point the way out of episodic fiction
alone. Joe Wilson was "a character largely based on self-portraiture,"[18]
as A. A. Phillips suggests, and a great many of the stories have the
ring of immediacy about them. Phillips speaks later of Lawson's fidelity to his locale, of "the exceptional power which Lawson has to
convey the feeling of Australia and the Australians. . . . His characters have a simple human universality; but they are nevertheless immediately recognizable, by those who know, as Australian; they could
never be anything else."[19] The effect noted by Nettie Palmer—

> A page of Lawson pulls you up with a delicious shock. This is what
> you've been looking for. Without apparent effort, Lawson takes you straight
> into his own intimate world and makes you free of it; his easy, colloquial
> voice has the incantation of rhythm.[20]

—is still one experienced by many readers.

Lawson the commoner and his semiaristocratic counterpart Banjo Paterson occasionally engaged in mock duels in the *Bulletin* over the merits and demerits of bush life. In these, Paterson took the romantic line, Lawson the realistic, both writing in verse. Paterson's prose, of which there is a considerable amount, is mostly journalism, but there are occasional stories collected in *Three Elephant Power* (1917) and two novels, *An Outback Marriage* (1906, station life in New South Wales) and *The Shearer's Colt* (1936, written to expose racetrack dishonesty). Rolf Boldrewood, not surprisingly, liked *An Outback Marriage* for its "original and effective" descriptions.[21] Lorna Ollif describes the outback sections as "bare, harsh, and convincing," adding that "Paterson was acquainted with this hard living and could describe a cattle muster or a buffalo hunt with all the energy of a man writing from familiarity and intimate knowledge."[22]

Neither Paterson nor Lawson lacked the background needed for realistic fiction. The social picture that emerges through Paterson has a generally broader scope, but the writing has not nearly so deep a resonance. George Nadel suggests that the Australian social classes were still so far apart that the *Bulletin* writers, in revolt, were finally too narrow, thinking that "universals were most readily explored through social satire redeemed by patriotism."[23] Perhaps "social realism *and* satire" might be nearer the facts.

Louis Becke (1855–1913), another *Bulletin* writer (and one closely associated with Rolfe Boldrewood, partly because of a notorious plagiarism case in 1894), had traveled extensively enough about Polynesia as a trader to become an early oracle on the South Seas. A book of stories, *By Reef and Palm* (1894), was followed by numerous others before his death at Sydney in 1913. Becke's characters, not unlike Jack London's from about the same time, are typically activists, sometimes heroic and sometimes not. The strength of his work, says A. Grove Day,

. . . lies in his self-confidence born of the early experience of a writer who not only responded to the call of adventure, but viewed the scene as a man does who looks up from his labor to wipe the sweat from his forehead. The glamor has faded under the pressure of work, sudden hardship, illness, and bitter monotony, and the islands of the Pacific are shown to be real places on our planet, not the dreamlands of more artistic craftsmen such as Conrad, Stevenson, and Melville. This is the way it was.[24]

With W. J. Jeffery as collaborator, Becke wrote a historical novel, *A First Fleet Family,* serialized in the *London Illustrated News* and pub-

lished as a separate volume in 1896. Other historical or quasi-histor-
ical works followed, but those for which he is best remembered came
from his own career as sailor, trader, and demi-buccaneer. He was
also one of the first moderns to contribute (as of 1901) to rehabilitat-
ing the reputation of Herman Melville.

The *Bulletin* was quickly successful enough to inspire imitations,
one of which, the *Boomerang,* appeared in Brisbane during the years
1887–92. For a time, the leading spirit of this journal was William
Lane, the labor leader whose socialist theories were espoused in its
columns and who produced one novel, *The Workingman's Paradise*
(1892). Propagandistic intentions are clear even from the title; it is
filled with earnest conversations but not very much real story interest.
Lane lived a much more dramatic novel than he or indeed anyone else
of his period ever wrote, when he led a band of followers all the way
to Paraguay to found a utopian colony, New Australia, which did not
long survive. Another socialist writer, for a time associated with the
Boomerang, was Francis Adams (1862–1893), variously poet, social
critic, and magazine journalist who wrote stories collected in *Australian Life* (1890).

Steele Rudd (A. H. Davis) for a time conducted his own magazine
and wrote voluminously on the Rudd family, headed by a patriarchal
Dad whose interminable misfortunes fell somewhere between movie
or television burlesque (for which they have been exhumed and ex-
ploited) and the more believable folk story. *On Our Selection* (1899) is
the first in an extended series, from which the mixture of serious and
comic in the following paragraphs is taken; the comment comes at
the time of the death of old Bob Wren, a bachelor neighbor:

> Dad couldn't make out the cause of death; perhaps it was lightning [dur-
> ing the violent storm immediately preceding]. He held a post-mortem, and,
> after thinking hard for a long while, told Mother he was certain, anyway,
> that old Bob would never get up again. It was a change to have a dead man
> about the place, and we were very pleased to be first to tell anyone who
> didn't know the news about old Bob.
>
> We planted him on his own selection beneath a gum-tree where for years
> and years a family of jackasses had nightly roosted, Dad remarking, "As
> there *might* be a chance of his hearin', it'll be company for the poor old
> cove."[25]

In all, Davis wrote some thirty books or more, including both stories
and plays, in addition to his journalistic efforts. The recent estimate
by his son, in a "life and times" volume, is fairly put:

Dad was imbued with a genuine nationalism. A Queenslander and an Australian, who wrote of the land and the people he knew . . . he dealt with situations in a humorous manner when occasions arose, and these were many; but he wrote with a sympathetic understanding of the struggles and the set-backs of those pioneers of this nation.[26]

Women Writers and the Social Scene

Mention of Lane and Adams as socialist writers of the 1880s, and later, recalls that as early as 1854 a novel entitled *Clara Morison,* by Catherine Helen Spence, was portraying the social effects of the gold rushes, commenting on British attitudes as contrasted with colonial ones, and looking closely at the class system of Australia along with other social and political issues of the day. Late in the story, Clara, a poor immigrant who has worked in a number of domestic situations and about whom the author has woven an emotional web not entirely evident from the following excerpt, receives a proposal of marriage which at length she accepts. As we meet the pair, she has just told her suitor (who, she believes, is engaged to another woman) that she intends to take up teaching: "If teaching is not my vocation, what else can I do? I am so unfortunate as to be a woman, and my sphere is very limited." She refuses, as she thinks, to accept a position as "companion to healthy people," and the exchange continues:

"Clara," said he, "I really want you for a companion at Taringa."
"No. Mrs. Reginald ought to be enough for you, and you for her. I will be a governess."
"Yes; and teach me many things. Mrs. Reginald would indeed be enough for me if you were she. Tell me, Clara, should I be enough for you? I am in earnest—Clara, will you marry me?"
"What would Miss Julia Marston say to such a proposal, sir?" said Clara, haughtily.
"Julia Marston is now Mrs. Dent, and has no right to give any opinion as to my affairs. I have been jilted, Clara. My handsome bride has been too happy to accept your cousin Margaret's rejected suitor, and, thank God, I am free. This declaration would have come long ago, but that I was bound to an indifferent and unloving woman. It is not from any caprice I ask your hand; it is from the deep conviction that you only, of all women in the world, can make me happy; and if you will trust me with your happiness, I will guard it as my own. You may find younger, and handsomer, and better men in the world, but I am sure you can never find one who loves you more. Do not refuse me, Clara."
Clara put her hand in his. "I am very proud of your love, sir," she said;

"and I will try to deserve it. You are young enough, and handsome enough, and good enough for me. I can trust myself entirely to you." Her eyes were full of tears, but she shook them off.[27]

Calling *Clara Morison* "decidedly the best Australian novel that we have met with," Frederick Sinnett, writing in the *Journal of Australasia* in 1856, goes on to say (in part):

Considered entirely apart from its Australian scenery and coloring, *Clara Morison* would be a book deserving careful criticism and much praise. . . . She has merely illustrated Australian life insensibly in the process of illustrating human life. Paul de Kock describes Parisian life because he writes novels and is a Parisian. Dickens describes London life because he writes novels and is a Londoner. The local coloring in each case is the accident— the portrayal of human life and interest being the essential.[28]

Spence, a friend of J. S. Mill, was a hard-working journalist before Francis Adams and William Lane were born, and she shared at least some of their social aims. In all, between 1854 and 1881 she published five novels, of which *Tender and True* (1856) and *Mr. Hogarth's Will* (1865) stand next to *Clara Morison,* which has recently been reprinted.

In the year following *Clara Morison* there appeared *Gertrude, the Emigrant; a Tale of Colonial Life* (1857), "by an Australian Lady," who was Caroline Louisa Atkinson, botanist and writer of light fiction serialized in the Sydney *Mail.* Daughter of James Atkinson, a substantial early N.S.W. pastoralist who wrote on agricultural subjects, Atkinson by publishing her novel at age 23 became the first Australian-born authoress. Ada Cambridge, who came to Victoria in 1870 as a minister's wife (her husband served several parishes outside the urban area of Melbourne), began writing not long after arrival in order to help improve the family finances. This was a time when a moderately capable woman writer (there were a good many such in Canada and the United States as well as in Britain) could succeed at popular fiction, and Ada Cambridge managed to do so. With her fifteen or twenty titles beginning in 1875 and continuing into the early twentieth century, she represents a quick response to an enlarged demand for romantic fiction about women, by women, and for women which has been with us for well over a century. Her books contain, for the most part, well-balanced and well-to-do people, some Australian, others English, who typify that part of Victorian society we associate with stability. In *A Marriage Contract* (1894), female opinion of the strength shown in the following passage was probably about as far as most novelists of the time preferred to go:

"You are perfectly free. You need not consider me at all. I have not the slightest objection. The mere writing of our names on paper does not bind us, except in a purely legal way; and you have broad views, I know; and men and women are different. Because I don't care to make ties, that is no reason why you should deny yourself, if others are willing to give you what I cannot. You certainly need not deny yourself on my account."

"Thank you very much. But, like you, I have no desire to make ties. I prefer to consider myself a married man."

"We are not married. We are simply a commercial firm. We entered into a business partnership to make money, and we made it. The end is reached. We retire upon our profits. It is expedient to keep our names over the shop door, but that is all. We have retired."[29]

Other notable titles in Cambridge's works include *A Marked Man* (1890) and *Fidelis* (1895).

Third in a more or less homogeneous quartet is Rosa Praed, or Mrs. Campbell Praed as her name appeared on title pages, of which there were upwards of fifty beginning with *An Australian Heroine* in 1880 and extending through 1916. Her second Australian title, *Policy and Passion* (1881), introduces a colonial prime minister (of Queensland), a self-made strong man, Longleat, whose career is broken by the revelation of his having been transported for murder (a crime of passion, it was). Longleat's daughter, in a subplot, escapes seduction by a treacherous Englishman and marries an honest Australian. Praed's novels are, as Hadgraft observes, "her tentative autobiography,"[30] which she produced, in part, in *My Australian Girlhood* (1902). The theme of the unharmonious marriage enters into her fiction (also as autobiography) as does that of a strong interest in hypnotism, astrology, and other forms of the occult. (H. H. Richardson's Richard Mahoney was similarly attracted.)

A passage from *My Australian Girlhood* (dedicated "To My Fellow-Australian Writers") may give some idea of her narrative style, but it is even more revealing of the degree of literary culture sometimes achieved even in the Outback. She is speaking of the station's library:

It was pathetic, the avidity with which we all devoured such as fell within reach. And one can't quite understand how there came to be so many books at Marroon [station]. Standard authors of thirty years back—there was a many-volumed set of the old-time black and gold Bentley edition. And besides fiction of all sorts, plenty of histories and travels and poetry and biographies, no lack of pasture of a curiously mixed kind for young minds to browse upon. . . .

It was a good thing that intellectual food abounded, though probably some of it was strong meat for babes, for of education in the ordinary sense there wasn't much to be had. Perhaps the *Marroon Magazine* [conducted a la Brontë by the station youngsters] may have helped a little that way. . . . and indeed, Mrs. Gaskell's life of Charlotte Brontë is responsible for arousing here in the bush much strenuous literary aspiration.[31]

Last in the group is Tasma (Jessie Couvreur) who wrote her best novel first, *Uncle Piper of Piper's Hill* (1888), and then published regularly in the 1890s until her early death in 1897. Like Praed, she was concerned with domestic strife, especially the sort in which the wife is quite evidently the superior partner and is made to suffer. Uncle Piper of the novel bearing his name is a widower-curmudgeon who makes life difficult for a cluster of relatives who themselves can be difficult in return. One of the women, Uncle Piper's stepdaughter Laura, is "an example of the New Woman, skeptical and unorthodox,"[32] and the men are not very congenial with either Uncle Piper or one another. In the long run, however, matters are made to work out and Uncle Piper is shaded into a less formidable ogre than at first he seems. In other Tasma novels, the outcome is not always so fortunate, though it is evident that if at all possible the woman is obliged to make things do, mismatched though she may be. Australia to this day can scarcely be called famous for male gallantry toward women, and the novels of a century ago, or nearly so, clearly reveal the earlier stages of a socially unhandsome tradition.

Chapter Three

From Federation into the 1930s

Confidence is surely one of the main things lacking in our writers up till now, particularly our novelists. They never seemed quite sure of themselves or their public, never were fully convinced of the validity of their own point of view, or that there were people to communicate with whose minds were as adult as their own.

—Nettie Palmer (1927)

In the Australian world of post-Confederation following 1901, we may observe two major divisions, two areas divided by the craggy watershed of World War II: first, the years 1901–50; second, the years 1950–80, with some overlaps. To each of these, two chapters have been assigned in order to emphasize certain trends, or tones, within a given time span. Too strict a boundary cannot always be defended after it has been drawn, for the divisions may turn out, finally, to have been a convenience as much to avoid congestion as to sort out writers ideologically. This chapter treats chiefly a group whose works fall comparatively early in the century; the next brings the record down to the decade in which World War II began. It will be noted, in the works of most writers included, that the earlier group is by and large more immediately involved with Australia, and more intensely, more personally so than many (but by no means all) in the later group, among whom appear immigrants, expatriates, and those deliberately seeking historical perspectives.

Alfred Deakin, making notes to himself on Henry Lawson's work in 1896, felt he could at that time say:

An indigenous literature is at last beginning in Australia. It contains of course traces of foreign influence but has subordinated those to itself and adapted them to its environment—Lawson and Paterson are the twins—complements—pessimist and optimist who mark this dawn.[1]

Lawson the pessimist, however, could not quite see the dawn in the same rosy tones:

> The Australian writer, until he gets a "London hearing" is only accepted as an imitator of some recognized English or American author; and, as soon as he shows signs of coming to the front he is labelled "The Australian Southey," "The Australian Burns," or "The Australian Bret Harte," and, lately, "The Australian Kipling." Thus, no matter how original he may be, he is branded, at the very start, as a plagiarist.[2]

Various opinions on the success of "native" writers are to be found at the time of Federation and afterward, ranging from the most chauvinistic of nationalist criticism to A. G. Stephens's wry comment in 1911 that "explorers in the interior of the Australian temperament bring back tales of a Great Emotional Desert."[3]

Women Writers and the Bush: Franklin, Baynton

There is an Australian mystique of the bush that goes far back into the nineteenth century, expressed most eloquently in poetical responses such as Bernard O'Dowd's famous long poem "The Bush," but attested to in the stories of Lawson, Paterson, and others of the *Bulletin* school as well. In a masculine world, it came to be associated also with mateship, since the admittedly hard-slogging type of life required mutual aid and companionship in adversity. Women novelists, not surprisingly, paid less attention to the bush per se. T. Inglis Moore takes note of the differently developed sociability among the women novelists discussed in the previous chapter:

> On the other hand, these three novelists [Cambridge, Tasma, and Praed] all did their best work in novels with the backgrounds of Sydney, Melbourne, and Brisbane. . . . Ada Cambridge, who came to Australia knowing nothing of "the mysterious Bush" which she thought of as "a vast shrubbery, with occasional spears hurtling through it," was mainly interested in criticizing social orthodoxy. Tasma and Mrs. Praed were concerned mainly with social relationships. So, too, was Catherine Spence, who passed shrewd comments on Adelaide's colonial customs in *Clara Morison*.[4]

Miles Franklin, by contrast, counted country living the supreme glory of Australia, and throughout her work—some of it under the pseudonym, Brent of Bin Bin—defended squatterdom and insisted upon the values and virtues imparted by active life in the open air, as did Henry Kingsley before her. Many Australians agree; and criticism of Miles Franklin's work tends to divide somewhat according to the critics' persuasions about rural living. *My Brilliant Career* (1901), published in the year of Australian Federation (and at just about the time of the author's birth centennial, 1979, made into quite a successful film), led to encomiums and expectations that a young author (she was twenty-two at the time) could hardly be expected to measure up to. Her next book did not appear until 1909, and her third (as Brent) in 1928. From that time until her death, she published steadily, and three of her books are posthumous. The sequel to *My Brilliant Career*—*My Career Goes Bung*—was written early but not published until 1946. The fact that she loved bush life did not blind her to some of its shortcomings, and there is a satirical inlay to much of her work, some of it employed in the service of feminism. On the whole, however, she represents the conservative station society (satirists are frequently conservative) in which she grew up but which by the time she wrote her last books had become largely a memory. The note sounded in *My Brilliant Career*—

I am proud that I am an Australian, a daughter of the Southern Cross, a child of the mighty bush. I am thankful I am a peasant, a part of the bone and muscle of my nation.[5]

—was sustained over half a century. In *Prelude to Waking* (1950), Merlin Giltinane, loyally Australian and feministically antimale, is unsuccessfully courted by a British intellectual, Nigel Barraclough, who tells the story. The time is the mid-1920s, when Australia was beginning to look abroad. As to that, Merlin feels that "there'll be no hope for my Australia in the new alignments unless the Occident will abandon war and the Orient will control its fecundity."[6] As the time settings of Franklin's novels progress through the nineteenth century into the twentieth, the background canvas narrows, moving toward urban settings. So, too, do the attitudes of the characters, who "seem smaller, not so much confined as more meager in emotional and spiritual outlook," says Cecil Hadgraft. "Some are almost querulous, and their arguments and complaints are a far cry from the early assurance of men easily able to deal with the world outside."[7]

Although always a readable and at times very brisk writer, Miles Franklin is memorable not so much for her style as for the content of

her books. Marjorie Barnard, a fellow novelist (see Chapter 4), says
of her:

> In her novels she summed up for Australians their pastoral age, the day-
> to-day life of the squatter and the small farmer, in a way that it has never
> been done before or since. She knew it at first hand, though only in her
> youth. Her parents, her grandparents, her uncles and aunts had been pi-
> oneers. She had a great fund of memories, experienced and related, to draw
> upon. She recreated an era that has gone and will never come again. The
> future historian, the student of economics, the sociologist, will read Miles's
> books for the living pictures of a time and place that they present. Others
> will read them for their natural verse and the lively stories they tell.[8]

Mention having been made of the filming of *My Brilliant Career,*
this may be the appropriate place to note that other "early" Australian literary figures (by current estimate) have furnished plot and/or
setting for Australian films of high quality (e.g., Henry Handel
Richardson, Joan Lindsay) or, as in the case of "Breaker" Morant,
have become film heroes. Readers are aware that much more of such
film-stuff exists among the earlier writers and may look forward to
seeing it gradually discovered and put to use.

Diametrically opposed to Miles Franklin, insofar as praise of the
bush is concerned, was Barbara Baynton. *Bush Studies* (1902) was of
course not written and published in rebuttal to *My Brilliant Career*
but it serves very much that function; and the two taken together
offer us a forceful demonstration of the ambivalences in Australian life
and thought. To Baynton, bush culture is what Thomas Hobbes
characterized as man's existence in the state of nature: "No arts; no
letters; no society; and which is worst of all, continual fear and danger of violent death; and the life of man, solitary, poor, nasty, bru-
tish, and short."[9]

In *Bush Studies,* this applies with double force to the life of woman,
who is consistently victimized. Nearly every one of its half-dozen stories reiterates and emphasizes the theme of masculine callousness or
overt brutality. But at the same time, as A. A. Phillips points out,
her use of the maternal theme "saves [her] work from the final effect
of pessimism, despite the grimness of her tone": maternal force is
strong enough to survive, in one way or another, the onslaught of
evil—but no thanks to the menfolk, for all that.[10] Her "intense
power," Hadgraft says, not overstating the matter, "is probably un-
rivalled in Australian short stories."[11] Her one novel, *Human Toll*

(1907), is consistent in tone with the stories. Two paragraphs, occurring near the breaking point of "The Chosen Vessel," illustrate the economy and directness of her style:

> She thought of the knife, and shielded her child's body with her hands and arms. Even its little feet she covered with its white gown, and baby never murmured—it liked to be held so. Noiselessly she crossed to the other side, and stood where she could see and hear, but not be seen. He was trying every slab, and was very near to that with the wedge under it. Then she saw him find it; and heard the sound of the knife as bit by bit he began to cut away the wooden support.
> She waited motionless, with her baby pressed tight to her, though she knew that in another few minutes this man, with the cruel eyes, lascivious mouth, and gleaming knife would enter. One side of the slab tilted; he had only to cut away the remaining little end, when the slab, unless he held it, would fall outside. [12]

Nor is this author one to exploit suspense to the hilt only to provide a last-minute rescue: the man with the cruel eyes, lascivious mouth, and gleaming knife *does* enter.

Joseph Furphy's *Such Is Life*

The high-water mark in Australian radicalism was reached in the 1890s, with Lawson, Lane, Adams, and a sizable group of other writers agitating for one or another of the then competing brands of socialism (not yet colored with the distortions and travesties of Marxism that our own century was to produce). All of it came out of Europe, ultimately, but some was refracted through such American writers as George, Bellamy, or Donnelly, all known in Australia along with British and other radical thinkers. One of the most resolute and at the same time independent republicans of the era was a self-educated mechanic and man-of-all-work named Joseph Furphy. Coming late to the literary scene (he was sixty when his first and in a sense his only book, *Such Is Life,* was published in 1903, as by Tom Collins), Furphy had a long life of reading and reflection behind him and was not one to spare the reader the pains of thought.

Many critics feel there is a strain of congenital long-windedness in Furphy, and they are at least partly correct. But we need to remember that *Such Is Life* is in the bushman's idiom, the fireside-yarn sort of delivery which is never in a hurry, and that the author is less an agitator than a persuader who wants his hearers to weigh the evidence for themselves. Throughout the history of fiction there has been an honorable place for the kind of deliberately inflated language we associate with Rabelais, Cervantes, Fielding, Dickens, Mark Twain; Furphy is one of that crowd. "Half bushman and half bookworm," he called himself; perhaps it would not be too much to say that he conceived the narrator of *Such Is Life* as half Collins and half Furphy.

Plot manipulation and setting as well call for a certain amount of masculine persiflage as supportive of the act: strands of the plot run parallel, or so we are led to suppose, and then suddenly veer off into one another. The bullock-track setting conspired to restrict characterization principally to men, but in any event Furphy was never very skillful with women characters. Cutting and rewriting to shorten the manuscript in several instances somewhat disturbed the original structural intentions, yet the story becomes, in part at least, entangled in its own complexities: its author seems overingenious, at times. The whole arrangement is overlaid with the tongue-in-cheek ironical detachment/involvement of Tom Collins, yarning along and pretending to grope his way through his own labyrinth.

Two other novels, or novelettes, in fact—*Rigby's Romance* (serialized 1905) and *The Buln-Buln and the Brolga* (1948)—were quarried out of the original massif at the insistence of A. G. Stephens of the *Bulletin,* who was midwife to publication of *Such Is Life.* The first of these carries most of the weight of Furphy's political thought, roped loosely on the back of a plot barely able to stagger along beneath it. The characterization, however, is entirely reliable, the language magniloquent if you like magniloquence (or are willing at least to put up with it, as most readers need to at one time or another). In *Such Is Life* there is no such restriction; the range of styles, themes, episodes, and personalities is a rich one; and Collins, the self-abasing "Deputy-Assistant-Sub-Inspector" of something or other, simply has to be trusted to see us through. Most of the action takes place along the roads of the Riverina (southwestern N.S.W.) country; many of the characters are bullock drivers (as Furphy himself was, for several years), and all of them have some authentic association with the territory. It is not easy to quote a short passage from Furphy, but this one is reasonably so, as well as representative of the hand-to-mouth existence of the teamsters and their beasts. We are at a night camp on one of the large stations, whose owner, Montgomery, is not very sympathetic with the problems of feeding teams from bullock drays when they compete—as inevitably they must—with his own stock.

My way led me past a small, isolated stable, used exclusively for the boss's buggy-horses. Nearing this building, I heard a suppressed commotion inside, followed by soothing gibberish, in a very low voice. This was bad. Priestly's bullocks were within easy view; and Jerry, the groom, was a notorious master's man. I must have a friendly yarn with him.

"What's up with you this hour of the night, Jerry?" I asked, looking through the latticed upper-wall. "Uneasy conscience, I'll bet." Whilst speaking the last words, I distinguished Montgomery's pair of greys, tied, one in each back corner of the stable, whilst Pawsome's horses—a white and a piebald—were occupying the two stalls and voraciously tearing down mouthfuls of good Victorian hay from the racks above the manger. Pawsome, silently caressing one of the greys, moved to the lattice on hearing my voice. "Sleight-of-hand work?" I suggested, in a whisper.

"Sort of attempt," replied the wizard, in the same key. "You gev me a start. All the lights was out two hours ago, an' I med sure everybody was safe."

"So they are. I've only been down for a swim. Goodnight, Possum."

"I say, Collins—don't split!"

"Is thy servant a dog, that he should do this great thing?"

"Second Kings," whispered the poor necromancer, in eager fellowship, and displaying a knowledge of the Bible rare amongst his sect. "God bless you, Collins! may we meet in a better world!"

"It won't be difficult to do that," I replied dejectedly, as I withdrew to enjoy my unearned slumber.[13]

On the question of Furphy's lingo, which puts some readers off, these remarks by Douglas Killam are relevant:

It is with novels such as Furphy's that we become aware of a problem which has become central to the evaluation of literatures in the new Englishes—the danger implicit in criticizing a colonial or commonwealth literature using criteria which are relevant to the mother country but little use outside it. Furphy was not an Englishman and his English is not British; he is consciously trying to present what it means to be Australian by using language which is distinctly Australian. Furphy remained the most innovative and successful writer until Patrick White began to publish in the 1940s; and his success is largely due to a fertile imagination and intense nationalism which found creative expression in his bold and experimental use of language.[14]

On this same topic Furphy himself had this to say, in a synopsis of *Such Is Life* written in 1903 for advertising use:

> Beyond all other Australian writers, Tom Collins is a master of idiom. There is no confusion of patois, nor exaggeration of grammatical solecism in his dialogue. As in actual life, the education of each speaker is denoted by his phraseology; the dialect of each European bespeaks his native locality; and, above all, the language of the most unbookish bushman never degenerates into "coster."[15]

Finally, there can be social barriers, as well, to a full acceptance. Speaking of the "Australian Cultural Cringe" (which he divides into two varieties, the "Cringe Direct" and the "Cringe Inverted, in the attitude of the Blatant Blatherskite, the God's-Own-Country-and-I'm-a-better-man-than-you-are Australian Bore"), A. A. Phillips remarks,

> Confronted by Furphy, we grow uncertain. We fail to recognize the extraordinary original structure of his novel because we are wondering whether an Englishman would not find it too complex and self-conscious. No one worries about the structural deficiencies of *Moby Dick*. We do not fully savour the meaty individualism of Furphy's style because we are wondering whether perhaps his egotistic verbosity is not too Australianly crude; but we accept the egotistic verbosity of Borrow as part of his quality.[16]

In the same volume, Mr. Phillips makes the interesting claim that Lawson and Furphy took Anglo-Saxon writing, for the first time, "out of the cage of the middle-class attitude," conducting "a Cook's Tour of the lower orders for middle-class readers, who were the 'foreigners.' "

> They wrote of the people, for the people, and from the people. In that task almost their only predecessors later than Bunyan were Burns and Mark Twain—and neither had the full courage of his convictions.[17]

However that may be, it is certain that Lawson and Furphy did have the courage of un-Sovietized socialistic convictions.

Sydney as Viewed by the Newcomer: Louis Stone

Reaching Brisbane in 1884 as a youthful immigrant, Louis Stone finished his education at Sydney, where he became a teacher. His novel *Jonah* (1911), descriptive of the street gangs (or "pushes") of lower-class Sydney, has been consistently praised for its careful realism: "smells and sights and sounds of the ramshackle area, garish at nights with the glare from the pub, raucous with the cries of the inhabitants, grimy with dirt."[18] Jonah (nickname for Joseph Jones), the hunchback leader of the Cardigan Street push, rises to wealth and power but remains unhappy, unfulfilled; it is the anatomy of the gangsterism he represents that renders the story so readable and still relevant. Ronald McQuaig, introducing a third edition in 1965, had this to say about the before-its-time quality of the novel:

> Pinkey [Stone's most sympathetic character] was published a year before Eliza Doolittle and four years before Doreen [of C. J. Dennis's larrikin poetry]; Jonah the larrikin businessman anticipated Frank Hardy's *Power Without Glory* by about forty years; and the Sydney setting in *Jonah* anticipated Lennie Lower's *Here's Luck* by nineteen years and *They're a Weird Mob* by "Nino Culotta" by forty-six years.[19]

Stone was not the first to present the larrikin in fiction, but his book is the classic on the subject, in which a new world was being revealed to startled readers from other social levels.

A second novel by Stone, *Betty Wayside* (1915), turns to another side of Sydney life in dealing with the arts, particularly music, and with a far politer grade of society than Jonah's. This book, however, was far less successful than *Jonah,* and Stone wrote no others. After pointing out the serious deficiencies of *Betty Wayside,* H. J. Oliver nevertheless concludes that the contemporary critic Bertram Stevens

> . . . was right when he said in 1919 that *Betty Wayside* was "the truest picture of Australian city life in the lower middle class that has yet been done"; it anticipated by many years Christina Stead's *Seven Poor Men of Sydney* and Katharine Susannah Prichard's *Intimate Strangers,* to mention only two of many.[20]

Vance and Nettie Palmer: Persons of Letters

To the outsider, distinctions between states and regions in Australia are not matters of very much consequence; and even to the later-twentieth-century Australian himself, who has often been in most of the principal cities of his own country as well as many others abroad, local geography is not paramount. It once was, however, and there will no doubt be lingering evidences of the old rivalries for years to come. Three vast areas—Queensland, Western Australia, and the Northern Territory—are still remote from the thickly populated coastal crescent having as its twin centers Sydney and Melbourne, with rapidly diminishing concentration past Brisbane to the north and Adelaide to the west. In this area live most of Australia's present-day 13.5 + million people, well over two-thirds. Naturally enough, the literary centers developed first in Sydney and Melbourne, with newspapers, magazines, and book publishers together with libraries, universities, and other public institutions taking the lead there. The gold rushes of the 1850s were chiefly responsible for the growth of specific places and for the rates of this growth, but it is also true that much of the best grain-farming and grazing land is in Victoria and New South Wales.

Melbourne was the adoptive home of Marcus Clarke, Francis Adams (for a time), Tasma, and some other early literary figures. Two native Australians, the Palmers—Vance from Queensland, Nettie from Victoria—married in 1914 and soon came to be identified with Melbourne. Nettie was a poet, biographer, and critic; Vance a novelist, playwright, biographer, and critic, the one Australian writer of the earlier twentieth century who emerged at length as indisputably a man of letters in the full sense. Both devoted themselves to fostering other writers and to a multitude of useful activities in behalf of Australian literature, such as the Commonwealth Literary Fund, established in 1938 (since 1974, the Literature Board of the Australia Council).

The cultural historian Geoffrey Serle gives us a dismal picture of the interwar years: Australians were "still almost entirely ignorant of and uninterested in their history"; only two publishing houses of any importance existed, and their production was small; no more than "about one-third of the more important novels were published in Australia and few of them achieved anything like adequate distribution"; there were no major literary journals; writers were isolated from each other; and "it was almost eccentric for an educated Australian to read more than an occasional book by an Australian."[21] It was into this near-vacuum that Vance and Nettie Palmer poured their combined talents for many years, working not only *as* writers but even more diligently *for* writers, as critics and advocates.

Vance Palmer's career as novelist began with the publication of a volume of stories, *The World of Men,* in 1915. Perhaps the title was prophetic; he was to write more convincingly of men than of women throughout his whole career, which included a chronicle novel, *The Swayne Family* (1934) and a political-industrial trilogy in the 1940s and 1950s, developing the career of a labor leader named Macy Donovan who becomes (in *The Big Fellow,* 1959) prime minister of Queensland. It was to his own Queensland background that Palmer turned in his first novel to attract wide attention, *The Passage* (1930). G. A. Wilkes assesses both the strength and weakness of Palmer's achievement in this analysis:

> Although in so many ways *The Passage* calls on Palmer's special powers as a novelist—his skill in suggesting the rhythm of existence in the fishing village, his insight into the vulnerable nature of little Peter Callaway—it also exposes certain of his limitations. The process by which Lew comes to marry Lena Christensen is never convincingly shown: Palmer typically holds back from the treatment that is demanded, and is not on safe ground again until he is dealing with the frictions of the Callaways' domestic life, their silent resentments and oblique tauntings. The same evasiveness is felt in Lena's relationship to Craig, and in Lew's feeling for Clem McNair.[22]

The Big Fellow is more accomplished in handling the romantic part of the plot, which is considerable. Macy Donovan, having risen from the position of water carter for the mines at Golconda to the highest office in his state, now faces opponents in plenty but is well able to hold his own:

> When he rose to his feet in the House they could feel confident that no matter how devastating the attack on the Government had been it would not only be met but repulsed. Even the men who opposed Donovan enjoyed listening to him. Starting in a low guttural voice he would seem to be digging up words with difficulty from a limited store, till gradually a flow of feeling was tapped and they poured from him with the violent rumble of steers through a stockyard gate.[23]

Political opponents try to damage him by reviving an old mining scandal. Surviving that attack proves easier than avoiding a much more damaging interest Macy cannot resist when he pursues an old romance with a sculptress, Neda Brouyet, whom he first met in Golconda. But his wife Kitty continues to be a steadying force, binding together the clan of relatives, including their grown son and daughter. Macy, says John Barnes, is "a figure representative of the contradictions in the human condition"; bluff and hyperenergetic, yet "aware of spiritual yearnings which can never be satisfied."[24]

Somewhat past the midpoint in Palmer's career (1948), Frank Dalby Davison praised him for having "got rid of our national inferiority complex by the difficult though simple-seeming method of dropping it": he "just took Australia for granted—like Lawson and Furphy in their more grown-up moods."[25] Also, Davison felt, the man's versatility was evident in the ease with which he "picks up the Swaynes and their circle with the same ease with which he picks Old Duncan [the Queensland cattleman of *Men Are Human,* 1930] and his children."[26]

The "big fellow" kind of novel is of course part of literature everywhere, especially after World War I. Somewhat of a curiosity in Australian fiction are D. H. Lawrence's two works, *Kangaroo* (1923)—the title is the name given to a powerful labor leader in Sydney—and *The Boy in the Bush* (1924, a collaboration with M. L. Skinner). Kangaroo has much the same charisma as that shown by Palmer's Donovan; Jack Grant of *The Boy in the Bush,* on the other hand, is the central figure of a growth-to-manhood narrative about a British immigrant. When Lawrence had finished his work, "style and atmosphere, except for the Australian colouring that Lawrence took over from Miss Skinner, had become markedly Lawrentian."[27] This included, for the mature Jack, "a rather daring development psychologically," as Lawrence informed Miss Skinner by letter, adding, "You may disapprove." Her disapproval, which she expressed firmly, came too late to allow further rewriting.[28]

Continuing Use of the Convict Era: William Gosse Hay

During much of the nineteenth and part of the earlier twentieth centuries, Australians avoided being too explicit in speaking and writing of the convict era because they felt that the "taint" of convict ancestry would be socially (or politically) ruinous. We have seen, for example, that the chief character in Praed's *Policy and Passion* (1881) was completely destroyed by the revelation of his convict past; and although it was an exciting time to read about, the convicts themselves, and their descendants for a long time, were all but indelibly branded. Thus it continued as a fictional subject, better left that way in the opinion of most citizens not yet ready to make light of "lags" in the family tree. Today it is at least as popular a subject as it was a hundred years ago; and with the approach of a First Fleet bicentennial in 1988, it will no doubt continue so.

Since most—virtually all—convict fiction emphasizes the well-known brutality of the system, it is worth pointing out that life for the transportee was not invariably an endless sequence of horrors, especially in the later years. On one convict ship sailing in April 1852, for example, with upwards of three hundred prisoners, the weekly "Pestonjee Bomanjee Journal," conducted by the ship's surgeon-superintendent, contained poems and essays by the prisoners.[29] Some of the less macabre aspects occur, as well, in the fiction of William Gosse Hay.

The one novel of distinction from Hay's pen is *The Escape of the Notorious Sir William Heans* (1919). In Hay's career as a novelist, it falls midway between his first book, *Stifled Laughter* (1901), and his last, *The Mystery of Alfred Doubt* (1937). By making his convict-hero a drawing-room type, Hay could deal with a different set of circumstances and people than in the chronicles of brutality we have from Clarke or Warung. Through a long, carefully narrated series of cloak-and-dagger episodes, Hay takes Sir William (who was transported for the crime of abduction) through two frustrated attempts at escape, foiled by his adversary and rival at love, a police officer named Daunt, before letting him succeed. "Though [Hay's] moral attitudes make him old-fashioned," says Fayette Gosse, "his unerring eye for detail and quite finicky polish look forward to modern Australian writers such as Patrick White or Hal Porter."[30] Also, she observes, the novel "presents points of view on the prison system, not one opinion," and "gives the reader the task of evaluating situation instead of taking instructions from the author."[31] This passage offers a fair sample of the convict as sophisticate:

Heans put in his eyeglass and leant over on his knee towards him.
"I will tell you," he said, swinging his cane slowly and speaking with a somewhat hectic air, "since you will have me even earthier than it is wise for me yet to believe I am. I was assigned as groom, or (let me be definite) 'pass-holder servant man' to this Charles Oughtryn sixteen months ago. I had been seen in conversation with Captain Stifft, of the schooner *Emerald*, too frequently for the police, and in the end—a humorous end of which you appear to have heard an echo—I was ordered by the police-magistrate to be assigned out as a servant. 'White-fingered men' were not then in demand, but some one told Oughtryn at Fraser's Club, and Oughtryn applied for me. Some time before, he had asked me if I would train his young miss to the

saddle. What would have become of me I don't know, but for this old fellow—himself a freed prisoner—who had often seen me riding for my pleasure. He was jubilant at obtaining for his own what he was pleased to
describe as 'a gentleman with some varnish.' . . .

O'Crone was glaring at him with his bearded face fallen and sinister.

"And now," he said at last, "it is cut and run at the first opportunity."

"And now," echoed the other, tapping his varnished boot with his cane,
"it is cut and run—at the first opportunity".[32]

Perhaps the term *elegant gothic* would best fit both style and plot, and
the period being described as well. All in all, thought R. G.
Howarth, it was "the most successful period novel that it has yet
been our good hap to produce."[33]

The Animal Story

Animal life, considered by itself, has not received from Australian
fiction the same attention as in British or Canadian literature, part of
the reason being environmental. Hard conditions of survival for both
man and beast (whether sheep or cattle) gave consideration for animals—particularly predators like the dingo or competitive pests like
the rabbit (introduced by hunters, not native)—little scope. One notable exception to this generalization is Frank Dalby Davison, in three
separate works: *Man-Shy* (1931), *The Wells of Beersheba* (1933), and
Dusty (1947). The first of these graphically describes the death, by
drowning in a muddy water hole, of an old red cow, then turns to
the fortunes of the orphan calf she has left, the red heifer who fights
her way out of numerous attempts at capture to remain a wild "scrubber"—"one out of the box," one of the branders admiringly calls her.
Davison's sympathy is evident in such a passage as these two paragraphs of comment following a cattle auction:

It matters little to the beast, scrubber or pure-bred, when the sale is over.
Bedevilled and bewildered and aching for the lost freedom of the western
country, they are driven to the slaughter-house. The smell of the blood
strikes terror into them, and their bellowing voices their fear.

The finish comes quickly. A blow that crashes consciousness into darkness; a body still quivering with life, that falls on the blood-slippery floor
of the killing-pen! In a short while, beef-on-the-hoof, gone for ever from the
wild runs of the back country, is beef-on-the-hook—beef for profit! And
that is the destiny of every beast that roams the cattle country—with occasional exceptions.[34]

The man-shy red heifer becomes one of the "occasional exceptions." *The Wells of Beersheba* is the story of men and their cavalry mounts during the Middle East campaigns of World War I. *Dusty,* a dog story, is set again in the *Man-Shy* country but is more complex in its methods, including human tensions.

A 1963 collection of Australian wildlife stories contains some twenty-five writers in all, from colonial narratives through Henry Lawson to the moderns. Among writers contemporary with Davison who have made notable contributions are Henry G. Lamond (*Tooth and Talon,* 1934), Leslie Haylen (*Big Red,* 1953), and Erle Wilson, whose *Corinna* (1953) describes the growth, limited survival, and death of a male Tasmanian wolf dog, named in the title. Corinna is supreme in his own world and for a time able to outwit a shepherd with a kangaroo dog and long-range rifle. Much other animal life is portrayed in the same volume.

Realism and Humor in the 1930s

We have seen that writers like Palmer and Davison were doing some of their best work in the Depression days of the early 1930s. That grim era did not, however, produce a very resolute or extensive fiction of social protest; no Australian Steinbeck arose to produce a *Grapes of Wrath.* Novels such as John Harcourt's *Upsurge* (1934), John Devanny's *Sugar Heaven* (1936), and Leonard Mann's *The Go-Getter* (1942) do give attention to social problems in realistic fashion, paralleling the work of John A. Lee in New Zealand whose *Children of the Poor* (1934) became one of the more enduring documents of the time and region. As Walter Murdoch pointed out in the early 1930s, the material was abundantly present, waiting to be used:

A great though gloomy book will someday be written about the Australian country town of our period. (Henry Lawson, I remember, in one of his short stories, gave us some Dantesque touches.) At its best our country town is a good place to spend a lazy holiday in—to vegetate in, as we say, but to vegetate there all one's life, to become part of the local flora, is an idea from which the mind recoils. At its worst it is what Cobbett was fond of calling the industrial cities of northern England, "a hell-hole."[35]

Until considerably later, however, no novelist of stature seemed ready to approach town life per se.

Humor fared somewhat better in the hands of Norman Lindsay and Lennie Lower. The *Bulletin*, by this time half a century old, had never been intended as light reading, but its editors were always ready to welcome stories with a humorous plot (Henry Lawson's "The Loaded Dog" is a hilarious example), and it abounded in graphic humor of a high order. One of its prize draughtsmen was Norman Lindsay, whose black-and-white drawings appeared throughout many years. Lindsay, one of an extraordinarily talented family, was proficient at whatever he undertook, and throughout a lifetime of ninety years he undertook a great deal. His fiction turned to the world of the young, boys in particular, and in *Redheap* (1930) and *Saturdee* (1933), he gives us early teenage thought and behavior as he knew it in the 1890s. The first of these was assisted into fame through being banned by Australian censors as "indecent and obscene"; it was not admitted into the country (having been published in London) until 1958.[36] From *Saturdee* comes the following somewhat comic-strippish episode:

Bulljo's powers of induction did not require to wait an investigation of action in Waldo, but stamped him into the house, with Waldo pounding after him, mouthing murder. Straightway within there exploded a pandemonium of yells, accusations, poundings, a crash, a bellow, a sharp crack, as of hairbrush hitting a skull, and Waldo burst out of the house again, applying a frantic poultice of friction to his scalp. All in one rush he crammed his pockets with pears, banged three stones at the house and vanished around it with a howl of rage.[37]

Thelma Forshaw, reviewing a reprint in the early 1960s, asks, "Guilty or not guilty of being obsolete?" and concludes that

. . . as we examine the concept of Boyhood he lays before us, the verdict is this: "Age cannot wither him, nor custom stale his infinite variety." He has hit the nail too squarely on the head for that.[38]

Age of Consent (1938) presents a painter, Bradly Mudgett, who seeks solitude in a beach shack on the South Coast (New South Wales) but doesn't get it; instead, all sorts of people show up including Cora, a young woman who becomes his model. Cora's grandmother—typically Puritanical, the embodiment of Lindsay's perpetual Australian adversaries—not unexpectedly makes trouble about this. *Halfway to Anywhere* (1948) returns once more to the theme of boyhood. A later novel, D. E. Charlwood's *All the Green Years* (1965), about adolescence in the 1930s and related in the first person, might be one to read alongside *Saturdee*. Still later, Phil Motherwell's *Mr. Bastard* (1977) deals with childhood and adolescence.

Lennie Lower was a newspaper humorist who published only one book, *Here's Luck* (1930), during his relatively brief life. His work, however, still has admirers—partly, it may be, because it is a link between the anecdotal bush humor of Furphy, Lawson, and Steele Rudd, and later urban humor by such writers as Nino Culotta. Like the cartoonists, Lower enjoyed burlesquing the "Australian legend," as for example in "Down Among the Wombats" which begins:

People who think that there are no more thrills to be had in our great open spaces have not heard anything. Why, only the other day a man was attacked by a six-foot kangaroo in the bush near Corinda, and fought with it for ten minutes. I have similar experiences with wombats. Not dingbats—wombats!

While camped on the side of a small nullah-nullah or waterhole I was startled by a loud roar. With true bushman's instinct I fell into the waterhole, and, on looking around, observed a huge wombat devouring one of my dogs. From tip to tip, its antlers were about eight feet across.[39]

Verbal humor per se has not been a thriving genre in Australian literature after the *Bulletin* days, perhaps because so much humor and irony are distributed among works that for the most part would be considered serious or at least not beneath the notice of literary historians. We shall encounter it again from time to time in the work of such varied novelists as Gavin Casey, Alan Marshall, Tony Morphett, Kylie Tennant, and Randolph Stow, none of whom very often undertakes humorous writing for its own sake. And when we reach the strictly contemporary scene, there will be found a strain quite different from anything seen before, borrowing as it does from black comedy and the theater of the absurd.

Short Stories (1)

The single most powerful early stimulus to the writing of Australian short stories undoubtedly came from the Sydney *Bulletin* at the end of the nineteenth century, but the local tradition had its beginnings far back in the century with John Lang (*Botany Bay,* 1859) and a little later with Marcus Clarke, who wrote about city life and bush life alike. (One of his stories even describes the effects of cannabis.)

The group of women writers including Cambridge, Praed, and Tasma published a great many stories including collections, but nothing to match the *Bush Studies* of Barbara Baynton. Mrs. Aeneas Gunn's *We of the Never-Never* (1908) is actually a series of related autobiographical sketches, but as Green says, "the events and people are re-created rather than described, so that it reads like a novel."[40]

Collection of aboriginal stories and myths was left mostly to later times, but not altogether so; the most important works of Catherine Langloh Parker began appearing in the 1890s. Probably a more comprehensive view of the Australian aboriginal can be achieved, for the average reader, from a group or whole collection of short stories than from novels, unless he reads a great many. A recent collection, *Aliens in Their Land* (1968), subtitled *The Aborigine in the Australian Short Story*, edited and introduced by Louise E. Rorabacher, presents stories from more than twenty writers, many of them novelists. The editor finds, she reports, that whatever the views of the general population may be or may have been toward the aboriginals, the attitude of Australian writers is uniformly sympathetic.[41]

That redoubtable artifact, the *Bulletin* story, may be studied in some detail through a representative collection, *The Bulletin Story Book* (1901). One learns from this collection itself, as well as from numerous discussions of the *Bulletin* school (Vance Palmer's *The Legend of the Nineties* [1954], is one of the best), that the usual story had a strong plot line, with necessarily laconic descriptions and dialogue (required by the editors' insistence on brevity), but occasionally there was room for fantasy, as in the stories of Hugh McCrae. To counter the darkness of Astley's "old regime" tales of the convict era, the *Bulletin* offered Polynesian adventure and romance by Louis Becke and a great amount of humor by Steele Rudd, Lawson (along with bush realism), Furphy (who contributed a few stories only), E. G. Dyson, Kodak (Ernest O'Ferrall), Frank Penn-Smith, and others. On the very strong influence of the *Bulletin*, not invariably for the best, John Barnes writes:

The Bulletin urged writers to be original, and this striving to be original produces frequent melodrama and farce. At least one of the readers of the day complained, in *The Bulletin* itself, of the poverty of imagination which these stories revealed. "The *Bulletin* short story," he wrote, "works up to 'He is dead' or 'He is dead drunk'—this being a generalization of the two favourite climaxes—one some 'novel' accident, the other a 'sell.' " Stephens, it is relevant to note, considered that Archibald's instinct was for melodrama; and certainly, *The Bulletin* stories include a surprising amount of melodrama, partly encouraged, perhaps, by Archibald's advice, "Boil it down," which led his contributors to over-value terseness, and effects of sudden surprise and revelation.[42]

The continuing appeal of the *Bulletin*'s original patterns may be gauged by the republication in 1966 of some twenty-three stories by James Hackston, who doubles as the cartoonist Hal Gye. Douglas Stewart's foreword praises the humor and concludes that, viewed as art, "such masterpieces of satiric comedy . . . will find a lasting place among the best short stories written in Australia."[43]

World War I generated quite a small fictional response, but two collections of stories, William Baylebridge's *An Anzac Muster* (1921) and Harley Matthews's *Saints and Soldiers* (1918), were part of it. Women writers, after the war, again took a leading role, especially in the stories of Katharine Susannah Prichard and Henry Handel Richardson. H. H. R.'s *The End of a Childhood* (1934) contains stories developed through a technique that places her alongside Katherine Mansfield, with characters and episodes also broadly similar in content and tone. E. O. Schlunke's *Stories of the Riverina* (1966) also hark back toward pioneering conditions: these are tales primarily concerned with settlers on wheat or sheep property or in small towns, ranging from hard-working German-bred settlers (the principal figures) to Italian POWs. Sharp (sometimes cruel) humor mingles with gentleness and consideration in Schlunke's depictions of gradual assimilation into Australian culture.

The range of early Australian storywriters is well illustrated in a comprehensive collection, *Short Stories of Australia: The Lawson Tradition,* chosen and edited by Douglas Stewart. Discussion of later writers appears in the concluding section of chapter 4.

Chapter Four
Through World War II

Miss Baker lit a cigarette nervously, looked up and saw him watching her. There was something that had to be said, but she didn't know what it was.

"And what part of Europe do you come from?" she asked, feeling the quicksand underfoot, the waiting bog.

Mr. Lenski glared at her, weighing her. He leant forward, pulled up his shirt-sleeve, mutely extended an arm for her to see, a slight, yellowing arm, the flesh growing flabby and already settling into the creases of old age. He thrust the arm under her nose, held it there so she could see the number, pulled it back, rolled down the sleeve. The effort had tired him, and he allowed his head to sink down a little on to his chest.

"I come from a labour camp," he said. "Anywhere in Europe."

—Lesley Rowlands ("And What
Part of Europe Do You Come From?")

Seeking to understand how Australia continued to reveal itself during the earlier twentieth century as something new both to old and to new Australians (the capitalized name "New Australian" is largely post–World War II), we shall have to look for clues in several directions. First of all is the entry of aliens into the social scene, helping to change it: from them, quite evidently, Australia evoked a strong sense of revelation. But turning back to history through chronicle-type novels was another means of reminding the present generation of how much change there had been and what directions it had taken. This kind of fiction, usually presented in realistic mode, has had a long and distinguished history in Australia. Expatriation provided another perspective, as did limited residence abroad, especially through participation in two world wars. All this will be reflected, variously enough, in the writers and works encountered in this chapter.

Chroniclers: Richardson to Herbert

Some historians of literature regard Henry Handel Richardson as the earliest Australian novelist worthy of note, but such a judgment is undoubtedly too constricted, unhistorical, and oversevere. At the same time, it was made evident in the 1920s that *The Fortunes of Richard Mahony,* a trilogy begun in 1917 and completed in 1929, was the achievement of a new major talent. H. H. R. had already published *Maurice Guest* (1908), drawing upon her own experiences as a music student in Europe but ending the novel tragically, as the Mahony trilogy itself ends. In *Mahony* she used her father's Australian medical career as a model for her protagonist but wove around it the social and commercial scene in and around Melbourne from gold-rush times through the remainder of the nineteenth century, or nearly so. There is a panoramic range of characters from all sorts of pursuits, Mahony meeting many of them as doctor but associated with them through marriage and business ventures as well.

Mahony himself varies both in mood and in the many subjects and objects of a restless life; his "fortunes" are good and bad alike. A typical snap decision on his part—not without parallel among other successful Australians of the day, it should be added—was to "retire" to England, where instead of a warm golden glow of rational culture he finds coldness, snobbery, and both social and intellectual frustration for a man of his inquisitive bent. How much of all this was invention, how much recollection? F. H. Mares insists that *Mahony* is not the unimaginative retelling of H. H. R.'s father's life:

Rather, she chose to subject her imagination to the hardest discipline of all: the discipline of a rigid adherence to fact; and her imagination triumphantly performed the task she set it. She took the whole of one man's life, and without suppression or distortion, imposed on it the order and significance of a work of art.[1]

The wide range of this remarkable trilogy, and at the same time the strict unity within that range, may be viewed in the following two passages:

In a shaft on the Gravel Pits, a man had been buried alive. At work in a deep wet hole, he had recklessly omitted to slab the walls of a drive; uprights and tailors yielded under the lateral pressure, and the rotten earth collapsed, bringing down the roof in its train. The digger fell forward on his face, his ribs jammed across his pick, his arms pinned to his sides, nose and mouth pressed into the sticky mud as into a mask; and over his defenceless body, with a roar that burst his ear-drums, broke stupendous masses of earth.[2]

Thus the shadows deepened. For still some time Mahony contrived to cover, unaided, the few yards that separated bedroom from sitting-room. Then he took to shouldering his way along the walls, supporting himself by the furniture. And soon, even this mode of progression proving beyond him, he needed the firm prop of an arm on either side, was he to reach his seat by the window. Finally his chair was brought to the bedside, and, with him in it, was pushed and pulled by the two women to the adjoining room.[3]

Nearly a thousand pages separate these two passages; yet the firm grasp of the fictional material so evident at the beginning is maintained throughout. There could hardly have been, in the author's mind, any conscious parallelism between the pitiful figure of Mahony in his last days and the digger caught by the cave-in at the gravel pits; yet the pattern of inescapable collapse and submission is strongly evident in both, as is the author's control of language and descriptive detail. It is a superb performance. Speaking a final word on her achievement, Leonie Kramer says that

. . . her searching analyses of human vulnerability, and her grasp of the nature of creative activity lend her novels a special distinction in a literature, which especially at the time she wrote, was for the most part content to exploit the environmental oddities of Australia, and neglected the exploration of those human dilemmas which recognize no geographical barriers.[4]

Later works were less successful. The judgment of Vincent Buckley, a Melbourne critic, on *The Young Cosima* (1939) is severe—"built upon novelese . . . a nonentity"—but justified, at least in comparative terms: this second musically inspired novel is hardly the equal of *Maurice Guest,* and far below the *Mahony* trilogy, the work that best demonstrates that "her power to develop convincing characters within the boundaries of the realistic method remains her chief contribution to Australian fiction."[5]

A second woman writer, whose career as novelist began a few years later with *The Pioneers* in 1915, was Katharine Susannah Prichard. Richardson set her trilogy in Victoria, whereas Prichard chose West Australia, thus recording a later period of development beginning with the gold discoveries of the 1890s at Kalgoorlie-Coolgardie which are explored in three novels: *The Roaring Nineties* (1946), *Golden Miles* (1948), and *Winged Seeds* (1950). In this series, a strong current of trade-unionist political-industrial sentiment imposes itself upon the story, as it does not in most of her earlier works. *Working Bullocks*

(1926) gives us energetic descriptions of timber harvesting in the beautiful *karri* woods of southwestern Australia in and around Karri Creek Mills. The book begins with a scene of bullock driving in the logging country, and as it progresses, we are made to understand that the men, too, might well be called working bullocks; in few novels, from any source, have we quite so realistic a picture of hard work being done. The principal male character, Red Burke, is the exponent of such labor, but has diversions in catching wild horses (brumbies), racing, and other sports. He falls in love with Deb Colburn, whose brother Chris dies in a logging accident while working with Red. The book as a whole provides a record of pioneering families treating their experiences of beauty, loyalty, and joy as well as of hardship and danger. A sense of the intensity of the work and the continuing threat to life is suggested by the response of Deb when she visits a sawmill for the first time:

She had held her breath from the moment iron dogs gripped the log on the truck, rolled it on to the platform and the saw, driven by an engine in a corner of the shed, set its cruel teeth in the raw wood. Then beat and throb of the engine, swiftly flying belts along the roof, attached to the saw, scream and moan of the log as the saw travelled through it, red dust which flew in a spray making the men's figures working at the wedges and saw, dim and unreal, went to her head, made her crazy with fear for them and for it.[6]

Coonardoo (1929) takes its name from its aboriginal heroine, who (not untypically in black-white relationships in Australian fiction) suffers degradation at the hands of ambivalent or frankly brutal white men. The life of a northwestern cattle station is carefully presented, including its decline as drought and gradual failure of nerve take their toll among whites and blacks alike. The final chapter, in which Coonardoo plods slowly back to her deserted home to die, is one of the most famous set pieces in all Australian fiction:

Very thin, and darker than the trees, the figure swayed and drifted, making an arrowy track, as a kangaroo goes to water, across the rough, hard ground, towards the hills. A gin, naked and wasted by disease, carrying her clothes in a little bundle on her back, she stalked on, and on, and on. . . .

Upon arriving she builds a fire, before which she crouches, singing, remembering, dreaming. Finally,

The fire before her had fallen into ashes. Blackened stocks lay without a spark.

She crooned a moment, and lay back. Her arms and legs, falling apart, looked like those blackened and broken sticks beside the fire.[7]

As a contrast with *Coonardoo*, the work of a visiting novelist from Britain, E. L. Grant Watson, is of no little interest. Between 1914 and 1936, Grant Watson published six novels in all after spending eighteen months with an archaeological expedition to the northwest in 1910–11. In the third of this series, *The Desert Horizon* (1923), J. J. Healy observes, "The paradise of the desert becomes a romantic creation to offset the inferno of the city," in which the aborigines have, of necessity, an artificial place:

They [the aborigines] are, in this context, the passive children of a strange Eden. But it is finally an Eden which is not theirs. They indicate the rapport and adjustment that is necessary before "the blue rim of the horizon" can yield up its sense of threat and become a sight of beauty. It is Martin and the shearers, however, "who are the true inheritors of the land. Through them, the soil and the bush which they love will ultimately speak. They are the new lovers of an exceedingly old land, through them it shall become articulate, upon them it puts this claim and this demand." Grant Watson recognizes that the aborigine moves across the same desert land but in a different world. They are present, aloof, strange, coherent. Any accommodation to the land which is an accommodation of self must accommodate the aborigine also. In this sense, the aborigine is meshed inextricably into the self-search of the white Australian. It is not a choice; it is an insistence. As Martin noted of the world into which he was sinking his fences: "these things were harmonious, gendering a sympathy for the brown, nomad people."[8]

Not unlike Henry Handel Richardson, Miss Prichard shows a falling off in later years, but not until after her goldfields trilogy. Here, there is already a heavy inlay of political observation, culminating in a view of the miners in *Winged Seeds* as proletarians under triumphant capitalism. On her political views, Jack Lindsay remarks:

Her work can in no sense be described as an intelligent application of Marxism . . . [but as] a creative development of the Marxist concept of what humanises and what alienates. . . . [This, moreover] could only occur in a country like Australia . . . for only in such a country would it be possible to observe and live through the rapid change from a pioneering man-to-man world into a world of capitalist monopoly.[9]

We may pause briefly, at this point, to note the continuing presence of women writers. During the fifteen-year period between 1925 and 1940, Geoffrey Serle observes, "it would be almost impossible to deny that most of the best novelists were women."

Richardson, Dark, Stead, Prichard, Barnard Eldershaw, Tennant and Franklin were backed by a strong second rank, which included Helen Simpson, Jean Campbell, Henrietta Drake-Brockman and Mary Mitchell; and they were soon to be further reinforced by Dymphna Cusack, Ruth Park and Eve Langley.[10]

When these names are linked with those of earlier women, we do not arrive at quite an unbroken continuity—at least not one of memorable excellence—but we do come close.

M. Barnard Eldershaw was the composite name for Marjorie Barnard and Flora Eldershaw, collaborative authors of a group of varied novels exploring social themes, first through a period novel, *A House Is Built* (1929), which relates the fortunes of a merchant family dynasty set up by a navy quartermaster, James Hyde of Sydney. At the close of this chronicle, Lionel, inheritor of the Hyde fortune, reflects on himself:

The Hydes had always taken the difficult road, they had been builders and makers. Lionel knew that it was not for such as he that his grandfather had striven. . . . He did not belong to the Hydes, and their wealth and power hung on him like a garment that is much too big. He was the mouse that the mountain had brought forth.[11]

Green Memory (1931), also historical (Marjorie Barnard wrote several notable historical and biographical works), is about the goldfields. Barnard Eldershaw's later works depart from the earlier pattern to scrutinize authorship (in *The Glasshouse*, 1936, and *Plaque with Laurel*, 1937) and to imagine a twenty-fourth-century Sydney (historians turned futurists) in *Tomorrow and Tomorrow* (1946). This talented pair formed a team, as the American critic Louise E. Rorabacher has said, to whom "illumination came not alone from any one kind of writing."

It came from the novels—notably the first and last [*A House Is Built* and *Tomorrow and Tomorrow*], but who could forget in *Green Memory* the description of the Rocks in Sydney, in *The Glasshouse* the nostalgic give-and-take of those two exiles, Stirling and the ship's doctor, in *Placque with Laurel* the

Australian countryside between Sydney and Canberra, and the atmosphere of the capital city?[12]

Another novel on somewhat the same theme as *Tomorrow and Tomorrow* at the same time is Mary Mitchell's *Servants of the Future* (1946). She is the author of several other novels and a "unique and poignant book," *Uncharted Country: Aspects of Life in Blindness* (1963), describing what she did in order to be able to continue successfully as a novelist, having resolved "not [to] let any talent . . . corrode into uselessness just because there are difficulties in the way."[13]

Ernestine Hill is likewise part-novelist, part-historian, whose fictionalized treatment of the explorer Matthew Flinders (1774–1814) gives us a story based on fact: *My Love Must Wait* (1941). This novel, vigorously narrated and memorable for its historical verisimilitude, expresses especially in its latter pages a pathos not unlike that of the last novel of the *Mahony* trilogy, *Ultima Thule*. Another historical novel of the same decade, Henrietta Drake-Brockman's *The Wicked and the Fair* (1947) is based on records of Dutch explorations off West Australia in the seventeenth century out of Batavia. After a shipwreck, the captain leaves to seek help, whereupon the survivors come under the tyrannous charge of an official whose misuse of his authority results in sadistic sexual abuse and murder.

Other reconstructions, mingling history and invention, use the stormy times of Governor Darling's term in New South Wales (1825–31), in Colin Roderick's *The Lady and the Lawyer* (1955); the South Australian vineyard country in Nancy Cato's trilogy, *All the Rivers Run* (1958), *Time Flow Softly* (1959), and *But Still the Stream* (1962), and also Colin Thiele's novels and stories; the Broken Hill mining boom of the 1880s in Donald McLean's *The Roaring Days* (1960); and the convict days again—or yet—in Catherine Gaskin's *Sara Dane* (1955) and *I Know My Love* (1962). To these names may be added those of several who have used historical themes in the popular novel (and who quite knows where the "popular" novel leaves off and the "literary" novel begins?) or short fiction: E. V. Timms, author of an Australian saga of many books, James Devaney, Ion L. Idriess, Helen Simpson, G. B. Lancaster (Edith Joan Lyttleton), Roy Bridges, and J. H. M. Abbott.

Brian Penton, newspaperman-turned-author of two-thirds of a Queensland trilogy—*Landtakers* (1934) and *Inheritors* (1936)—begins his chronicle in Queensland in the 1840s by bringing into a very rough-hewn society (ex-convicts and unscrupulous fortune hunters) a young Englishman, Derek Cabell, who survives and is himself heavily influenced by his surroundings. What was said earlier of the world portrayed by Barbara Baynton in *Bush Studies*—the Hobbesian tooth-and-claw world of nature even out-Darwinizing Darwin—applies to Penton with equal force. A reviewer, Keven Margery, sees *Landtakers* as giving expression to "Australian Nietzscheanism or nihilist-vitalism . . . the transporting to, and flowering in, Australia of a certain vigorous under-current of English life."[14] In the closing chapters of the second volume (the two together form a fairly tight unit despite the fact that Penton did not produce his intended three), Cabell has lapsed into senility, with the result that a "superlative comedy" (but still with cruel overtones) is played out: James, the most orthodox and conventional of Cabell's three sons, manages to whitewash his father's reputation into an image of pioneering unselfishness and public spirit. Hadgraft comments:

Part of Penton's motive in writing this volume, one suspects, was a sardonic impatience with public reputations, . . . a sort of debunking of the pioneer legend, as though he had remembered all the foundation stones and obituaries with exasperated patience and then had said to himself: This will show them.[15]

Parallels from other sectors of English writing come readily to mind: Galsworthy's Forsyte novels, for example, Marquand's *The Late George Apley* or Faulkner's Yoknapatawpha world, Mazo de la Roche's extensive Jalna series or the prairie novels of F. P. Grove in Canada, and Nell M. Scanlan's Pencarrow novels in New Zealand.

Eleanor Dark, who began publishing at about the same time as M. Barnard Eldershaw and Penton, has elements of both in her work, at the same time surpassing both. In *Prelude to Christopher* (1933), hereditary insanity dogs a family; and though such a somber pattern is not repeated in her other novels of the 1930s (*Return to Coolami*, 1936, *Sun Across the Sky*, 1937, *Waterway*, 1938), they are at times heavily introspective as well as retrospective (through the use of flashbacks, for example). One other contemporary family novel (*The Little Company*, 1945) appears in the midst of her masterwork, a three-volume historical sequence—*The Timeless Land* (1940), *The Storm of Time* (1948), and *No Barrier* (1953)—dealing with Australian colonial experience from First Fleet days through Governor Macquarie, approximately a quarter-century.

A. Grove Day's recent study of Eleanor Dark speaks of "the melody of her prose," citing a passage from *The Timeless Land* that is part of "a moving tapestry, a panorama of scenes and people that for many readers evokes the best vision of early Sydney":

> Here it was as if the pulse of life in plant, and beast, and man had slowed almost to immobility, taking its beat from the land itself, which had all eternity in which to change. Here life was marooned, and Time, like a slowly turning wheel, was only night and day, night and day, summer and winter, birth and death, the ebb and swell of tides. Nothing showed for the passing of the ages but a minutely changing coastline, an infinitesimal wearing away of mountains, a barely discernible lifting of coral reefs. Still the ancient grass-tree thrust its tall spear towards the sky; still the platypus laid its eggs and suckled its young as it had done in primeval times; and still through the high tops of the gum-trees the blue thread of smoke from the black man's fire wavered into the uncorrupted air. [16]

Describing this writer as "an intellectual romantic," H. M. Green goes on to say that "while in her earlier novels emotion predominates, in the later novels reflection gains upon it, though neither is without elements of the other" and that "as with the typical poet, her emotions are intellectualized and, at the same time her ideas are felt in the blood." [17] Best of all, such feeling is transferred to the reader. That the taste for historical fiction has not entirely waned may be suggested by the appearance in 1979 of *Southern Cross* by Terry Coleman, a British journalist turned novelist, whose work traverses somewhat the same territory as Eleanor Dark's. Bicentennial fiction in the late 1980s, one may safely predict, will give the genre further impetus.

Covering a later time segment, but in some respects hardly less primitive than the earliest days, Rex Ingamells's book, *Of Us Now Living* (1953), reports roughly a century (1850–1950), tracing family backgrounds, touching on convict life, developing personalities through several generations. The aborigines are sympathetically dealt with and enter into the lives of the settlers, several working on the stations. The method uses excerpts from the diary of Miss Singwood, a retired teacher, whose reflections on history and memory include commonplaces such as "How inextricably involved with the Past are the lives of us now living" together with wider ranging ideas:

> What is unique is an *authenticated* Chain of Memory. My investigations with regard to the stories that so occupy me convince me that chains of

memory exist, unsuspected, all around us. Unperceived, their links rust and crumble away; yet, at any moment, if we knew how, apart from happy accident, to pick them up, we could recover for present interest and instruction much of the intriguing vitality of buried generations. Here, I doubt not, could lie a vast new field of historical and sociological science.[18]

The final figure among this large group of chroniclers, writing for widely varying purposes as we have observed, is the redoubtable Queenslander Xavier Herbert. *Capricornia* (1938), together with Prichard's *Coonardoo,* Dark's *The Timeless Land,* and other works such as Ingamells's *Of Us Now Living,* presents a case for the aboriginal as the most abused part of a generally much-abused land. Most of the action takes place in the Northern Territory, where the worst in life is to be expected and more often than not, as Herbert sees things, occurs. The book is crowded with characters and episodes, a thesaurus of outback life, from which emerge a few dominant figures. Herbert's approach to his material resembles, in many ways, that of Fielding or Dickens: fascinated and at the same time outraged by life, he rummages in it with prodigious vigor, never hesitating to let us know what he, as narrator, thinks about what he is narrating. Vincent Buckley sees *Capricornia* as not merely a social document but a metaphysical work, whose author "is concerned not only with the social injustice done to aborigines and half-castes, but with a cosmic injustice done to all men."[19] It "performs among others the important service of putting the central issues of life vividly before us, all the more vividly since it is done with such enormous and comic liveliness."[20] Agreeing with this estimate, Hadgraft calls *Capricornia* "the most readable long novel of importance in Australian literature."[21]

In *Seven Emus* (1959), twenty years and a second world war after *Capricornia,* Herbert still feels that the aborigines have been wronged, but that they are most probably immune to "progress" and/or assimilation. *Soldiers' Women* (1961) is a mixture of comedy (at times even farce) and tragedy, with women inevitably the victims though not always the clowns. *Poor Fellow My Country* (1975), dedicated ironically "to my poor destructed country," is a leviathan novel of nearly fifteen hundred pages structured into three books: (1) Terra Australia, "Blackman's Idyll Despoiled by White Bullies, Thieves, and Hypocrites," (2) Australia Felix, "Whitman's Ideal Sold Out by Rogues and Fools," and (3) Day of Shame, "A Rabble Fled the Test of Nationhood." There is a printed list, almost a catalogue or directory, of principal characters running to seventy-four names, varying both racially and occupationally. For so large a cast, the scenario might seem restricted in time: it is emphatically not a historical novel in the ordinary sense, but rather a study in what Herbert considers loss of national nerve and purpose during the late years of the Depression and onward through World War II. The target of his indignation, as originally in *Capricornia,* is the dispossession of the aborigines and the despoiling of the land (this time by mining), which of course are closely linked. Confronted with all this, critics have not been notably generous; but whether or not *Poor Fellow My Country* is to be written off as a technical failure, it may well continue, like *Capricornia,* to be read for its sheer power to describe both places and actions, to irritate (when irritation may not be an entirely useless exercise), and even to entertain.

Laurie Clancy, writing in *Southerly,* concludes that it must be conceded that *Poor Fellow My Country* is "a very ambitious novel written out of a deep sense of pain and outrage at the failures and abuses of the author's fellow countrymen," but that "the real novel that is buried somewhere inside this one" could never emerge, and that ". . . its status in the country's national literature will in the years to come be primarily that of a curiosity, a kind of literary brontosaurus, *Poor Bugger My Book.*"[22] Not all responses were quite so negative, however; Herbert's fellow novelist Randolph Stow, writing in England, had words of praise for the book.

Expatriate Voice: Martin Boyd

The chroniclers whose works we have just surveyed have lived and written in Australia, for the most part, although some have spent significant periods overseas. (*Capricornia,* for example, was written in London, under quite interesting circumstances, and K. S. Prichard worked there as well in the earliest years of her long career.) But Australian writers, whether at home or abroad, were not deprived of access to new modes and methods. In the 1920s, for example, Chester Cobb was to be found (as an expatriate) experimenting in two novels (*Mr. Moffat,* 1925, and *Days of Disillusion,* 1926) with stream of consciousness as a technique. (But over the years Australians, much like New Zealanders, have been less hospitable to literary experimentation than some of the older, supposedly conservative countries. When in 1944, for example, Max Harris in *The Vegetative Eye* attempted a new fictional mode, he was put down with a satiric severity that possibly discouraged others from trying, very hard, to break the sound barrier for another fifteen or twenty years. Coupled with the Ern Malley poetic hoax and an obscenity trial into the bargain, the literary reception accorded Mr. Harris in the forties began to resemble a convict flogging at Norfolk Island more than what Australians like to call a "fair go." Australian criticism, including some in the later work of Harris himself, can be at times unnecessarily rasping and shrill, in addition to being not invariably well-informed.) Those who remained away long enough to be counted expatriates came to display a different concept of Australia, especially when writing of contemporary or near-contemporary life there.

Martin Boyd left Australia as a young man and lived first in London and afterwards in Rome, paying occasional visits to his homeland. Expatriates have never been very popular with Australians (who resemble Americans in this and a good many other particulars); and Boyd endeared himself even less by supporting the ideals of a natural aristocracy—"civilized" people, frequently religious, wishing to live with independent grace if not necessarily at more than moderate expense in whatever place might suit them. His fictional people do not always achieve this ideal; indeed, many of them rather consistently fail. In *Lucinda Brayford* (1946), for example, which Boyd himself considered his best novel,[23] there is a balanced account. In this four-generation study, Lucinda, a sensitive, beautiful woman from Melbourne, marries Captain Hugo Brayford, an Englishman, and becomes one of the socially elite. She fits into English society well enough, but family misfortunes overtake her: her husband, after his affection to another woman is revealed, is severely wounded and deformed in World War I, after which she takes care of him. Their son, Stephen, is also thwarted in love and is a conscientious objector in World War II, though he assists at the evacuation of Dunkirk. At the conclusion Lucinda finds herself far away indeed from the Australia in which, as a young woman, she was to be found commenting on a man who, unbeknownst to her at the time, was to be her future husband:

"Captain Brayford's awfully funny," she said. "This afternoon he said to me, 'D'you jump wahheah?' I thought 'wahheah' must be a New Zealand dance, so I said we weren't New Zealanders. He said, "Do they jump wah [wire] in New Zealand?' I was terribly embarrassed, but I couldn't help laughing, and he said I must give him two dances to make up for it, and show that I didn't dance like a Maori. But he's taken three. Still, it doesn't matter."[24]

Commenting on the melancholy situation at the close of this novel, Dorothy Green writes:

The final section is, among many other things, a celebration of the spirit of Cambridge and its celestial music of sound and stone, which so moved Boyd while he was writing the novel. Against this background is enacted the drama of the disappearance from public life of those who possess the three convictions which make a true civilization possible: the sense of "trusteeship," of duty to the past and responsibility for the future; the belief that life is meant to be enjoyed and that beauty, both natural and man-made is its chief enjoyment; the faith in the ultimate, if painfully slow, prevalence of reason and justice.[25]

The Langton tetralogy—*The Cardboard Crown* (1950), *A Difficult Young Man* (1955), *Outbreak of Love* (1957), and *When Blackbirds Sing* (1962)—follows various members of the Langton family through eighty years. The first three novels use a narrator, Guy Langton; the fourth is concerned less with the family saga and more with the personal anxieties of its central figure, the pacifist Dominic. Boyd once suggested, as a cover title to the series, the phrase "The Past Within Us," recalling what Ingamells was thinking at about the same time.[26]

Boyd's work has been differently assessed by Australian critics. For Vance Palmer, *Outbreak of Love* was an inaccurate account of Australian society; "Government House society" was not, as Boyd seems to have thought, "a gracious and cultured one." On the contrary, the characters show "a queasy self-consciousness," in which

. . . their brilliant conversation is no more than the twittering of returning tourists in an Orient liner; there is a nostalgic pawing over memories; even the two lovers seem less moved by passion than by sentiment about the places they had once visited in Europe.[27]

Nor was Norman Ashbolt, writing in *Australian Book Review* about *When Blackbirds Sing,* impressed: Boyd's "aims are beyond his abilities," and he "writes far too much about self-centered people, without exposing them for their self-centeredness."[28] Brian Elliott, on the other hand, felt that *The Cardboard Crown* and *A Difficult Young Man* were "reflective and meditative, even ruminative" works which afforded opportunities to see both England and Australia from such perspective. Elliott sees "a certain pattern of evolution in his mastery of subject and style" and calls him, finally, "A novelist of a most sensitive quality."[29]

A Canadian critic, W. H. New, placing Boyd in a group including Hal Porter, Randolph Stow, and Patrick White, emphasizes the religious content of his fiction, revealed as well in his sequence of autobiographical volumes: *A Single Flame* (1939), *Much Else in Italy* (1958), and *Day of My Delight* (1965). "He sees religion," says New, "as an accommodation of man's imperfect nature, an adaptation to this world as much as a guide towards a world to come." The classical tradition in Italy, both religious and secular, attracts Boyd at the same time that he contemplates "the timeless possibilities and pagan soul of the Australian continent"; thus,

The European link is as ineradicable a part of the Australian identity as is the landscape. And because of that implicit connection with the world of linear time, the world of the historically verifiable, life in the new world can never be perfect. The "convict" fact intrudes yet again on the vision of the South Seas paradise, and the pugnacious middle-classness that substitutes for the ideal becomes at once a mask across the face of Australian class tensions and, as Patrick White and Randolph Stow were openly to declare, a tempting invitation into cultural mediocrity. Yet the fact that the *status quo* is preserved also allows the preservation of the knowledge (often unadmitted) of the society's imaginative depths.[30]

Further Expansions of Outlook: War Novels and a Few Others

Two world wars could not fail to produce new areas and modes of thought and feeling for Australian writers, as indeed for those everywhere else, and the uneasy two decades between them included a world depression bringing parallel results. Although the major responses did not come until after World War II, we may end our account, in this chapter, by looking at some war novels marking both ends of the period as well as at certain other works produced in between.

Two novels about World War I have survived as specially notable: Frederic Manning's *Her Privates We* (1930) and Leonard Mann's *Flesh in Armour* (1932). Manning, who died in 1935, served with an English rifle regiment through World War I. His alter ego, at least in some respects, is Private Bourne, who along with all his fellow soldiers is finally a casualty. Battle itself is not the main theme; rather, the emphasis falls on the boredom and personal erosions of military life, and the book is structured to keep this in view. All the maneuvering and pointless busywork, the filth and vermin, the slow degeneration of some men's minds, contrast with the few and short moments of actual battle. During the conversation leading up to the following utterance, the infantrymen are reacting to an order from headquarters forbidding attacking soldiers to stop and help their wounded.

"A don't mind tellin' thee, corporal," said Weeper, again lifting a large, flat hand, as though by that gesture he stopped the mouths of all the world. "A don't mind tellin' thee, that if A see a chum o' mine down, an' a can do aught to 'elp 'im, all the brass-'ats in the British Army, an' ther's a bloody sight too many o' 'em, aren't goin' to stop me. A'll do what's right, an' if a know aught about thee, thal't do as A do."[31]

Stephen Murray-Smith, who calls the novel "a profoundly democratic book," observes that the author's resolute objectivity—as filtered through Private Bourne, the Australian volunteer who might be termed a "democratic aristocrat"—corresponds with the objectivity of war itself, which renders it all the more horrible and in fact insane. However,

Manning's almost fatalistic acceptance of the horror of it all doesn't prevent him painting some telling pictures of the officers, old and fat and short of breath; or of pointing out that "all responsibility, for the errors of their superior officers, is borne eventually by private soldiers in the ranks"; or of remarking on the side that what the British Army needs to ginger it up is a few thousand Australians in the ranks. Manning himself said that his concern was mainly "with the anonymous ranks," and it is like a breath of fresh air to see the British "officer and gentleman" class treated, for a change, with something of the laconic superciliousness with which representatives of this class normally write of the "other ranks."[32]

Leonard Mann, like Manning, was a soldier in World War I but attached to an Australian infantry battalion. *Flesh in Armour* ("the flesh of each soldier enarmoured itself" with the necessary virtues of warfaring) presents, as does *Her Privates We,* the viewpoint of the common soldier, and there are slaughter scenes here too (as no World War I novel could readily avoid), but the battlefront activities are contrasted with scenes on leave in London—somewhat after the rhythm of Hemingway's *A Farewell to Arms,* including even a tragic romance not quite like Hemingway's but broadly similar in its urgencies and in the way it alternates with military affairs. As for judgments on the war itself, says Green,

The impression made on them by official England, cold, formal, condescending, as distinct from private individuals, who are friendly enough, is exemplified in the entertainment of "other ranks" by the duchess in the Lower Servants' Hall; and the widespread distrust of the British generals and staffs, Blount's refusal to accept promotion from the ranks for the reasons he gives, the casual "affairs" of men segregated from almost all womenfolk: all these, with the final quotation from Monash, go far beyond individual and platoon and shadow forth better than any other novels the characteristics and experiences of the ordinary members of the first A.I.F.[33]

Mann's other novels include a much-praised crime story, *A Murder in Sydney* (1937), *Mountain Flat* (1939) which is centered upon a land dispute, and *Andrea Caslin* (1959). The heroine of the latter novel, who grows up under privations in a country town near Melbourne during the closing years of the nineteenth century, becomes resolutely amoral. After the birth of her illegitimate son Adrian, in Sydney, she enters business and by 1913 (the end of Part II), has become wealthy. In Part III Adrian's growth to maturity, Andrea's great love for him, and his death are recounted; at the end, Andrea is alone and feeling deeply her loneliness. Similarly, postwar society provides the background for Dal Stivens's *Jimmy Brockett* (1951), a first-person-plus-documents narrative which paints, ironically, the "portrait of a noble Australian." Jimmy, not unlike Andrea and other go-getters of the age, beats his way to the top only to find the view an empty one.

The democratic spirit shown in the war novels, contrasting with growing inequalities at home, is paralleled later, just after World War II, in a novel by Alan Marshall. Although Marshall's most appealing work is his serial autobiography, his one long work of fiction, *How Beautiful Are Thy Feet* (1949), yields realistic description of home-front work in a shoe factory not very much different from industrial work thirty or forty years earlier. For example:

There are four of you in the team . . . side by side you stand . . . the pace maker is on your left . . . what he puts on, you pass on with something added . . . for there is the toe piece to be put in and a few more tacks . . . and you can only work while the sole leather is mellow and damp . . . and they have to be second lasted right side out before the knock-off bell . . . so keep up with the pace maker on your left or out you go . . . and he's fast . . . he's a picked man . . . and you've got to be fast too.[34]

Between wars, Australia (like New Zealand) began developing responsibilities of her own in the Pacific, including administration of

New Guinea and assistance to other Pacific territories and emerging nations. The experience of one Australian who found himself teaching for several years in the Philippines, T. Inglis Moore, resulted in an early exploration, via fiction, of that part of the world by a non-Filipino. Of Moore's *The Half Way Sun* (1935), Green's semi-prophecy that, as "the first Australian novel to be set in an Eastern country and written from the point of view of its inhabitants," it "blazes a track that may become a road,"[35] has not quite been ful-filled; Australians have not yet written extensively about the Orient or on Oriental themes. All the more credit, then, to the author who nearly a half-century ago used Philippine history as the background for his hero Kalatong, whose life and death are sympathetically and graphically presented.

World War II produced its fictional response in larger measure than World War I as well as sooner, much of it related to campaigns in the Pacific and to captivity in Japanese prison camps. T. A. G. Hungerford's *The Ridge and the River* (1952) is set in New Guinea and deals with one section of men and their patrols. The race question is not much handled (in contrast with later New Guinea novels), though one half-caste character, Malise, is presented as "hateful as possible at all times."[36]

Short Stories (2)

In the first section of this continuing brief survey, *Short Stories of Australia: The Lawson Tradition* was cited as a comprehensive guide to the early period. These stories more often than not, it was found, were closely related to the land: they came out of a time when the towns and cities did not contain, as now, an overwhelmingly large portion of the population. By contrast, the companion volume *Short Stories of Australia: The Moderns,* shows considerably less than half its stories set in the country or the bush, and most of these are not painstakingly local. "Becoming more cosmopolitan," says the editor, Beatrice Davis, "the modern short story is often no longer unmistak-ably Australian as Mark Twain's stories are unmistakably American and Turgenev's unmistakably Russian."[37] Shifts in form and tone (e.g., from conquest of environment to personal relations; "mateship" and social comedy to loneliness and individual tragedy; cruelties of the convict system to cruelties of the industrial system) do not be-come abundantly apparent until after the 1940s. The "Lawson tradition" had pervaded the popular mind well down into the 1920s and 1930s and even beyond, although the new voices of Prichard, Davison, and Palmer had begun to be heard. On the special topic of aboriginal life probably a more comprehensive view can be obtained, for the average reader, from a group or whole collection of short stories than from novels, unless he reads a great many.

The range in style is so wide among nearly any set of modern writers (Australian or otherwise) that a series of illustrations is likely to seem unnaturally restricted; but the reader will be able to judge for himself, from the following half-dozen samples, how fundamentally different from one another a geographically homogeneous group can be. Beginning with the broken, reportorial rhythms of vernacular speech in Dal Stivens (or Gavin Casey, to name one alternative choice that might have been made), we move to the simple, direct statement of fact in Peter Cowan (or Alan Marshall) and onward to the poetic rhythms of Judith Wright (or David Campbell). Close attention to sensuous detail is apparent in John Morrison (or Cecil Mann); symbolism appears in Douglas Stewart (or Patrick White); and finally, humor/irony in Thelma Forshaw (or Margaret Trist). The work of the most recent writers to appear (in the 1960s–70s) is discussed in chapter 6.

Dal Stivens, "The Pepper-Tree"

I read over her elbow. There was only one page. There was nothing about the pepper-tree. Dad was well and making money but he was thinking of returning soon. Only a few lines.

I couldn't understand it.

On the next Tuesday there was no letter. Nor on the Wednesday. On the Thursday my father came home. He turned up at breakfast-time. He gave us a surprise walking in like that.[38]

Peter Cowan, "The Tractor"

He seemed to step backwards. His movement was somehow liquid, unhuman, and then she thought of the natives she had once seen in the north, not the town natives whose movements had grown like her own. But with a strange inevitability he moved like an animal or the vibration of the thin sparse trees before the wind. She did not see him go. She looked at the boles of the trees where he had stood, and she could hear her own sobbing.[39]

Judith Wright, "The Ant-Lion"

In their minds the ant and its arena of battle enlarged, filled the whole world. Under the sand at the pit-bottom crouched the lion, big as a real lion, waiting for the ant to slide down a little farther. But this one was so big, bigger than the ant-lion itself. Max said, "Now we'll see some sport."[40]

John Morrison, "Goyai"
The air became cool, and the dry-sweet smell of living scrub gave place to an odour of rotten wood tinged with eucalyptus. The deep car ruts in the track lost themselves on a hard sour soil littered with bark and dead leaves, sprinkled with faded sundews, and blotched with patches of moss that had withered in the heat of summer. All the trees staggered northward as if violent winds often blew here. Cinnamon bracket fungi glowed on trunks charred by bushfires and ravaged by disease.[41]

Douglas Stewart, "The Three Jolly Foxes"
Yet it might, indeed, be a mad fox who thinks he can catch Joe Packet asleep. Joe is like a fox, too; he lies snug with his vixen in the warm burrow of the bed, but all night long he leaves his mouth out in the paddock to catch the rabbits; his spare mouth, his dozen spare mouths, all gaping, waiting, with sharp steel teeth. Joe Packet has caught two rabbits while he sleeps. Broken, they lie in his spare steel mouths—fast shut these mouths are. How warm, how appetising they smell! How inviting is the thought of pink flesh under that soft grey fur! The red fox lolls his tongue. He whines with pleasure.[42]

Thelma Forshaw, "The Wowser"
Then from the tree there thrust a delicate new branch, as I felt born in me a quick revolt, a refusal to be drawn down into the Halloran underworld; but, more than that, a sure divining-rod tremor towards other magics.

I put the cup down. "I think—I might like—looking at things—the way they are." The mint-new heresy came faltering, but once said, was as palpable as the stake thrust through the heart of a witch. I smiled timidly to soften it.

Auntie Dee stared at me, aghast, gorgeously scornful. She levelled at me the whole ethos of a clan.

"You bloody little wowser," she cursed. "*You'll* never be one of us."[43]

Chapter Five
Postwar: Exile and Hope

Was Ireland the "old sow that eats her farrow"? There is about Australians something uncomfortably Irish. In London, Australians congregate and talk about Australia, compulsively, with derogation, with contempt and love or with love and contempt. In Australia, Australians talk about England—with indignation and yearning. We have not yet realized that England is not what we imagine her still to be; we have not yet discovered that we are free to be British or not, as we choose. We are caught up in the old nineteenth-century split of consciousness, the stunned shock of those who cross the seas and find themselves, as the Australian ballad puts it, in "a hut that's upside down."

—Judith Wright (1961)

The Australian critic A. A. Phillips speaks of "an Australian way of writing English." Does this mean only language, in the phonetic and lexical sense of an Australian variety of English ("Strine" or some other descriptor), or something else? Questions like these can yield us widely separated answers. A whole large *Dictionary of Austral English* (Austral meaning Australia and New Zealand) was published as early as 1898, but we may be reasonably sure that Mr. Phillips's phrase does not refer to linguistic variation, or not at least to that alone. Closer to his meaning may be the idea that an Australian "way" of writing is the use of English—with some minor linguistic differences between Australian and British or American English—to interpret the country and its people. That is the sense in which it has been taken here, and from what is to be said the reader may judge for himself how far the process has gone. Since the end of World War II, writing in English throughout the British Commonwealth and elsewhere has shown a phenomenal growth, which in itself is a factor in helping the language consolidate its position—not to "standardize" itself in accordance with the dictates of an official academy but nevertheless to ensure that a worldwide audience will continue to read and enjoy English writing.

If language is becoming less a problem, however, the perennial difficulty of the writer's market still remains. This has been stated plainly, with figures, in the recent *Australian and New Zealand Writers Handbook,* under "Fiction," by a literary agent, Tim Curnow:

> A writer of quality fiction in Australia and New Zealand has a special marketing problem. By "quality" I mean fiction whose aim is to do more than just entertain. He must publish to survive and to achieve any real success, in other than Australian and New Zealand terms, he must publish in London or New York. Ignoring the jibe that publication in London gives the "colonial" writer the feeling of having "made it," there are good economic reasons for these writers to continue to look to London and New York for publication. The market for fiction in Australia and New Zealand is so small as to be, in most cases, uneconomical for a publisher with no more market than this at his disposal. An average print run for a piece of fiction in Australia and New Zealand would be 2–3000 copies. If the book sold for $4 and the royalty for the author was 10% he could expect $800–1200 if the book sold out. It must also be remembered that it could take five years to sell out.[1]

All this reminds us that hope and exile, the twin themes of all Australian literature, as Judith Wright sees it, still commingle in the outlook of Australian writers.

Continued Story: Aboriginals and Outbackers

For many years, well into the twentieth century, the *Bulletin* carried on its masthead the slogan "Australia for the White Man" (emphatically not the "White Person"); and although the "White Australia" policy it espoused has taken its time in disappearing, it is now proportionally more history than fact. That does not mean there is total integration and equal opportunity between "black-fellers" and "white-fellers," but the trends at least have been set in that direction. In Cecil Mann's *Venus Half Caste* (1963), for example, both principal characters, male and female, are part aboriginal, and numerous other examples are to be encountered. Along with the publication of fiction and other works by aboriginals themselves has come an effort to record actual personal experience—not altogether a new idea, of course, but with improved recording apparatus more effectively pursued. One recent result is *The Two Worlds of Jimmie Barker* (1977), a study of transitions during the lifetime of a man in his seventies, in his own words.

Recalling what was said in the preceding chapter about the treatment of such matters by Prichard, Herbert, Ingamells, and others, we may refer again to *Coonardoo,* written more than fifty years ago, not only to show what then was a massive wall of prejudice or indifference but to suggest what still is an unresolved social difficulty. Part of a conversation in that novel pinpoints the formidable problem of reaching a rational understanding between whites and aboriginals. When Mollie Watt is told by Saul Hardy that "no black ever did to a white man what white men have done to the blacks," she ("Coming from one of the coastal towns, she had acquired the belief that it was a divine right of white men to ride rough-shod over anything aboriginal which stood in their way") replies in amazement: "But Mr. Hardy . . . the abos are filthy and treacherous. I thought you had no time for them." He stares at her incredulously.

> Hugh stared at Mollie too. He did not know why she had interrupted. She knew nothing about the black really. She had wished to assert herself, he decided. She often spoke like that quite irrelevantly and off the subject, in a way which made you hopeless of reaching her mind, combating what she had said.
> "No, girl," he said quietly, "they're not treacherous—except when they've been treacherously dealt with. And filthy? You never saw a wild black look as dirty as a native about the towns. And cripes, when Coonardoo's done up Warieda's white moles [moleskin trousers], you'd hardly call him filthy, would you?"[2]

That there *is* as well as *was* unresolved difficulty may be learned from a comment by Marjorie Barnard on a novel by Joe Walker, *No Sunlight Singing* (1960): "Almost all the aborigines are drawn as gentle, good, long-suffering, brave. The whites, almost without exception, are brutal, lecherous, and hard-hearted."[3] This criticism might also be applied to much of the later work of Xavier Herbert. Clearly, we can still find, in some places, more propaganda than art. But aboriginal culture today is taken seriously: painting, dancing, storytelling (both religious and secular)—and (of necessity) tennis! Among the collectors and interpreters of aboriginal legends are the fiction writers Alan Marshall (e.g., *Ourselves Writ Strange,* 1948) and Roland Robinson, author of *Legend and Dreaming* (1952), *The Feathered Serpent* (1956), and later works. Books such as these relate in one way or another to a movement focused in South Australia and extending from the late 1930s into the 1950s, known as Jindyworobak (from the aboriginal word meaning "join, link up"). Like many other movements of its kind, it generated thought waves that continued to vibrate after its launchers were gone, or at least dispersed and forgotten as Jindyworobaks per se. Rex Ingamells, its leader who died early in an accident in 1955, wrote one novel, *Of Us Now Living* (1952), which we have already considered. His chief work, however, was done in verse and criticism. His *Conditional Culture* (1938), which pleads for what we might today term an ecology-oriented national literature, was the manifesto of the movement; the linking up emphasized by the name was between man and environment, for which the aboriginals were a prototype.

The far western outback (which we will encounter again in the fiction of Randolph Stow) is the scene of Mary Durack's *Keep Him My Country* (1956). Here, on Trafalgar Station, white and aboriginal cultures collide when the manager, Stan Rolt, becomes attached to an aboriginal girl, Dalgerie, and yet tries to avoid remaining on the station. Also in her *Kings in Grass Castles* (1959), a sociobiographical saga of the family from which she is descended, Mary Durack writes with special authority about West Australia. In one of her stories, "Pilgrimage," a very old aboriginal man, ill and sensing that his life is nearly over, is impelled to seek out a holy place for whatever final word might come, through him, to his people from the spirit world. After a painful effort, he reaches his destination, pauses, and waits for the enlightenment which he fears may be too long delayed for him to receive it. Night comes, and with it the message:

Breathlessly he listened, for now at last the Wondjina spoke of his people, spoke of them as they had been in olden days, living in thought and deed within the close-knit pattern of the law, rich in a faith that made them a part of all creation. It spoke of them as they were now, the wandering remnants of broken tribes, living on sufferance in the country of their forefathers, the spark of faith too feeble in their hearts for the dreaming of spirit children that became men.

"Am I not to sing them, then?" the old man asked, the tears hot on his shrunken cheeks.

"Sing them," said the Wondjina. "Sing them the spirit of life with your last strength, and they will dream again."

The old man raised himself, trembling now with the weakness of his starved, emaciated body, from which in his ecstasy he had drained the life blood onto his stones. The spirits bore him no farther now than the entrance to the cave, through which he saw the rugged outlines of his "little country" in the white radiance of the moon, and there he sang—or so it seemed to him, though no sound came from his lips. A dark shape swooped and hovered towards him, and as the strong wing brushed his cheek he knew by its pungent odour that it was [his dream totem,] a flying-fox.

"I know you, brother," he whispered and then its shadow passed across the moon and the world grew dark.[4]

Tom Ronan's fiction—*The Vision Splendid* (1954), *Moleskin Midas* (1957), and other novels—combines many of the elements typical of the pioneering cattle station, as well as the extremes. Much of what is said about the men who opened up the country remains at least partially true:

"They had a tough spin. They gave up everything that civilization values for the sake of extending a civilized way of life and all the reward that most of them got was a fatal dose of fever, or a spear through their kidneys while they were asleep."[5]

By contrast, when World War II sent the price of beef sky-high, another speaker summed things up like this: "I don't know how the fighting men are doing, but there's a lot of other people having the time of their lives."[6] And in the figure of Tony Yates of *Moleskin Midas,* the rough-and-tumble squire of holdings in outback Queensland, Ronan portrays the epitome of what it took to survive in the cattle business.

Another side of the question, one that we encounter very early in Australian history and also very late, is the attempt by public officials to maintain justice for the aboriginals and half-castes. F. B. Vickers, in *No Man Is Himself* (1969), develops a situation in which an officer named Quinton, in charge of native welfare, has established quite good relations with the natives as well as among his staff, but feels nevertheless that he has failed in his job as well as in his personal life. In the isolated small town where he is quartered, irregular social situations develop and gossip is widespread. The "right" people get away with virtually anything. In the following passage, Quinton is making a visit to an aboriginal camp:

Only the old folk and the children lived permanently in the headquarters camp; and they, recognizing Quinton and Somerset as friends, gathered round them eager to shake their hands in welcome. And while the doctor asked this one and that one about that fella sore leg or aching bingy, others among the old folk urged their friend Arthur not to worry "'bout that fella Ian. Yarri fix'm that fella," they said. "Yarri him law-giver. Him talk'm-up

proper that feller white law-giver." Quinton had to smile. He would have
liked to have heard Yarri debating points of moral law with Sherwood.
Though just as well it would never happen, he thought, or Sherwood would
be likely to have that coronary that would take him off the bench.[7]

(In contrast, one of Vickers's later novels, *Without Map or Compass,*
1974, takes place in the author's native England where a boy grows
up, as the title suggests, amid the confusions and frustrations of poverty at the turn of the century. As he leaves for Australia, his mother
speaks hopefully about the life he may have a chance to lead there
and pleads, "Don't let it be all brass.")[8]

Donald Stuart of West Australia has written consistently about aboriginal people and their problems since his first novel, *Yandy* (1959).
Reviewing this book, John Barnes wrote:

Although the narrative flags in places, Stuart does capture the spirit of the
natives in their struggle against white oppression and exploitation. Stuart is
uncompromisingly on their side, but his portrayal of the white men is not
coloured by his own feelings. Stuart succeeds in giving the effect of truthful
reporting, because he is able to sustain the aboriginal manner and point of
view.[9]

Yaralie (1962) is told from the viewpoint of a mixed-blood aboriginal
girl who fights off the "whitefellers" to wait for a man "of her own
people" and at the end is serenely expecting his child. The *"real* people of the Nor-West," Yaralie believes, will be mixed-bloods like
herself, not Europeans. Between *Yandy* and *Yaralie,* Stuart published
The Driven (1961), in which the central event is a cattle drive in
Northwest Australia of the 1930s. In addition to collections of stories, the 1970s have seen the publication of Stuart's *Ilbarana* (1971),
relating the growth of an aboriginal boy to manhood and into a position of responsibility and tribal authority. *Prince of My Country*
(1974)—the first in a projected series of six novels to be called, col-
lectively, *The Conjurer's Years*—is another growing-up story, this one
of a half-caste, Davey Redman, maturing and learning the art of station management in the Northwest. In this passage, Davey is rumi-
nating on the hard fact of a current drought:

He shakes his head, feeling the idea of a drought closing in on him, feeling
the idea settling itself in his thinking, crowding in, pushing out all thought
of work. . . . Can a man lay hands on drought and bend the red marauder

to breaking point? Can hands, strong as steel traps, cunning with all craft so patiently taught, so willingly learned, hands backed by strength of arms and deep-muscled back and tireless legs; hands; he holds them in front of him, and looks at them, his eyes hot with this new bewilderment; hands, inches across, inches long, in a country of hundreds of miles; can hands, however strong and able, handle a drought, bring forth feed without rain, put flesh on the ribs of wasting cattle, turn the years faster, change the slow progression of the months and the years, make the land wholesome again as it had always been in his father's time? He knows now that he is . . . minute, insignificant, in the face of the hot dry days and nights, the dry weeks, the months without rain, the years.[10]

This leads him onward into a reflection on the work of termites building their cities—for what?

Before turning to a novel by an aboriginal himself, we may note a few other titles that indicate the continuing use of the outback theme by Australian writers: Lyndon Rose, *Country of the Dead* (1959), Frank Kellaway, *A Straight Furrow* (1960), Nene Gare, *The Fringe-Dwellers* (1962), John Patrick, *Inapatua* (1964), Max Brown, *The Jimberi Track* (1966), John McGarrity, *Once a Jolly Black Man* (1973), and David Ireland, *Burn* (1974). Nancy Cato and Vivienne Rae Ellis present in *Queen Trucanini* (1976) a fictionalized but extensively researched biography of the woman who died in 1876 as the "last of the Tasmanians." Her death is narrated as follows:

"Soon me never wake up no more," she told Mrs. Dandridge. "Missus, you look after mine little bird, give-im your son. What you do without Trucanini, Missus? You all alone too."

"You stay in bed today, dear, if you're not feeling the best," said Mrs. Dandridge comfortingly. "I'll get you your lunch on a tray." She did not believe in these premonitions.

Early in the evening Trucanini gave a scream. She held out her arms as Mrs. Dandridge came rushing in, alarm on her face.

"Missus! Missus! Wurrewah catch me. Wurrewah bin catch me!"

Mrs. Dandridge gripped her hands, but she sank back unconscious, her eyes rolled up in her head. Her voice had been full of fear. The spirits of the departed ones had come for her as she knew they would.[11]

Also on the last days of the Tasmanian aborigines is Robert Drewe's *The Savage Crows* (1976): the phrase *savage crows*, originally applied to blacks by whites, in this account far better fits the whites. And with Donald Stuart's West Australian novels might be compared Richard

Beilby's *The Brown Land Crying* (1976), on the deteriorating Myunga tribe living near Perth, told through two half-caste characters: Milton Odel, an ex-prisoner, and Myra Colton, a young prostitute looking for the good things of life.

Although these novels are not uniformly and completely depressing, it might not be altogether inappropriate to recall Thomas Hardy's melancholy observation that "happiness is but the occasional episode in a general drama of pain." Countering that impression—in the realm of the imagination, at least—is the famous fictional half-caste Inspector Napoleon Bonaparte in the detective novels of Arthur Upfield. One of these, *Man of Two Tribes* (1956), will serve as a sample. In this story, Myra Thomas, following her acquittal of the crime of murdering her husband, disappears from a train crossing the vast Nullarbor Plain in Southern Australia. With two camels and a dog, Bony sets off into the desert, not only to find Myra Thomas, but to become imprisoned for a time with her and two male murderers, one of whom is already a corpse. The return trek gives us a vivid picture of the vast, desolate country, and the solution inspires admiration for the writer as well as for his hero. Toward the end, the detective rises to eloquence in discouraging a companion from further searching for a man still missing:

"Not now, Clifford. We're on the Nullarbor. Not in, but on Australia, the real Australia known by the aborigines, the old time sundowners, the stockmen and waifs like us. For people in cars who follow the roads, for politicians who come inland only when winter coolness is here, Australia puts on a disguise. You and I see Australia without any disguise, see Australia as it really is. You have a great deal to be joyful about.

"Come on, lift your feet. That's better. You will come to love Australia, as I do. You have to get down on your stomach, press your face into the sand and against the hot gibbers, smell the land and feel through your empty belly its closeness to you, woo it with a voice clogged by lack of saliva. And then, Clifford, as with many men, this naked fair Australia will become the great love of your life."[12]

Wild Cat Falling (1965), by Colin Johnson, is the first novel to be published by an aboriginal writer. The book's three divisions mark points in an only too familiar cycle: I, "Release" (from prison); II, "Freedom" (of a limited kind); and III, "Return" (to prison). After reviewing her associations with Colin Johnson, Mary Durack comments in her foreword:

The honesty of his approach floodlights a sinister and dangerously expanding area of the post-war world that few outsiders can begin to understand. His "make-believe-they-are-alive kids," convinced that they have plumbed experience and added up the sum of life, haunt a juke-box limbo of abysmal boredom, their only aim to flout accepted morals and behaviour and to provide themselves by theft and violence with the ritual trappings of their cult. [13]

This leads her to conclude that the story is "an unconscious appeal and an imperative challenge to the society that breeds his kind." [14] Another commentator, Derek Whitelock, adds to an otherwise enthusiastic review this cautionary paragraph:

It is, of course, a splendid thing that a writer of Aboriginal blood has at last appeared to voice the degradation of his people. We have had it coming for a long time. But it will be deplorable if *Wild Cat Falling* is a success, not because of its intrinsic merit, but because the ancestry of its author is used as a gimmick. I suspect that the latter will happen: the literary bleeding hearts will seize on it, just as the Edinburgh bon ton once vapoured about a ploughboy—Robert Burns—writing verse, and as English gentility was diverted to learn that a lunatic farm labourer, one John Clare, was actually writing poetry. [15]

Healy's recent work (1978) on the aborigine in Australian literature from the beginnings to 1975 provides the opportunity of examining, both in critical depth and considerable narrative detail, this topic that continues to occupy Australians writing in all the literary genres. Current novels include Christine Townsend's *Travels with Myself* (1976), which touches on aboriginal urban life, and Thomas A. Roy's *The Curse of the Turtle* (1977) about Queensland aboriginals.

The Ultimate Outback: New Guinea

Before Papua New Guinea recently (1973) undertook independent self-government, Australia had been the administrative authority. World War II, of course, brought soldiers and airmen from literally everywhere into the island to repel the advance of the Japanese, and after the war there was nothing even barely resembling the somnolent prewar times: an insistent independence movement, troubles with Indonesia over West Irian, "Cargo cult" disturbances, and much else had to be faced. Through all this there began to emerge what today is already a surprisingly extensive literature associated with New Guinea which is still increasing. First came war novels: Peter Pinney's *Road into the Wilderness* (1952), for example, or Lawson Glassop's *The Rats in New Guinea* (1963), together with Hungerford's *The Ridge and the River* (1952), mentioned in chapter 4. Edward Lindall's *A Time Too Soon* (1967) and G. C. O'Donnell's *Time Expired* (1967) are stories about Cargo cults, with tensions written even into the titles. A Polish-English writer, Lesek Szymanski, in 1967 published in London *On the Wallaby Track,* consisting of three novelettes and a story set in Australia and New Guinea. Then in the 1970s appeared Ian Downs's *The Stolen Land* (1970), in which black-white friendship turns to violence of politics; Vincent Eri's *The Crocodile* (1971), the first novel to be published by a New Guinea writer; and in the same year, Maslyn Williams's sardonically titled *The Benefactors: A Novel of New Guinea Conquest.* More native writing appeared in a 1972 collection, *The Night Warrior and Other Stories from Papua New Guinea,* by a dozen different authors, and in the same year, John Bailey's *The Wire Classroom* described the crack-up of an Australian teacher in the tropical bush. From 1974 there is Geraldine Halls's *The Voice of the Crab,* a cult thriller about a small group of outriders living on Kipi, an imaginary island strongly reminiscent of Papua New Guinea of the 1950s. Paulias Matane's *Aimbe the Pastor* (1979) uses its central figure to explore the total history of New Guinea as a developing nation.

Australians have written fiction about lesser Pacific islands as well, and about Pacific islanders "blackbirded" to the sugarcane plantations of Queensland; Nancy Cato's *Brown Sugar* (1974) is a recent title, but the tradition goes all the way back to the turn of the century with Louis Becke and others. Nancy Phelan's *Serpents in Paradise* (1967) describes exploitation of the hypothetical Peaceful Islands by a swarm of whites in the Pacific Islands Development League—satiric acronym, PIDL. One needs to read New Zealand fiction as well—late works, including novels by Polynesian New Zealanders—to enlarge one's view of the South Sea Island world, now far more in the realm of realism than of romance.

New Australians

Among host nations to the many millions of refugees after World War II, Australia was one of the leaders. Her Central European and Southeast European immigrant population increased dramatically both in the cities and the countryside, adding much-needed manpower which was actively recruited to make up for natural shortages owing to falling birthrates during Depression years. Writing of the comparative effects wrought by massive immigration into the United States and Australia, Rorabacher states:

> Again the younger sister relives the experience of the elder. The United States had received immigrants in large numbers throughout her national history, but only in the late nineteenth and early twentieth centuries, when the character of her newcomers shifted from northwestern to southeastern Europeans, did assimilation become a serious national problem. And not until a half century later with these waves of postwar New Australians (various, but predominantly non-British) did Australia, whose early migrants had been even more homogeneous than those of the United States, begin to feel the real stresses and strains of growth by melting pot.[16]

Immigrants figure prominently in the several novels set in Australia by the British writer Nevil Shute as well as in the short stories discussed at the end of this chapter.

One of the most prolific writers among a growing number with immigrant backgrounds is David Martin, originally from Budapest. His earlier novels and stories, from the 1940s and 1950s, contain chiefly European characters although one, *The Stones of Bombay* (1950), is set in India. Having migrated to Australia in 1949, Martin produced in 1962 *The Young Wife,* a story of marital jealousy involving Anna and Yannis Joannides, in which the innocent Anna is murdered by Yannis. This novel recalls also Hugh Atkinson's *The Reckoning* (1965), describing the search for a Polish farmhand who has murdered his boss's wife and fled to the bush. *The Hero of Too* (1965), by contrast, is not about immigrants, or at least recent ones, seeing that *Too* is short for *Tooramit,* a Victorian wheat-belt town on the Vossler Highway (named for an eccentric German explorer—a sendup for Patrick White) which in 1950 is celebrating its seventy-fifth anniversary. We learn more about the local bushranger celebrity Dick Grogan (alias Ned Kelly?) than romance really wishes to know, as well as about a famous Australian painter who has chronicled his exploits. *Where a Man Belongs* (1969) narrates the wanderings in Europe and Asia of a Jewish writer from Melbourne, Max, and a similarly aging Aussie named Paul, who at fifty-nine sets out in search of romance or at least sympathetic female companionship, neither of which is to be found.

A translated author, Herz Bergner, produced two novels in Yiddish about Jewish refugees: *Between Sea and Sky* (1946), in which refugees from Poland are loaded onto an old Greek freighter making for Australia, and *Light and Shadow* (1963), also about a Polish family, the Zelings. Since the experience of the Zelings is fairly typical, some attention to the story line is in order. Settling in a small town near Melbourne, the Zelings prosper and begin orienting to the Jewish community, but the wife (with minimal English only) withdraws from even her immediate neighbors. Moving their business to Melbourne, they become involved even more deeply in Jewish organizational affairs. Their children separate from them, one going to Israel, and the clash of cultures as well as generations becomes more acute. In the following excerpt, Morry, one of the grandsons, is the observer on the way to Melbourne Cemetery where the grandmother is to be buried:

He kept his eyes on the black wagon which moved swiftly along the highway as though he were looking to it for an answer to the mysteries of death. Everything around was golden. But this gold was reflected in the black of the wagon. Even though it was winter, everything strove for life. The grass which had become dry and parched during the summer heat now swayed gently in the breeze as if newborn after the winter rains. Even the grey eucalyptus trees were covered in a silvery shimmer. Only the uprooted trees which lay on the ground with their roots in the air and brittle branches on the earth, were reminiscent of death. The trees lay stretched through the sparse forest, like horns of some pre-historic monsters. The black stumps of the fire-ravaged bush bowed to the dark earth.[17]

Chronologically earlier than the Zelings and other such refugee families came the Germans, who have been chronicled by Colin Thiele and the storywriter E. O. Schlunke. Thiele's *The Sun on the Stubble* (1961) portrays a teenager at home, at school, and in the South Australian countryside of the German settlements, together with "the special customs, the special idiom—even, one suspects, the special personalities of these German farming families."[18] *Labourers in the Vineyard* (1970) presents again the German population, in the wine-growing section of South Australia: stern, suspicious of strangers (as, for instance, of the chief character, Kurt Neilson: "Dis Neilson! Is he really a Lut'eran at all, I vonder?"), but gossipy, and at times, tragically passionate.[19]

Also of an earlier immigrant culture is Judah Waten, who came to West Australia from Russia as a child of three in 1914, later establishing himself in Melbourne. *The Unbending* (1954) is based upon the experience of his parents; the sturdy "unbending" one is the mother. After contemporary social studies in two novels (*Shares in Murder,* 1957, and *Time of Conflict,* 1961), Waten returned to the immigrant theme in *Distant Land* (1964), the story of Joshua Kuperschmidt and family. Of this novel, Blake writes:

The difficulties of adjustment by migrants—especially on the part of sensitive, tradition loving Joshua—and their struggles to succeed in an alien community are finely resolved. Joshua's creed is surely akin to that of a writer in the beginnings of a movement that will one day be looked on as the tradition of migrant literature: he believes that "a Jew was one who respected all mankind, loved justice, and believed in intellect. He would give expression to his ideals."[20]

Waten's *So Far No Further* (1971) is about the intermingling, not without difficulties, of second-generation Italians and Jews in Melbourne.

Most recent of all is Iris Milutinovic's *Talk English Carn't Ya* (1978), the story of a Yugoslav migrant, Boris Mihailovic, who in his own words explains:

At first [1949] I think it is too different and I cannot live here and my country where I am born much better but now I know this is not true. Australia is the best country in the world now, and I am Australian with an Australian wife and a fine brick home and some money in the bank. Not much money but enough if bad things happen. But at first everything is very hard. To begin with, I have no English at all, and still make plenty mistakes. My wife says this is because my memory is no good and I have no ear for sound. This, I think is wrong for I hear everything very good, I mean very well.[21]

Lack of communication, as the author explains in her preface, "has nothing to do with such qualities as intelligence, courage, money sense, and the will to achieve."

If you look around, you will see many many Borislavs—people who know only too well what they want to say but cannot quite manage, so that it comes out sounding too simple, almost childish—not very bright. Yet most of these people have succeeded not only in enriching this country, but in successfully managing their own lives.[22]

At the same time, Boris's simple, downright English is often refreshingly effective for social (including domestic) narrative.

Not all the difficulty, of course, befalls those migrants who are not native to the language; those coming from Britain have their troubles too, as explored in R. A. Nicholls's *Almost Like Talking* (1978), which brings an English couple into the Australian culture of the late 1960s and early 1970s. On the assumption that something resembling a "tradition of migrant literature" already exists, especially in English, a reader might find ample room for comparative study in the fiction on that theme that has been produced in Canada (Susanna Moodie, F. P. Grove, Laura Salverson, A. M. Klein, Henry Kreisel) and the United States (Willa Cather, Hamlin Garland, O. E. Rölvaag, Mari Sandoz, William Saroyan) to mention only two other countries in which substantially the same patterns of massive migration and assimilation have taken place. Australia has also a story, still to be told by the migrants themselves, of involuntary Polynesian labor (the Kanakas) introduced into the sugarcane fields of Queensland, just as laborers of other racial strains were brought into North America.

Hope in New Social Theory

Postwar socialists in Australia could look back, as we have seen, to a strong tradition of radicalism in the latter nineteenth century. The war itself was treated extensively by one socialist advocate, Eric Lambert, in a quartet of novels: *The Twenty Thousand Thieves* (1952), *The Veterans* (1954), *The Dark Backward* (1958), and *Glory Thrown In* (1959), dealing with the North African and Asiatic sectors as well as wartime Sydney. Interspersed with these came two historical novels, *Five Bright Stars* (1954) and *Ballarat* (1962), which view the Eureka Stockade episode as a kind of fountainhead of Australian reformist thought, and *Watermen* (1958), which describes the struggle to establish a fishing cooperative. "Togetherness" is presented without political theorizing in *The Tender Conspiracy* (1965), a short novel among several others by Lambert. In a Queensland setting, about 1930, an illegal immigrant from Austria, Herman Hart, is nicknamed Toowoomba by the children at whose school, for a time, he is caretaker. The affection they have for this kindly, independent old man—very well presented—is put successfully to the test when he is in danger of losing his job as garbage collector because of increasing blindness: in a "tender conspiracy" they combine to serve as his eyes on garbage days.

Industrial society, with varying shades of social opinion expressed or implied by the novelists who present it, appears increasingly in the novels of the postwar period. In chapter 6, we shall be looking at several categorically violent protests against both industry itself and all its products, but here we are concerned with examinations of specific types. Mining, as one of the earliest, most persistent, and most profitable among all Australian industries, is treated extensively by Gavin Casey both in stories and novels. *Downhill Is Easier* (1945) is the first-person narrative of a man who quits mine work to become a gold stealer with disastrous consequences. *The City of Men* (1950) and *The Man Whose Name Was Mud* (1963) both relate to the West Australian goldfields (Kalgoorlie, Casey's birthplace), the first as a chronicle-narrative. *Snowball* (1958) looks at aboriginal-white relations and *Amid the Plenty* (1962) at the crisis generated by unemployment. Mining in a different region is treated by Betty Collins in *The Copper Crucible* (1966), which describes operations at Mt. Isa (Queensland), including industrial action. Considerable attention is also given to migrants and their families.

Three women writers—Mena Calthorp, Dymphna Cusack, and Dorothy Hewett—have likewise given attention to labor and labor difficulties in Australian industry. Mena Calthorp's first novel, *The Dyehouse* (1961), was praised for its skill in characterization as well as its exposure of abuses in the textile industry (Sydney). On the other hand, *The Defectors* (1969), which described the subtle corrupting of a trade unionist by the blandishments of industrial power, struck one reviewer as "curiously ineffective, when viewed as fiction" (rather than social commentary), because of its being "put in such stark and staring black and white that she repels rather than attracts the reader's sympathies."[23]

Dymphna Cusack's fiction, as well, takes risks such as these and for similar reasons does not always succeed. *Say No to Death* (1951), in the view of fellow novelist Eric Lambert, is more convincing in its criticism of underbudgeted tubercular sanitoria than in its love story, which in effect says no to life.[24] *Southern Steel* (1953) deals with the industrial city of Newcastle at the time of Japanese entry into World War II. The war atmosphere is rendered impressionistically, with characters not following a very well-defined plot line. In *The Sun Is Not Enough* (1967), a solicitor's family in a Sydney middle-class suburb become slowly aware of neo-Nazi ideas and activities among German immigrants, some of whom have become their close associates.

The leader, Carl von Rendt, is at length exposed as one of the most virulent Nazis during the invasion of Vienna and—not without tragic consequences—is deported from Australia. The political tones of black and white (too commonly a failing in proletarian writing everywhere) are quite evident in numerous passages, as for example this one in which the crypto-Nazi Uncle Carl is berating Australians to his nephew, Johann:

> He leaned back picking his teeth:
> "They say they are a weird mob. They boast in your face that they are eighty per cent British stock and they are indeed British in the worst way. They have inherited all the English arrogance and because they are Colonials they have strengthened it with their own provincialism that makes them harder to live with than the English themselves, who are so sure they are superior that they tolerate other people's peculiarities. Here while they think we are trying to assimilate ourselves it's fine. But let them see that you have other ideas, then they show another face."
> Johann looked at him, bewildered: "Why do you hate them so?"
> "I don't hate them, I despise them. They think because they're a big continent they're a big nation. I wish they were. They have the highest general standard of living in the world. No question of that. But what a standard!"[25]

A Bough in Hell (1971) has as its central figure a naval officer's wife, Roslyn Blackie, who slips gradually but firmly into alcoholism. A friendly doctor helps her as much as he can, but at the close of the story her future is uncertain. One of this author's most attractive books is an editorial collaboration, *Caddie: The Story of a Sydney Bar-Maid* (1953). Ms. Cusack's introduction places Caddie for the reader and sets the story, which has been made the basis of a recent film.

The final novelist of this trio, Dorothy Hewett, is as resolutely prosocialist, prolabor as the other two, but in her novel of a Sydney textile mill, *Bobbin Up* (1959), her social interests do not overwhelm the story—or rather stories—of fourteen women workers, seen as they return home from working their shifts. Interspersed with this content is a political theme, communist in emphasis, dealing with labor organization. This tends to dull somewhat, but does not blunt, the "tender, vivid and sensuous description" of the personalities, expressed often in their own language and from a maturely feminist viewpoint.[26]

Frank Hardy, whose *Power without Glory* (1950) was something of a sensation at the time of its appearance (Australia was not believed, by many readers, to be open to the influence of Chicago-style rack-eteering), is the author of two modern-day cautionary tales for week-day as well as Sunday reading. *Power without Glory* traces the career in Melbourne of John West through the late nineteenth century and the first half of the twentieth. All out for money in any unscrupulous way, West when finally rich is confused by his apparent helplessness: quite literally he does not know what to do with his money. The novel uses a wide screen, with many characters associated at one time or another with West. Domestic life is not very convincingly por-trayed, nor are dialogue and description very lively or convincing; the main quality is in "the tenacity and ruthlessness in which the writer pursues his theme of a corrupt and degraded society."[27] *The Four-Legged Lottery* (1958) turns its sights upon racecourse gambling and bookmaking. Somewhat in *Robbery under Arms* fashion, a man in prison writes about what happened to his friend Jim Roberts, re-cently hanged for murder, at the hands of racecourse professionals. Hardy's melodramatic style, as well as his political viewpoint, is ev-ident in this passage from the concluding chapter, in which the hero Jim becomes a berserk murderer:

> For Jim, they did not exist [Pittson's wife and partner]; only Pittson ex-isted as a symbol of dreadful memories. Cissie and Tom Roberts quarreled in Jim's mind; Kathleen took a lover; he wanted to be an artist and could not; a woman lay on a dirty bed and Kathie wept; his dead son came to life and kissed him; hostile adults surrounded an adolescent boy and mocked his love and ambition; leering mouths shouted at him "you are unemployed, a susso!" A hostile society crowded in on him to frustrate his pursuit of hap-piness—and he struck out at it.[28]

More recently, Hardy has published *The Hard Way* (1961), explain-ing the background of *Power without Glory; The Unlucky Australians* (1968), on the aborigines; three books of yarns and legends; and *But the Dead Are Many* (1975), which "submits a lifetime experience in radical politics to the complex discipline of the fugal form."[29] An apology for social realism by Mr. Hardy appears in *Literary Australia,* edited by Semmler and Whitelock (1966), under the title "Environ-ment and Ideology in Australian Literature, a Personal View."[30]

Change and Acceptance of Change

Both exile and hope are closely tied to change, which in Australia (not unlike North America) has been rapid in the past and continues so. Many base their future hopes upon the prospect of change—immigrants, for example, or at least the younger ones among them, since for the old so drastic a shift may seem more like exile. Those who feel themselves to be exiles, expatriates—either those entering Australia from abroad, or Australians having left it—sometimes think of themselves as victims of change, for whom exile has become either a forced or voluntary condition. Moreover, there is a long tradition of the casually employed person (usually but not always male) in Australian society: the swagman, jolly or unjolly, who is "on the wallaby" looking for whatever may turn up. This was strong among the *Bulletin* writers, as we have seen, and it has continued so, joined with occasional echoes of the aboriginal "walkabout," undertaken for not the same set of reasons. All this emphasizes Australia as a land infused with change.

Neither hope nor exile, as a theme, appears very often in a black-or-white presentation. Many writers, probably most, have mixed feelings: they know that change, some of it sudden and socially disruptive, must come but are not very happy to see it. This is emphasized by T. Inglis Moore, whose *Social Patterns in Australian Literature* contains a chapter on "The Great Australian Dream."

We of today, disillusioned by two world wars and a depression and living uneasily under the threat of an atomic armageddon, find it very hard to project ourselves into the enthusiastic optimism of the eighties and nineties and to recapture that first, fine careless rapture, but we must recognize in all fairness that the Great Australian Dream had, after all, some reasonable foundation in the hard facts of a phenomenal expansion and unprecedented political advancement.[31]

Technical advancement was, and is, no small part of the general movement, with none more spectacular than that applied to Australian mining for well over a hundred years. We may recall here what has already been said about the response to mining itself, and to the subsidiary industries it creates, in the fiction of Boldrewood, Prichard, Casey, and Cusack. Other, later kinds of industrial change appear in the novels of Calthorp and Hewett. Much of this is social criticism to some extent, as well as fiction, and it is no more than fair to ask whether all Australian novelists view the products of science and engineering as dubiously as most of these (not all: Boldrewood, as one of the eighties-nineties "optimistic" school that Moore mentions, is an exception).

One novelist who reflects not only acceptance of change as wrought by science and technology but joy in it is John Iggulden. In *The Clouded Sky* (1964), he gives us through his central figure Ritchie Harrington the exhilaration to be felt in flight as he sails about hunting and finding thermals to lift his glider *Virago* and bring it into a winning position during competitions. (Iggulden is a former Australian national gliding champion.) The beauty of the Australian countryside, seen as mosaic-carpet, and the thrill of gliding through the space above it can be strongly sensed in the book; and the depth of emotion revealed in the human relationships helps create a well-balanced story. Danger, as well, is present:

Flying fast, I headed back. This was a day to fly fast; to be wary every second for a twist of air that might dump you in a stall by blowing suddenly behind, and watchful as I was, there was a moment as I came in low over the fence when I could have been in trouble. For a second Virago became uncannily silent. The life went out of the stick. For one beat, the calm nerves that stroked the muscles of my heart gave a sharp bound; and then Virago was mine again, the air waived this quick chance to put us down, and blew again from the right place. In seconds I had touched down lightly where I meant to, and nothing had happened that I could have explained to anyone.[32]

Iggulden's other novels include *Breakthrough* (1960), *The Storms of Summer* (also 1960), about fishing communities on the south coast of New South Wales, and *Dark Stranger* (1966), in which white and aboriginal characters clash over crucial legal matters.

Mobility, in one guise or another, is a dominant pattern in the fiction of five other writers, G. M. Glaskin, Geoffrey Dutton, Eve Langley, Shirley Hazzard, and Kylie Tennant. Glaskin's work has been produced partly in West Australia, partly in such other places as London and Malaysia, and reflects the writer's changing subjects as well as residences. *A World of Our Own* (1955) is about the experiences of three men and two women immediately after World War II, from which the author turned, in *A Minor Portrait* (1957), to the liaison of a teenage youngster with the Countess, a rich Frenchwoman whose attentions bring him close to self-destruction. Later titles include *A Change of Mind* (1959), in which experiments with hypnotism result in a bizarre transposition of personalities; *A Lion in the Sun* (1960); *The Beach of Passionate Love* (1961, the name is a genuine geographical one, of a beach in Malaysia); and *O Love, O Loneliness* (1964), consisting of two short novels, one of which uses a novelist as one of the characters, to explore the human relationships associated with an elegant old house.

Geoffrey Dutton's *Tamara* (1970) also crosses international borders readily, from Australia to Russia, where there is a festival honoring the 800th anniversary of Shota Rustaveli, the Georgian epic poet, author of *The Knight in the Tiger Skin*. (There was, in fact, such a festival held.) Angus James, an Australian agronomist invited to the festival, has been recently widowed; but Tamara, a beautiful woman as well as a very successful popular poet, proves to him that his emotions are not, after all, completely dead. Among much feasting, rhetoric, revelry, and intrigue, a romance develops, around which is woven much of Soviet culture: ideals as well as problems and injustices. Following is Angus's reaction to one of the festival speeches delivered by a poet-critic:

> Like all shrewd doctrinaires, he was an expert at making anything fit into his doctrine, and like all good orators, an expert at making nonsense sound convincing. He explained that there was no real conflict between socialist realism and the romance of *The Knight in the Tiger Skin*. Angus liked the explanation so much that he wrote it down. "The principle of socialist realism is so broad and all-embracing that it gives art grounds for speaking both with the language of reality and with the language of romance, while nevertheless remaining the art of socialist realism." He thought of the jargon of scientific papers, and gave it second best to this verbal fog pulled down over a whole country.[33]

Dutton is also the author of *Andy* (1968), in which a World War II flying instructor—undisciplined, fond of women, free *only* in the air—cuts a figure much in the picaresque pattern.

Fiction with overseas orientation was to become more frequent in later years, as for example a number of Patrick White's short stories, or Thomas Keneally's *Gossip from the Forest* (1975) and *Season in Purgatory* (1976), both war novels set in Europe, together with one on the American Civil War, *Confederates* (1979). Christopher Koch's *The Year of Living Dangerously* (1978) deals with a coup in Indonesia; Richard Beilby's *The Bitter Lotus* (1978) is set in contemporary Sri Lanka; Blanche D'Alpuget's *Monkeys in the Dark* (1980) and *Turtle Beach* (1981) mix women's liberation with social observations on Southeast Asia. Murray Bail's *Homesickness* (1980) takes a party of thirteen to present-day Africa, England, South America, New York, and Russia.

Eve Langley's *The Pea-Pickers* (1942) was favorably received at the time of publication, but except for one other book (*White Topee*, 1954), the writer did not continue her career as novelist. In *The Pea-Pickers*, two girls in their late teens, the narrator and her sister, assume boys' names and clothes to become migrant farm laborers. They not only enjoy getting acquainted with the Southeastern Australian countryside (beginning in Gippsland, their mother's girlhood home) but making many new friends with varying backgrounds and languages. Frequently on short rations, they filch food when they can and share rough accommodations in a harking back to the pioneering "mateship" aura of an earlier age. In addition to controlled abandonment and pranksterism, there is a good bit of sentiment that by comparison with the next generation seems archaic in itself, as for example:

Drunken with joy and love, I walked beside him, my strong limbs scarcely able to move, so stumblingly thick were they with the mystical glory of life and love, and that untouched and unhoped for portal of sex. My heart and mind swam ignorantly around in their circumscribed ecstasies, knowing that there was a gate through which all could pour, but not daring nor desiring to flow through it and lose the beauty of the earth.[34]

Shirley Hazzard, whose views of love and romance are less ecstatic but at the same time less circumscribed, uses settings outside Australia. *The Evening of the Holiday* (1966), in which the attempted renewal of a love affair does not succeed, takes place in Italy; and *People in Glass Houses* (1967) describes an "Organization" very much like the United Nations, which has reached the state of bureaucratic petrifaction and in which its officials can "relate" or "coordinate" but can no longer feel. John Colmer, who reviewed the volume, concluded that it should be "compulsory reading for civil servants and sociologists," and speaks well of the author's other works. R. G. Geering praises her style, especially that of *People in Glass Houses*, for "a wit and delicate irony that are ideally adapted to [a] satiric stance."[35]

Kylie Tennant, on the other hand, sets all her novels in Australia—in New South Wales, in fact, either Sydney or various rural or coastal districts. Some of her people move in and out of the city, but almost all of them do move, the exceptions being those in *Lost Haven* (1946), who are violent enough at times but in a static setting. Dorothy Auchterlonie, comparing Miss Tennant with George Eliot (who wins this competition), praises her work for "a broad humanity . . . a sympathy that issues not merely in a diffused compassion, but as a social conscience,"[36] together with a descriptive gift which, exercised to its full power, is poetic. In the diverse settings within her own geographic area, she stays closely within the chronological limits of her own personal experience, broadly from about 1935 onward through the 1950s, with one exception: *Foveaux* (1939) develops the theme of change as it affects a Sydney suburb over the years (beginning just before World War I and extending into the 1930s), and even here she is within the bounds of her own lifetime. This novel introduces such grim social realities as slum landlordism, war, and depression, carrying into suburban life the panoramic view of social strata in conflict, small-town pettiness, and the rejection of romance already blended in her first novel, *Tiburon* (1935).

The Battlers (1941), a strongly realized study of the nomadic unemployed during the late 1930s; *Ride on Stranger* (1943), in which Shannon Hicks undertakes a spectrum of occupations in Sydney in an effort to find her right place as she sees it; *Tell Morning This* (1968, first published in short form as *The Joyful Condemned*, 1953, to comply with paper rationing), with wartime Sydney in turmoil; *Time Enough Later* (1943), in which a second heroine, Bessie Drew, seeks a place in Sydney but deliberately decides to return to the country; *The Honey Flow* (1956), the odyssey of a group of beekeepers—all these are evidently powered by a kind of adjustable picaresque design. In *The Honey Flow*, the narrator-heroine Mallee Herrick, a scriptwriter, wishes to get away from the city, and so, with her stepfather and a group of others gradually assimilated into a caravan, she ranges through New South Wales and into Queensland. The group are a pioneering breed willing to struggle against drought, flood, and fire for their beloved bees—which, notwithstanding, are finally lost. This passage shows Mallee's intense concern with the work:

When Joe let me help with the queen cells, I realized that as far as good old Joe was concerned I was passing my final test. One of the worst things I ever did was to drop a queen cell. When Joe saw my stricken face, instead of calling me a ham-handed half-wit, he said gently, "All right, Mallee, it has to happen to everyone. We can't risk putting her in a hive, so I'll show you how she looks."

The queen cell is always a curious, elaborate big cell, like an acorn made of coral, and packed with royal jelly so that the tiny anonymous larva may eat and become royal. There she lay in her jade coffin, the sleeping beauty, white as a ghost in a wrapping of silk, snow white with eyes of a red cornelian, dreaming for what must have seemed to her a hundred years. I had seen nothing so lovely as that poor queen Joe showed me; and I had destroyed her, deprived that little Cinderella of her one ecstatic hour when she would have danced a measure on air with some strong-winged prince.[37]

"The story Mallee has to tell," says Frank Dalby Davison, "exists quite successfully on two levels": the serious and the comic. Whether or not the events are serious, or sometimes even tragic, the style carries them along easily. Among all her novels, Davison placed this one first: "It conveys her highly idiosyncratic talent in purer distillation than any of its predecessors. In that connexion alone it is very happily titled."[38] Turning directly to humor (which in one guise or another is almost always present in her fiction), she wrote *Ma Jones and the Little White Cannibals* (1967). Ma Jones is a self-appointed private investigator who, with help from two other middle-aged ladies, looks into a variety of situations in politics, education, the arts, and other topics good for the rise and resolution of a plot within ten or a dozen brisk pages. Kylie Tennant's latest novel is *The Man on the Headland* (1972), the title deriving from a hermit, Ernie Metcalfe, who lives on Diamond Head, northern New South Wales. The book evokes the spell of north-coast landscape, but does not do as much with character or plot as several of its predecessors.

A skillful variation on the theme of enforced change through exile appears in David Malouf's *An Imaginary Life* (1978). Here the one exiled is the poet Ovid, who (history tells us) did suffer banishment from Augustan Rome but to what place and for what cause we do not know. Malouf, a poet himself, imagines the place to have been a primitive village on the border of Dacia, scarcely yet removed from savagery. Ovid's responses to his new surroundings (presented in first person) are developed with fine sensibility, and the story is given additional depth through the figure of the Child, a wild boy taken out of the animal world into the village under the protection of the poet-exile. Through Ovid's eyes, "old" Rome, already decadent, is compelled to face its imagined future at the hands of its own frontier. Nearing his own end, Ovid wonders if the Child is

. . . already moving away from me in his mind, already straining forward to whatever life it is that lies out there beyond our moment together, some life I have not taken into account, and which he will be free to enter only when our journey together is done. I have tried to induce out of the animal in him some notion of what it is to be human. I wonder now if he hasn't already begun to discover in himself some further being. Is he, in fact, as the villagers thought (their view was always simpler than mine, and perhaps therefore nearer the truth) some foundling of the gods? Is it his own nature as a god that his body is straining towards, at this edge of his own life where any ordinary child might be about to burst into manhood, and into his perfect limits as man?[39]

Returning briefly to the opposing themes of exile and hope with which the chapter began, we have not encountered literal, geographic exile as a nostalgic theme among recent Australian writers to the degree that we might have expected to find it—least of all, exile from Europe (such as the earliest Australians certainly felt), except among some of the immigrants. But a strong sense of separation between aboriginals and Europeans remains, with the charge being made repeatedly that hope has been denied and old injustices continued, extending even outside the boundaries of Australia proper, to New Guinea. Alienation there certainly is, but it does not go unnoticed and unprotested as once it did. For a counterbalance, the element of hope—even of optimism at times, or at least good cheer—is present too.

Much of all the foregoing is implicit in a novel by Donald Horne, *But What If There Are No Pelicans?* (1971). This work, teeming with ideas and emotional responses, might be summed up as a kind of latter-day Australian *Candide* wired up to computers (of various colors), which concludes not "Let us cultivate our garden" so much as "Let us try to find our garden if we can, and cultivate it if the state of the world will let us." Amid oceans of talk, perhaps the following comes as close to being a representative statement as any:

"The characteristic that destroyed you on Earth was a simple heroism of the playground," said the red computer. "You were not concerned with serving anything except your sense of comradeship. Perhaps you represent the type of self-acknowledged adventurer—the man who admits he thrills to the chase—who used to be common enough, both in politics and in war, but who in the present age usually has to conceal his real motives so effectively that he may cease to be aware of them."[40]

The inhibiting mask of any such concealment, as we shall see in portions of the following chapter, is now beginning to drop away.

Chapter Six
Postwar: The Moderns

"Fiction we publish as a gesture to the cultural heritage, though there is little money in it unless a novel is translatable into the wider media of film and television."

—Peter Mathers (Thomas Wort of
The Wort Papers, 1972,
addressing a luncheon meeting)

The novel—*the* novel, generically, in its broadest terms—is being currently viewed in two ways: either as well on its way to extinction, having served its purpose and now being replaced by other forms, or else as undergoing profound change which in itself may seem the end of fiction as we have known it. Such change involves the absorption of social realism into new modes more akin to poetry, drama, and painting than to traditional "literature," laying also heavy stress upon individual psychology, as of course much fiction has always done. As such, it is more a mode of exploring experience than a means of re-porting upon experience by re-creation. The first of these views is well represented for Australian fiction in this statement by Geoffrey Serle:

> The decline of the novel . . . is a world-wide phenomenon, for the visual media have attracted away the potential audience. The cinema has been a major rival; although people may not read much less than formerly, the highly literate give less attention to literature and everyone's attention-span has shortened. That Keneally is almost the only younger serious novelist who can live by his work is an indication of the novel's declining appeal; only the most optimistic and dedicated can continue to write in such a sit-uation. At least half a dozen of the more promising novelists of the 50s have abandoned the task.[1]

If on the other hand we see the novel as in mutation, not at the end of its whole life cycle, we can turn with a little more confidence to an admittedly confused situation, trying to sort it out on some kind of tentative basis.

Every novelist, as we quickly recognize, must be a psychologist at least in some degree, if not in the treatment of his characters, then in gauging the capacities and expectations of his audience. No chapter, therefore, can pretend to isolate any one set of writers as exclusively psychological novelists or whatever. Those included here have been selected first, because virtually all of them are still writing and thus represent Australian fiction as it continues to emerge in our day. But they also represent a wide spectrum of themes and modes; and one group, the second, is directly opposed to what might be described as an established trend, since the other writers—all quite different from this group of social and aesthetic dissidents—have been publishing over a considerable span of years and their reputations are already on record. Such an arrangement allows for display of the latest and, comparatively speaking, the old-line novelists side by side. It should be pointed out, as well, that the latter 1970s and early 1980s saw the republication, locally, of many novels originally appearing outside Australia together with republication or reissue of Australian "classics." There were also numerous critical studies of single writers, including "notes" on certain volumes apparently being used as school textbooks.

Explorers of Variety in Personality

The work of older writers such as H. H. Richardson, Martin Boyd, Eleanor Dark, and Katharine S. Prichard reminds us of how wide-ranging and well-crafted Australian fiction had become before the present generation appeared. We do not look so much for radically different themes as for extensions, and applications from our own point of view, of the familiar. In the work of the first novelist to be introduced, for example, the use of the convict era for setting and plot is scarcely unprecedented; yet he has contrived to "make it new."

Hal Porter. Hal Porter, says John Barnes, writing in 1974, "recognizes more completely than any other Australian writer how we create our own reality through our use of words."

He is alert to the "deliberate disguises" by which we live, the faces we show to the world, the voices we assume, the manners by which we create our identities as social beings. But he is not concerned merely with surfaces.

Neither is he concerned merely with Australia alone, or with present-day culture; his novels and stories range from convict times to the latter twentieth century and from London and Venice through both urban and rural Australia to Japan. Leonie Kramer has pointed out that his characters are constantly in motion, that the journey is the single most dominant image.[2] In this he relates closely to the group of writers discussed in the last section of chapter 5. This motif appears as well in his two vividly written autobiographical volumes, *The Watcher on the Cast-Iron Balcony* (1963) and *The Paper Chase* (1966). His first novel, *A Handful of Pennies* (1958), examines postwar Japan and its impact on the lives of some of the Australian portion of the occupying forces: "too flimsy a work for a writer of his abilities," one critic believes. The Australians in the book, Mary Lord writes,

. . . never quite lose their civilized veneer, but the culture they reflect seems brutally coarse and primitive. It becomes exaggeratedly so in their Japanese environment, and in their relationships with the impeccably polite Japanese."[3]

Porter was to return to the Japanese theme more than once.

Meanwhile, *The Tilted Cross* (1961) uses also a situation in which one group is subservient to another. This novel, set in Tasmania during early days of the convict era, is far more than a historical reconstruction; the grotesque characters who inhabit it, one feels, would still be grotesque against a less lurid background. Some critics do not care for Porter's style; H. P. Heseltine, for instance, speaks disapprovingly of recherché diction and "dandyism"[4] and calls *The Tilted Cross* "a monstrously parodied version of Christian myth and morality" in "overheated prose" and a "shuddering search for the moral and sensuous *frisson*."[5] Those less offended might view the style as well suited to the subject: an outwardly stable but inwardly decadent society, isolated in the novel almost as for biological study, except that psychotheology is the method employed. What shall we make of a culture, Porter seems to be asking, that can be so ambivalent with respect to the official Christian virtues and vices as well? The episodes and the imagery alike are sensational, as if to meet the expectations of reality that fiction (of that period and for a long time after, not excluding our own time) so often overlooks. Porter makes this point through the thoughts of Rose Knight:

She held a novel; she had even been reading in a novel, oh, a silly, for it told of people who were not people, of events beyond reality . . . of renunciations, noble sacrifices, sweetnesses florid and scented as dahlias. . . . murders recurred like dinners but with less trouble; there was a wife like a paper rose; a husband like a sirloin; a hero with a brow and brain of ivory; a heroine whom the villain never ravished after a hundred opportunities. There was not a sour privy, or a privy at all, no bum bore a boil, no tooth decayed, no stays creaked, at a time of sacred silence, like a red-coat's boots.[6]

The Right Thing (1971), as the title suggests, is about the force of social codes, seen here in the Ogilvie family of Erradale, rural Victoria. Told partly through the diary of Gavin Ogilvie (an ex-actor returned home to anticipate his inheritance), the story explores and drives hard against destructive futility of the sort of provincial ritualism the Ogilvies represent.

Christina Stead.   The next author in this grouping, Christina Stead, shares Porter's liking for eccentrics. Her first two books, *Seven Poor Men of Sydney* and *The Salzburg Tales,* appeared the same year (1934), and in the more than forty years since then, she has become an international novelist in a very broad sense of the term, having lived abroad for most of the period and using a number of different settings for her fiction: Paris (in *A House for All Nations,* 1938), Washington, D.C. (in *The Man Who Loved Children,* 1940), London and other English locales (in *For Love Alone,* 1945, and *Cotters' England,* 1967). She is, as the critic Brian Kiernan observes,

. . . the first major Australian novelist to take the city as a setting and to create from it an image of the metropolis, an image of the great city as the focus of contemporary life.[7]

This she does in *Seven Poor Men of Sydney,* set among the harbor area of Woollomooloo and Fisherman's Bay. Here, postwar unemployment and accompanying poverty lead to socialist gatherings and long conversations of imaginary happenings, together with the tormented sexual attraction between Catherine Baguenault and her half brother Michael, both wanting a simple life yet complicating their existence by withdrawal into soul-searching and fantasy. Such entanglement is symbolized, at one point, by a painting:

Joseph often went home with Baruch for tea. He looked noncommittally for a long time, the next evening, at the drawing which Baruch was working at, called, "La Femme s'échappe de la Forêt," showing a naked woman with agonised contortion of body and face bursting through a thicket, tearing her thigh on a splintered tree, while a boa constrictor and a tropical vine loaded with large lilies hung before her and impeded her.

"Queer," said Joseph; "what does that mean?"

"Woman escapes from the forest. It means, the middle-class woman trying to free herself, and still impeded by romantic emotions and ferocious, because ambushed, sensuality."

"I don't understand."

"Your cousin Catherine, for example."[8]

Of the four novellas in *The Puzzleheaded Girl* (1967), three are about unhappy and/or unfortunate women and a fourth about an alcoholic writer and his family whose rural cottage is, reputedly, haunted by the ghost of a madwoman who thought she was Pocahontas reincarnated. To this writer, thus, "spiritual realities" were rather consistently somewhat grim ones.

Contrasting Christina Stead's work with much that has appeared alongside it, R. G. Geering writes:

Christina Stead's fiction continually reflects [a] disturbed and disturbing world as a matter of course, but it does not subordinate the individual to society in any simple, determinist way. Even Letty Fox, who is more a victim of society than the other heroines, asserts herself in a struggle against the forces that deny her freedom and fulfillment. The people who are overwhelmed, like Michael and Henny, go under because they will not, cannot, surrender their individuality. The most memorable of Christina Stead's characters, both the attractive and the unattractive, remain stubbornly unique; Raccamond and Léon, Teresa and Crow, Sam and Louisa, Nellie Cotter—whether succeeding or failing they are, as individuals, bigger and more interesting than the environments that have shaped them. For such apparently old-fashioned literary virtues we may still feel grateful in an age which has made a fetish of novelty and experimentation, and which has presented so many "novels" that turn out to be propaganda, confessions, reportage, pornography, tracts for the times, typographical jokes—anything, indeed, but genuine fiction.[9]

Commenting more directly upon Stead's Australian experience, Clement Semmler says:

There is no question that her best work reflects her own experience: *Seven Poor Men of Sydney* has elements of her home life; *For Love Alone* is even more autobiographical—Teresa (Christina) enduring poverty, saving money by walking the stifling streets of Sydney to pay her way to London. Teresa, like

Louisa, like Nellie Cotter—as did Christina—"flew the nest." Here we have various portraits of the artist as a young woman. The autobiographical aspects of these novels, coloured by her remarkable literary imagination, make up Christina Stead's most consistent and enduring theme—her escape into literary emancipation from the soul-destroying shackles of an Australian environment as she had experienced it—and from which self-imposed exile she had no wish to return, nor ever did.[10]

For the most direct parallel to such pressure into exile, the examples of three women writers from New Zealand come to mind: Katharine Mansfield, Jane Mander, and Robin Hyde.

George Johnston.   A much less stylistically complex novelist, George Johnston, began his writing career as a war correspondent, then wrote three novels with settings outside Australia: two in China (*High Valley,* 1949, with Charmian Clift, and *The Far Road,* 1962) and one in the Middle East (*The Darkness Outside,* 1959). The last one of these is the story of an archaeological exploration on the Euphrates River with overtones of natural disaster and human engulfment by overpopulation. (As Shane Martin, Johnston also wrote several mystery novels whose controlling character is an archaeologist.) *The Far Road,* in which two journalists (one Australian, the other American) view the devastations of a Chinese famine in 1945, is another story filled with portents of disaster. *My Brother Jack* (1964) and *Clean Straw for Nothing* (1969), both of which won the Miles Franklin Award in their years of publication, form part of a trilogy; the third, *A Cartload of Clay* (1971) was left unfinished at Johnston's death in 1970. The first of the three was widely admired at the time of its publication, and later, as a "miracle of memory"[11] in its ability to recreate Melbourne of the 1920s and 1930s. The narrator David Meredith, the younger brother, develops into a journalist and free-lance writer; Jack remains what he wants to be, a plain man speaking and doing exactly as he pleases. *Clean Straw for Nothing*—"to some degree similarly pegged to a background of autobiographical experience" but at the same time "a very free rendering of the truth," says the author's note—takes place in Sydney, Greece, and London chiefly during the 1960s, chronicling David's subsequent career and the stresses of a second marriage. *A Cartload of Clay* finds Meredith old and ill, given to reminiscing, still able at times to view life with the reporter-novelist's eye, but wondering about final meanings:

When you boiled it all down the real importance of Empedocles the Sicilian was his masterly contention that life was based on the rule of conflict between Strife and Love. This was the thing that one had to have quite firmly fixed in one's mind. This was what it was all about. Except that it did not really dissipate the confusion.[12]

Thea Astley. Thea Astley, whose fiction has had much harder going with critics than Christina Stead's or George Johnston's but who persisted and has now produced half a dozen novels or more, began writing primarily as a satirist and social critic. Her first two novels, *Girl with a Monkey* (1958) and *A Descant for Gossips* (1960), offer unflattering pictures of small-town life (the setting is Queensland but the judgments would fit many other localities). The observers are women teachers (as is Astley herself), whose positions make them singularly vulnerable to censorious and gossipy behavior. Turning to men characters in her next two books, *The Well Dressed Explorer* (1962) and *The Slow Natives* (1965), she portrays first an inadequate personality, George Brewster, city dweller and roué, who facing age and death "at last comes alive in weakness less boastful and sensational than lechery";[13] then a sympathetic character, a gentle and affectionate parent, Bernard in *The Slow Natives,* exploring the polarities between Catholicism and social permissiveness.

In *A Boat Load of Home Folk* (1968), a group of failed, frustrated people brought together on an island somewhere near Port Lena are put through a hurricane, emerging somewhat chastened but not exactly redeemed. The central figure is a failed priest, Father Lake, symbolic of the collapse of organized religion. *The Acolyte* (1972) enters the world of art through Paul Vesper, who having ditched a career in engineering to follow art, becomes acolyte to a blind composer-genius, Holberg, until he is finally convinced that "it's all a mess, a highly organized garbage-tip of human relationships and pardon the stinking journalese of that,"[14] and rebels. What, the novelist seems to be wondering, should be the rational relationship between a "great man" and his associates, or can it ever be such? *A Kindness Cup* (1974) recalls a massacre of aboriginals in Queensland by whites in the 1850s and—years afterward—the persecution of their protectors at the hands of a "hate-pack" when the truth is revealed. At a climactic moment:

The crowd is embarrassed now. It has been told things it did not wish to hear—not now, not when it has been softened into a spurious amity once again. The champion of their mediocrity is twitching on stage before their astounded eyes, and even their mediocrity by this turn of events has been belittled. . . . Arguing and shouting break out. The crowd is two-headed. Everywhere people are standing and pushing from their seats in an animal perplexity.[15]

These novels contrast with less serious treatments of the social scene, of which Lesley Rowlands's *A Bird in the Hand* (1965), Lola Irish's *Time of the Dolphins* (1972), and Dusty Wolfe's *The Brass Kangaroo* (1973) offer three examples out of many—with the added caution that the label "popular fiction" is always elastic.

Elizabeth Harrower.   Another woman writer, Elizabeth Harrower, began writing at the same time as Thea Astley and published four novels during the 1950s and 1960s. Of these, *The Catherine Wheel* (1960) and *The Watch Tower* (1966) have received the most attention. The first, comparable to "that other expatriate Australian novel of destructive romantic love, *Maurice Guest*"[16] studies the destructive power of love. Clemency James, the first-person narrator, an Australian studying in London, meets a failed actor, Christian Roland, who is now an odd-jobs man in her boarding house. Against everyone's better judgment, she falls in love with him, and as he degenerates into dishonesty and alcoholic viciousness, she comes near to her own crisis, a nervous breakdown. In *The Watch Tower,* Laura Vaisey, expensively and protectively educated (in Australia), falls victim (as wife) to Felix Shaw, a paranoiac businessman. Laura's sister Clare becomes the "watch tower" character, leaves, and at length, a young Dutchman, Bernard (Felix's protege), brings decency and hope to Laura. R. G. Geering feels that although Elizabeth Harrower "has not yet been completely successful in dramatizing her vision of the evil and the good in human life," this novel "in its unsparing concern for the dilemmas of life itself is, arguably, a better novel than some of the more Australia-conscious and widely acclaimed prize winners in literary competitions of the last two decades."[17]

Thomas Keneally.   The two remaining writers in this group, Thomas Keneally and Randolph Stow, have more than once been compared with one another and—inevitably—with Patrick White. The basis of comparison is psychological, or "poetic" as sometimes stated: both are frequently concerned with characters whose inner states are approached as the thing of most interest about them, and whose fortunes, misfortunes, and conflicts are at the same time of symbolic significance to many others. Thus we encounter the fable or other metaphorical device used for both the development and the extension of character.

Thomas Keneally's first resounding success, *Bring Larks and Heroes* (1967), came after two previous novels, *The Place at Whitton* (1964) and *The Fear* (1965). In the comparatively few years of his career, he has written and published with remarkable speed, not quite a novel a year but approaching that momentum: *Three Cheers for the Paraclete* (1968), *The Survivor* (1969), *A Dutiful Daughter* (1971), *The Chant of Jimmy Blacksmith* (1972), *Blood Red, Sister Rose* (1974), *Gossip from the Forest* (1975), *Season in Purgatory* (1976), *A Victim of the Aurora* (1977), *Confederates* (1979), *Passenger* (1979), and *Schindler's List* (1982). Stow, a man born the same year as Keneally (1935), by contrast has been a slow producer (but occupied with poetry as well): *A Haunted Land* (1956), *To the Islands* (1958), *Tourmaline* (1963), *The Merry-Go-Round in the Sea* (1965), and *Midnite* (1967).

Keneally's *The Place at Whitton* is an account of murders at a Catholic college for the priesthood (Keneally himself is an ex-theological student) near the New South Wales country town of Whitton, with involvements as well in a coven of witches at King's Cross, Sydney. Max Harris, noting that the story "develops an increasing gothic quality," welcomed Keneally, perceptively, as "a remarkably fully-formed talent."[18] *The Fear* describes the state of mind of a young Australian, Danny Jordan, when his country was threatened by invasion in World War II. *Bring Larks and Heroes* returns to that seemingly never-ending fountain of inspiration for Australian fiction, the early convict era. The title is from a poem written by the hero, the convict Halloran, shortly before he is hanged for his part in a prisoners' rebellion. There is plenty of realism in the story, but aspiration too, and even comedy at times. Brian Kiernan, who ranks Keneally's achievement with the novels of Furphy, Richardson, Herbert, Stead, and White, views its central concern as "the need of the individual to seek salvation *within society*" (not in retirement, for instance, to a pastoral paradise).

In the emphasis [Keneally] places on this concern, in the imaginative force with which he conceives society, and in the directness with which the conflict between personal and institutional values is dramatized there is apparent a creative originality. The constant imagery of extremism—the insistence on the precariousness of the characters' hold on life at the world's edge, on the oblivion beyond and within them, and on their preoccupations with insanity and death—reinforces the characters' dependence on each other. The novel probes life at its extremes; but fundamental to its form is that Halloran and Ann represent the possibilities of life, and social life, unattainable in such a denatured society.[19]

Writing on the moral problems raised by *Bring Larks and Heroes*, in which the protagonist Halloran joins a prisoners' rebellion, Frances McInherny concludes:

> Halloran's naive desire to please God, or at least fate, by aiding Hearn is credible in view of his character. His execution is the final ironic demonstration of the moral and emotional inversion of the "world's wrong end," so that the potential saviour, the only upright man in [the] community, is so corrupted by the system he serves and the religion he reveres that he wilfully abandons his personal responsibility and casts himself into the oblivion of despair.[20]

After this peak, the next two novels, particularly *The Survivor* (set in the Antarctic) and *A Dutiful Daughter* (problems between parents and teenage offspring), were understandably something of an anticlimax. History came again to the rescue in *The Chant of Jimmy Blacksmith*, which derives its plot from an episode occurring July 1900 in rural New South Wales, in which an aboriginal named Jimmy Governor took revenge upon his employers. After Jimmy Blacksmith's slaughter of the Newby family comes hubris: "Jimmy was the master. In him the night was vested, and the gift of swift action. He decided he should enjoy it while it was there, this possession and being possessed."[21] From here onward, the flight-and-pursuit pattern of action takes over. Almost as if in response to Kiernan's critical comment in 1972, that Keneally was much better at the "historical fable" than at contemporary life, the succeeding novels were historically based: *Blood Red, Sister Rose* (Joan of Arc), *Gossip from the Forest* (the Armistice makers of November 1918), and *Season in Purgatory* (Yugoslavian resistance to German occupation, World War II). *A Victim of the Aurora* (1977) returns to the setting of *The Survivor*. This time, during a pre–World War I expedition, one of the members, a reporter named Henneker, is murdered. The victim's private journal, though it mercilessly pinpoints the human failings and errors of the whole company, including high-level scientific researchers, offers no conclusive evidence but the narrator (Anthony Piers, an artist who can capture the unusual light effects of the region) comes up with the murderer's identity, precipitating a solution that seems to epitomize what the century is doomed to become. The effect of the Antarctic itself upon its explorers is well described, as for example in this passage:

We had been gone a mere three and a half days but the refinements of the hut dazzled us as the Savoy might dazzle a farm-labourer. We sat for a long time with hot mugs of cocoa in our hands. The flesh of our palms gratefully took in the heat, while AB Stigworth, as a concession to our small winter journey, laid the table around us. If I hadn't been surrounded by colleagues I would have groaned like someone sexually aroused as the heat of indoors took over my extremities and crept towards my core.[22]

Randolph Stow. Randolph Stow's first novel, *A Haunted Land* (1956), was reviewed appropriately enough by the poet-novelist David Martin who called it "a poet's novel, both positively and negatively"—positively because it shows richness in feeling and intuition, and negatively because the lyrical element dominates characterization. It is not realistic, but not surrealistic either; there is a balance maintained between the average and unaverage character, Martin thinks. How to sum it up?—"a poet's study of the deviousness of love."[23] Although slighter than Stow's other books, it does introduce the setting and general thematic tone of works to follow. Andrew Maguire, owner of a farm near the West Australian coast at the end of the nineteenth century, is a family tyrant who precipitates evil upon his children. *The Bystander* (1957) brings to West Australia after World War II a young Latvian woman, Diana Ravirs, who accepts the post of helping care for a mentally retarded youth, Keithy Farnham, while his parents are away. She soon marries a neighboring farmer, Patrick Leighton (son of two characters in *A Haunted Land*), but the marriage is loveless and neither Diana nor Patrick can quite relate fully to Keithy, who in his simplicity and innocence is a charming person: all are "bystanders," with tragic results.

The loneliness explored in the first two novels is given further treatment in the figure of the aged and failing missionary, Heriot, of *To the Islands* (1958), the novel that brought Stow international acclaim. After some preliminary action during which Heriot believes he has killed a man, a long journey begins "to the islands"—an exterior narrative of hardship and at the same time an interior quest for peace out of tumult and self-hate. Both landscapes are carefully developed and in a climactic fashion. In the "country of caves, where bluffs and cliffs of rock were split with dark holes," for instance, Heriot finds cave-paintings,

. . . the crude figure of a man without a mouth, his head outlined with a horseshoe shape like that of the rainbow serpent.

"I know you," he said. "You are Wolaro. God. What does it matter what you are called."[24]

And at the end of the journey he stares at the ocean, still looking for "islands" which he cannot see:

His carved lips were firm in the white beard, his hands were steady, his ancient blue eyes, neither hoping nor fearing, searched sun and sea for the least dark hint of a landfall.

"My soul," he whispered, over the sea-surge, "my soul is a strange country."[25]

Tourmaline, published in 1963—there is a break in the rapid productivity at the beginning of Stow's career—takes its name from an old mining town which is very nearly a ghost town, at the dead end of a desert road through "no stretch of land on earth more ancient than this." Into the town comes—is brought, rather, half-dead from exposure—a young man, Michael Random, who describes himself as a diviner. Both mystical and mysterious, he encounters an adversary in Kestrel, a realist and unbeliever. These two intersect with other characters, and all the characters in fact seem to blend into the setting, which is made to represent—as the people themselves do, in their variety—both desolation and potentiality, as for example in the description of the abandoned church:

The church is of tender brown and rose stone. Beside it, an oleander impossibly persists in flowering. Planks are falling from the wooden bell-tower, but the bell is there still; and in dust-storms and on nights of high wind its irregular tolling sweeps away over Tourmaline to the south.[26]

Of all the novels, perhaps this one is the most resolutely "poetic."

Childhood, as shown by *The Bystander,* has interested Stow very much; and in *The Merry-Go-Round in the Sea* (1965), the chief figure is a boy, Bob Coram. Bob's cousin Rick, to whom he looks as an elder male, goes to war and after a period of years returns, changed and still changing as of course Bob is too. The relatively small amount of action provides room for description both of place and of mood. Finally comes *Midnite: The Story of a Wild Colonial Boy* (1967), which is at the same time a children's book and, for adults, a burlesque of Australian folklore, most particularly the long-lived desperado portion of it. A seventeen-year-old orphan boy, good-natured but none too bright, sets himself up as Captain Midnite and enlists a band of animals—cat, cow, horse, sheepdog, cockatoo—as his accomplices and, more than once, his rescuers.

In discussing sense of place in Stow's novels, Ray Willbanks points out how setting—often used as a determinant of character—adds uncommon strength:

It is not so much that a character is inescapably molded by his immediate environment, made victim by it in the sense that philosophical naturalism would have it, as it is that a character is strongly conditioned by his surroundings. Malin is to *A Haunted Land* what *Wuthering Heights* is to that novel. Heriot's personality, his sense of spiritual isolation and loneliness, is heightened through his long years of geographical isolation at the mission. The people of Tourmaline, cut off from the rest of the world by their desert isolation, interact in a way that a people with the possibility of communication beyond the limits of their town would not. As an influence on character, one might add that setting is also important to Stow's work because of his own interest in the particular Australian nature of his places. While his concerns are universal enough that an isolated place might serve as the setting for *A Haunted Land, The Bystander,* or *Tourmaline,* and any small town and its environs might serve as a background to play out his insights into childhood, his interest in communicating a sense of what is specifically regional, uniquely Australian is what, given his descriptive powers, makes his fiction outstanding.[27]

A recent novel by another poet-novelist, *Johnno* (1975) by David Malouf, may be cited as a bridge to the next section, in which Malouf chronologically as well as ideologically belongs. Sympathetic treatment of the young is common both to Stow and Malouf, and we see in the following passage a rather Stow-like realization of change, from the young person's viewpoint. Surprisingly, to his friends, the larrikin-like Johnno begins to become interested in his studies— geology most of all—and is "about to settle, after all, for the *predictable*":

It was, I suppose, a kind of meanness in us to insist that the old Johnno should not die. . . . If Johnno was not Johnno where did any of us stand? But changes can't be resisted, and we might have observed, if we had bothered to look, that he had ceased to be an ugly duckling, all arms and legs, with a head too big for his body, and had developed, as if to match his aspirations, the long hard lines of an athlete. He was tall, well-built, relaxed as he jogged round the oval in his spiked shoes; and girls, if they hadn't been scared off by the tales they had heard of him, might even have found him good looking. He had simply outgrown our idea of him, and we found it difficult to accept the fact without making allowance for commensurate changes in ourselves.[28]

Continuing "Popular" Fiction

Before passing on to the overt experimentalists, we need to make room for a sizable group who are commonly consigned to an elastic purgatory called "popular" fiction. This is neither a very satisfactory term nor—divisive as it is—a very generous concept, but it is still widely in use and tends to govern the availability of informed opinion. Somehow, critics (especially academic ones) seem to feel that *creative* and *popular* are descriptors somewhat analogous to *pure* and *applied,* as in mathematics and science, most often to be distinguished by the fact of success in the marketplace. That the best-seller *is* quite often superficial is shown by the way it so frequently fades from attention within a few years of its appearance; yet commercial success, in itself, is surely not invariably an absolute qualification, as the reputations of writers like Scott, Dickens, Mark Twain, and more modern figures remind us. Recognizing the unsatisfactory operation of this distinction but still instructed by the broad drift of critical opinion, we should accord such writers at least the courtesy of honorable mention, wondering if in some instances that is really enough.

The occasional writer, of course, makes his or her way slowly into critical acceptance after having been branded as "merely" popular. This has been true, as suggested, of Thea Astley, whose gifts, says H. P. Heseltine—a little cautiously—"are much more for social observation, often recorded with wit and a pungent satire."

Her characters are usually middle-class, their problems sometimes petty, but [her] books . . . bring an urbanity and intelligence in their comments on society and manners hitherto little known in the Australian novel.[29]

A quartet of veterans—Jon Cleary, D'Arcy Niland, Olaf Ruhen, and Morris West—are mentioned by Serle as inheritors of a "new professionalism . . . which enabled skillful writers . . . who shaped their work for a popular market, to make reasonable incomes."[30] Of these, West is by far the most wide-ranging in his settings, having used Australia only once, and that under a pseudonym in 1960.[31] His stories are set, for example, in places as widely separated as Italy,

(*The Devil's Advocate,* 1959; *The Salamander,* 1973), the Middle East (*The Tower of Babel,* 1968), and Indonesia (*The Concubine,* 1958). Cleary and Niland, by contrast, remain mostly at home, as does also Ruhen—home being interpreted, for him, as the whole Southwest Pacific. Some of the early novels by both Niland (now deceased) and his wife Ruth Park are currently being reprinted; and in a large, chronicle-type novel, *Swords and Crowns and Rings* (1978), Park explores the 1920s and early Depression by bringing to Sydney two young people who have grown up in a country town.

James Aldridge, whose war novels (especially those with flying scenes) and stories of outdoor sports and exploration have drawn praise for their vigor, has been like West an expatriate, with only the occasional attempt at the Australian setting.[32] Barbara Jefferis's *The Tall One* (1977), like *Time of the Unicorn* (1974), is set in medieval England, where Mary Mary Harney and her twin brother Dickon, born to poor parents, struggle to improve their lot. Mary Mary's narrative, in first person, is a picaresque account of her matings, childbirth, life in a traveling freak show (she is six feet tall) and a convent, and finally her return full circle to her original home.

A highly successful newcomer, Colleen McCullough, produced in *Tim* (1974) a story developed with sensitivity and understanding both of the gentle side of man's nature and the beauty of his surroundings. The title character, Tim Melville, twenty-five, a handsome but mentally retarded unskilled laborer, meets Mary Horton, in her mid-forties and in most respects his opposite: a keenly intelligent, wealthy spinster. A platonic friendship develops, each giving the other a richer life but also plummeting toward an inevitable problem and a surprising solution. In this passage, Tim and Mary regard a cicada in Mary's garden:

"Oh, don't be afraid of him, Mary," Tim begged, smiling up at her and stroking the cicada softly. "Look, isn't he lovely, all green and pretty like a butterfly?"

The golden head was bent over the cicada; Mary stared down at them both in sudden, blinding pity. Tim seemed to have some kind of rapport with the creature, for it lay on his palm without panic or fear, and it was indeed beautiful, once one forgot its Martian antennae and lobsterish carapace. It had a fat, bright green body about two inches long, tinted with a powdering of real gold, and its eyes glittered and sparkled like two big topazes. Over its back the delicate, transparent wings were folded still, veined like a leaf with bright yellow gold and shimmering with every color of the

rainbow. And above it crouched Tim, just as alien and just as beautiful, as
alive and gleaming.

"You don't really want me to kill him, do you?" Tim pleaded, gazing up
at her in sudden sadness.

"No," she replied, turning away. "Put him back in his bush, Tim."[33]

The Thorn Birds (1977), by contrast, uses the traditional format of the
family chronicle, applying it to a set of characters whose strong personalities take them inexorably away from the familial center, Drogh-
eda, the N.S.W. sheep station owned by the Clearys through half a
century and more. Meggie, the only girl among seven children, becomes the central figure. Meggie's great love for a priest, Ralph de
Briccassart, winds in and out of her life and those of her two children, Dane, who follows in Ralph's footsteps, and Justine, who becomes a well-known London actress. Toward the end of this sizable
novel, the explanation of the title phrase is given during a conversation between Meggie and Ralph.

> Her hand stole along his bare arm, tenderly. "Dear Ralph, I do see it. I
> know, I know. . . . Each of us has something within us which won't be de-
> nied, even if it makes us scream aloud to die. We are what we are, that's
> all. Like the old Celtic legend of the bird with the thorn in its breast, sing-
> ing its heart out and dying. Because it has to, it's driven to. We can know
> what we do wrong even before we do it, but self-knowledge can't affect or
> change the outcome, can it? Everyone singing his own little song, convinced
> it's the most wonderful the world has ever heard. Don't you see? We create
> our own thorns, and never stop to count the cost. All we can do is suffer
> the pain, and tell ourselves it was well worth it."
>
> "That's what I don't understand. The pain." He glanced down at her
> hand, so gently on his arm, hurting him so unbearably. "Why the pain,
> Meggie?"
>
> "Ask God, Ralph," said Meggie. "He's the authority on pain, isn't He?
> He made us what we are, He made the whole world. Therefore He made
> the pain, too."[34]

Is this the stuff of which "popular" novels are made? What will it
look like in five years, or in ten? Time will tell us. Meanwhile, this
author has published another novel, *An Indecent Obsession* (1981). Perhaps there is merit on the current scene for at least some degree of
the extensibility suggested in a recent statement (in *New Currents in
Australian Writing,* 1978) by a prominent Australian critic: "By fic-

tion I mean anything that calls itself fiction—and in these days that is a pretty elastic label"—a concession that applies with double force to the pages immediately following.

"A Wild Ass of a Trend": Business as Usual and Unusual

In 1963 Barry Oakley published a novel called *A Wild Ass of a Man,* from which title the heading of this section derives. It was not the first fictional expression of the counterculture, Australian strain, but it was fairly early and, as well, conveyed its message in a "fast word-tumbling, image-jumbling prose [which] is warming, high-spirited, and very infectious."[35] It is likewise, when taken too much at a time, rather exhausting to the reader. The novel of the counterculture, one could say if he wanted to be uncharitable, has its own electronic amplifier which puts it in a class with the discotheque: louder is better, loudest is best.

The rise of this species in the 1960s[36] coincided with a re-examination of the Australian commercial and industrial world by writers, including poets and dramatists as well as novelists, which was even less sympathetic than that of earlier observers such as Alan Marshall (*How Beautiful Are Thy Feet,* 1949, an unbeautiful view of shoe manufacturing), or as far back as Edward Dyson's *Fact'ry 'Ands* (1906). We have already noted that Calthorpe, Cusack, Hewett, and others took unflattering views of postwar industry in Australia; and to the titles of their works might be added such others as D. H. Crick's *Martin Place* (1964, a study of several intersecting lives in Sydney's world of business, which at length is rejected, the central character having despaired of coming to terms with the big three—politics, business, religion). The newspaper world, as generally supportive of the business community, was examined by Tony Morphett (*Dynasty,* 1967) and T. M. A. Graham (*The Paper Men,* 1969, which described the Melbourne newspaper world as thoroughly depraved). Morphett's *Mayor's Nest* (1964) was one of the earlier productions of the "mad" school, in which the easygoing sawmill owner and mayor of Parramatta, Jack McDonald, suddenly becomes dictator of Australia by virtue of a tardily discovered decree of George III. Chaos ensues, and the whole Australian establishment exposes its underpinnings of clay. "Young man's satire," it was appropriately called; "friendlier and more boyant [than that of elder Australian satirists like Cyril Pearl]," with a plot describable only as "a sublime piece of nonsense."[37] Morphett's *Thorskald* (1969), by contrast, is the life story of a painter, told chiefly through the life stories of numerous people who knew him; Thorskald may have been unorthodox, but the method by which he is presented is largely sober and coherent, comparable with Thea Astley's *The Acolyte* a few years later. So is Dan Reidy's *It's This Way* (1964), though *sober* might be too neutral to characterize this account of a schoolteacher who sees himself comically—in picaresque, laced with Thoreau, Tolstoy, Spinoza, and others. It is an antidote to some of the more febrile fiction of about the same time or a bit later, yet it partakes of its mood to a degree. For example, this tongue-in-cheek bit of self-criticism:

Like Paul on the road to Damascus I had seen a light and things could never be the same; no longer could I continue persecuting and flogging; a pale Galilean spirit had got me and was driving me forward to the New Jerusalem. Life was great. I had my bow of burning gold, like Blake, and also my arrows of desire and it wasn't long before the clouds unfolded and delivered me of my chariot of fire.[38]

Quite another brand of academic cat (this time a fat one) appears in Keith Leopold's *My Brow Is Wet* (1970). Dr. Steve Hinton, lecturer in comparative literature at Queensland University of Technology (familiarly known as Quot), turns to making money through crime— kidnapping (with the collusion of the student victim, a millionaire's son from Singapore), a faked libel suit, and so on—and does very well. At the close, he is in the hospital but on the mend and calculates his take thus far as being well over $100,000. Here we meet him in mid-career:

Forty minutes later I was opening a cheque account with twenty thousand dollars in a large bank in Queen Street in the heart of the city. I gave my name as Victor Sartre. Ten minutes later I opened another account with twenty thousand dollars at another large city bank. This one was in the name of Paul Hugo. . . . I returned to Quot and spent the rest of the day waiting for students who didn't come and thinking about my new wealth. To people like Doug [a colleague, the professor of petroleum engineering, another operator], Monty, and George the Graze forty thousand dollars was undoubtedly chickenfeed. To me it was an incredible fortune.[39]

Academic life in Australia receives further examination at the hands of D. A. Aitken (*The Second Chair*, 1977), Michael Wilding (*Scenic*

Drive, 1976), and doubtless several others. Novelists are not infrequently academics themselves, and several university presses are active in publishing recent fiction.

Having now forecast the main thrust of the wild-ass school of fiction and before going on to illustrate it, we should ask why it arose and what its significance may be. For help we may turn to an instructive summary, written also in the mid-1960s, of tendencies that not all of us may be as yet completely alive to, or at least may feel that our struggles to come to terms with them have not been notably successful and therefore must continue to occupy our time and attention. Jack Lindsay, in a *Meanjin* article on Patrick White's short stories, asks, "What then are the issues in art or literature that came with the new century and are still with us?" and goes on to point out that as the result of a major break that was "more decisive than previous efforts to gain a new start," existing methods of construction fell under suspicion and social relations were subjected to "quite new factors of dislocation," not least among them the advent of the highly centralized State. Faced with all this,

The inner division of the individual reached a new intensity; no "real life" was less and less the life one lived. To express this deepening alienation the Bergsonian formulation was found the most useful, and through Joyce and Proust it has passed into general circulation in endlessly modified forms: the opposition of clocktime (habit, the workaday world, the abstracting intellect, all that divides, oppresses, and reflects the fragmentation of man in a mechanistic world) to inner time, the intuition of the timeless moment of concrete experience. With the revolt against the clockworld and its habitual (false) constructions, the old forms of characterisation and narrative lost their virtues and appeared as forms for deadening and disguising human reality. The novelist (poet, artist, etc.), faced with such a disintegrated and delusive world, felt the need for new methods capable of grasping the concrete moment in its fulness and of breaking down the false appearances.

These comments are highly generalised, but they state briefly what have been the preoccupations of serious art for the last couple of generations. (Socialist writing has in general so far failed to solve the problems because it has assumed that the restoration of social purpose makes it possible to carry on with pre-1900 forms and ignore all that has since been done; it attempts a contemporary art without a contemporary sensibility.)[40]

With this much to steer us, we may grasp our ball of string and enter the limbo of the Great Australian Inback, as seen by a number of licensed guides.

The year 1966 saw publication of two novels introducing resolutely
conceived antiheroes, Peter Mathers's *Trap* and Morris Lurie's *Rappaport*. The second is set nominally in Melbourne, but Lurie shortly
thereafter moves the production to London in *The London Jungle Adventures of Charlie Hope* (1968) and continues it there in *Rappaport's
Revenge* (1973), a spectacle somewhat in the mode of Mordecai Richler's farce-novels but not as skillfully done. *Trap* and its successor *The
Wort Papers* (1972) are both as aggressively Australian as the flies in
Canberra. Jack Trap of Melbourne, forty, a compound of "Squatter
English, convict Irish, Tierra del Fuegan Yahgan, and First Australian," is a wild man and general public nuisance—something of a dis-
solute but at times convincingly engaging Gulliver among a great
crowd of Yahoos, his contemporaries. The story ranges from 1830 to
the present, breaks down conventions of fiction, assaults White Australia (or WASP Australia, perhaps): in short, "with the emergence
of Peter Mathers, a terrible talent is born."[41] L. J. Clancy, who sees
affinities with Herbert's *Capricornia* in the "savage ironic chronicling," describes the form of the novel as being "roughly the shape
of a cone":

At first it concentrates solely on Jack himself, but as it proceeds its vision
steadily widens to include, eventually in the discussion of Jack's forebears,
the whole savage history of the Aboriginal race: the shooting down and poi-
soning by white settlers; exploitation by businessmen and missionaries;
abuse and mistreatment by foremen and fellow-workers; and finally, assaults
by police and gaolings by magistrates.[42]

The Wort Papers fulfills the expectations inspired by *Trap*, confirming
the prediction of a "terrible talent." The "papers," which appear out
of a butter-box from Uppersass, chronicle an Australian stickywork-
saga through both rural and urban situations, with improbable jour-
neys and even more improbable journey makers, quite often in such
mood as "I kept going because I was too damn frightened by what I
was thinking about to stop."[43] It is crowded with description, rendered at times with Rabelaisian exhilaration. In the words of the concluding sentence, "We move on."

Barry Oakley's James Muldoon of *A Wild Ass of a Man* (1968) is
a lapsed Catholic whose endlessly adaptable personality enables him
to change roles in the manner of the other antiheroes we have already
encountered. *A Salute to the Great McCarthy* (1970) is a left-handed

salute to still another facet of Australian big business known as football, told in first-person narrative by McCarthy himself. Are the games a mirror of the national character? McCarthy says of one club he played for:

Kingswood is a tough suburb, an inner industrial area, and the Depression of the thirties moved through it like a fire. Football in this suburb isn't a sport, it's a way of venting your hate. Overbearing when they won, sullen when they lost, . . . they were on the way up again, because they hated so well.[44]

In *Let's Hear It for Prendergast* (1970), Prendergast—the "world's tallest poet" and messiah of the absurd, promises his audience:

> O lost people
>   wandering through labyrinths of merchandise
> Follow the thread of my argument
> Hang on to my words
>   all genuine
>   not artificially coloured or flavoured.
> I'll lead you past the snapping jaws of the cash registers
>   and the cold-eyed floor managers
>   to the pure, free unpackaged land—[45]

And in the words of Huck Finn, "he done it, too": after numerous rude pranks that tear things up on a small scale, he reaches at last the pure, unpackaged land in a fire-bombing gesture of a Melbourne exhibition, during which he is consumed along with the frippery he sets ablaze. Other "poet-hero" novels of the time include two satires: (1) Juliet Rolleston, *In My Lady's Chamber* (1963): feminism takes a farcical twist when a failed poet from Canberra decides to write a novel about women and, in search of authentic material, poses as a woman and takes a job as nursemaid; and (2) Colin Free, *Carbon Copy* (1972): one poet writes bad verse in the name of another and becomes instantly popular—the Ern Malley hoax redone as a rivalry, with complications over sex partners, and so on, and both poets emerging, at last, as ridiculous.

David Ireland is much less of a carefree Katzenjammer than his immediate predecessors. His first novel, *The Chantic Bird* (1968), describes a psychopathic boy in his late teens, who experiments with a wide range of violence and loves it all. Having taken up with a writer (interested in the boy as a subject) whom he kills and dismembers, he undertakes to continue the unfinished book about himself and finally—not a moment too soon—is removed from society by a heart attack. *The Unknown Industrial Prisoner* (1971) lays down its battle plan in the first chapter, "One Day in a Penal Colony":

> "Fight 'em! Every step of the way!"
> "They've got the whip hand. What do you fight with?"
> "Smiles, a quick wit, sex, alcohol, and never say Yes to the bastards. Once you recognize the place is a prison, you're well off. The best that can be said is everyone draws an indefinite sentence. The final horror of a life behind barbed wire is mercifully withheld." He glanced out at the high wire fence they were passing then, topped with several strands of barbed wire. "You see, the battleground where they beat you is in here." His long, friendly brown hand lay relaxed on his own high, resonant chest.[46]

To this end, there is provided a disjunctive mosaic of episodes varying from a brief paragraph to several pages, each with a catchword heading—One Good Turn, Assembly Line Love, Shadows in the Cave, Gotcha, The Will of the People, Replaceable Parts, Ship of Fools, and many more. Characters bear names like The Glass Canoe, Grey Goldfish, Samurai, Great White Father, Canada Dry, Good Shepherd, Cement Head, and Whispering Baritone. One of these "bipeds" named Far Away Places looks at the industrial ugliness of the "squat control room with its flat roof already scarred by well-aimed bolts and metal droppings from the welders," its air "gauzy with gas," and fantasizes an alternative:

> If only a man could get away. A small farm somewhere. . . . A few sheep, fruit trees, bit of a garden. Christ, it was a glorious dream! It was freedom.
> Freedom? It was isolation and that was better. Feel of the wind on your face, the sun warming you, . . . A dream. A man wakes up one day, realizes the world was made for other people and knows he's going to be at the arse end all his life. Nothing here for a man to live on. A pay packet stops you from dying, it doesn't teach you to live.[47]

Does such a saturation pattern work? Yes and no; a good many readers may feel rather badly flogged after a hundred pages or so of such unremitting ambivalence, but there is no doubt of the gusto and technical brilliance of the writing.

Ireland's *The Flesheaters* (1972) is another social satire with one of the central figures, Clayton Emmet, constantly remarking, "All that is not Industrial Production is therapy." Tongue in cheek? "Progress," he also says, "is the worst flesheater of all."

"Our existence depends on the death of other organisms and the despoiling of the planet. In a jungle only the strongest animals survive. The higher animals—denoted by their capacity and desire for war—survive by slaughter."
He seemed so anxious to persuade that his tone became bullying. She looked up at him with clear eyes, not understanding why she should be scolded.[48]

The Glass Canoe (1976), set in a Sydney pub, the Southern Cross, is a series of tales related by Meat Man, one of the habitués. It blends humor, bawdiness and violence, with futility and wastage as final precipitates.

Frank Moorhouse began publishing at about the same time as Oakley and Ireland. When his *Futility and Other Animals* first appeared in 1969, it was thought to be so avant-garde in content that booksellers were reluctant to display it, although it was not banned by the Australian censors. The book explains itself in these words (in a prefatory note):

These are interlinked stories and, although the narrative is discontinuous and there is no single plot, the environment and characters are continuous. In some ways, the people in the stories are a tribe; a modern, urban tribe which does not fully recognize itself as a tribe. Some of the people are central members of the tribe while others are hermits who live on the fringe. The shared environment is both internal (anxieties, pleasures and confusions) and external (the houses, streets, hotels and experiences). The central dilemma is that of giving birth, of creating new life.[49]

Moorhouse's *The Electrical Experience* (1974), published after a book of stories, *The Americans, Baby* (1973, fantasy escapes into paranoia, grotesque sexuality, and soon, with American commercial clichés and travesties of American moderns like Hemingway—fallout from Vietnam, perhaps?), has as its central figure T. George McDowell, whose experiences occur in "discontinuous narratives" which appear to be the author's continuing mode. McDowell, a soft-drink manufacturer from New South Wales, is a contradictory semithinker trying to place himself in the general plan of things but never succeeding. Besides its discontinuous narrative line the book contains illustrations and other embellishments along with "helpful hints" of varying helpfulness. (Is the novel, too, headed for the coffee table? One may wonder, after looking at this one and others—some Canadian ones, for example—expensively got up.) Also in 1974 appeared Michael Wilding's *Living Together,* a "dump-the-whole-load" exercise at removing any lingering vestiges of inhibition. "Why," exclaims one of the characters (evidently a newcomer) on page 189, "are you all so neurotic here?" Well, if she had slogged her way through the previous 188 pages of graffiti, she wouldn't have needed to ask. The drug culture appears in such works as David Foster's *Escape to Reality* (1977) or Helen Garner's *Monkey Grip* (1978). At latest word, society was not yet off the hook: David Foster's *Moonlite* (1981) is an Aesopian satire on Australian history.

Predictably, writing so contrivedly and consistently *sansculotte* invites (and doubtless must obtain, to flourish) criticism ranging somewhere between polite indignation and impolite outrage. The mid-seventies supply us with these two paragraphs, which may be enough to suggest one type of response. Instead of crying "foul!" the critic cries "fake!"—as probably more wounding.

Certain dicta spring forcibly to mind as a result of reading these four books—to be fashionable is not to be original; to talk about dullness or stereotypy is not necessarily always to evade those vices oneself. There is a plethora of currently saleable, trendy clichés, and a rather indulgent dwelling on a life-style just barely beyond the borders of respectability. There is less ennui, desperation, and art than in Beckett, less genuine assertion and assault than in Genet, and the lovingly considered sexual curiosities are distinctly sub-Sadean.[50]

Like science fiction come true, our writers give us robots, humanoids, the automatons from distant galaxies inheriting the earth we have failed to love, gimmicky dreams arranged mechanically, methods of fictional composition which will one day be performed with greater thoroughness by a computer. Whatever experimentation there has been in our fiction has been imported and acclimatized to middlebrow demands: Australian anti-intellectualism has finally found its accommodations in fake intellectual guise.[51]

One can hope, and in a few cases at least can probably expect, that the best work (still to come) of this energetic young group will settle somewhere between their early experimentations (which almost always tend to excess) and the traditions against which they were directed. Perhaps a swing has already begun to take place, if one can judge by such a novel as Geoff Wyatt's *The Tidal Forest* (1974). This is the first in a projected cycle of novels, intended to follow the career of an observer, here an orphan boy named Roddy. Set in the decaying town of Meteora, south-central Victoria, the episodic plot seems less important than the evocations of atmosphere both past and present—descriptively rich and semipoetic—keyed to excerpts from Dylan Thomas which are used to establish mood. Not that this pattern would be more interesting or acceptable, perhaps—only that the tempo and volume of what has been appearing for the past few years are so extreme that some kind of modulating reaction seems inevitable.

Whatever the response in Australia may be (and there is no difficulty imagining what the squares, the "Ockers," must think of it all), one thing is plain: the view of life these writers represent is worldwide, not by any means localized in Australia but showing similar (and simultaneous) manifestations (or epiphanies, in the more stylish way of putting it) in English-speaking North America, Europe, and elsewhere. So far, it has generated more dichotomy than dialogue: structure vs. amorphism, sequence vs. simultaneity, discernible level vs. free flotation, verbal decorum vs. verbal assault, shaped component vs. undefined containing-envelope, graded evolution vs. mutation, and so on. Are we in fact approaching—or perchance have we already reached—a point at which rebellion is already old hat, way-out no longer in, thumbing the nose only one more way of scratching it? If so, these writers are merely redundant and must very quickly fade. At least they do give at times the incongruous impression of anxiety, of wishing to establish antiestablishmentarianism, of cult construction, of newfangled exclusiveness. Are they indeed no more than too many cooks for some new brand of marmalade?

For comprehensive lists of new writing as well as interviews with the writers, the October 1977 number of *Australian Literary Studies* is very useful; and Brian Kiernan's introduction to *The Most Beautiful Lies,* a 1977 collection of stories by Bail, Carey, Lurie, Moorhouse, and Wilding, offers a genetic account of the movement. *The Outback Reader: A Collection of Australian Contemporary and Experimental Short Fiction* (1975), edited by Michael Dugan and John Jenkins, is a sampler of some two hundred pages by eighteen authors, in which experimentation ranges all the way from automatic writing (or what sounds like it) through concrete poetry, film sequences, patheticism, and surrealism onward to Zen Buddhism. "It is implicit in the nature of experiment," say the editors in their brief introduction, "that there is a greater chance of failure, although the more radical the experiment the more difficult it is to establish a standard by which to make a qualitative assessment." There we may as well leave it.

Patrick White

Any attempt to classify, to categorize Patrick White's fiction is useful chiefly to show how stubbornly his work resists classification. Is it usefully divisible on any geographical basis, for instance? No; most of the settings are Australian but by no means all. Do any discernible differences in theme, in ideology, offer a basis for division? Again no; the novels are about the condition of Mark Twain's "damned human race," often in far darker tones than Twain's blackest pessimism ever invoked, touching all classes. Is there then a bias of emphasis between certain kinds of characters, most obviously, perhaps, male and female? Here it can be said that in some novels and stories men do tend to dominate *(The Tree of Man, Voss, The Vivisector, The Solid Mandala)* and in others, women *(The Aunt's Story, The Eye of the Storm, A Fringe of Leaves)*, but closer inspection soon shows us that both sexes are in fact omnipresent and any emphasis on one or the other is not finally significant: heroes and heroines share the stage about equally. In *The Twyborn Affair,* indeed, they become interchangeable. Is White social or antisocial, religious or irreligious, democratic or aristocratic, aesthetic or psychological or anthropological? Are his characters (like a good many in current fiction) chiefly reflections of himself? Brian Kiernan answers such a query by saying:

The attempt to find some correspondence between the world within (of ego, memory, aspiration) and the world without (both the social world of other selves and the natural world) involves the major characters in all his novels. Each might be defeated, but the variety of inner worlds that White has created for them must counteract the impression from individual novels that he has withdrawn into solipsism.[52]

The magnitude of his achievement, suitably recognized by the Nobel Prize for literature in 1973, can be sensed all the more through our failures to affix any such boundaries or separations. (In all, he has published, through 1979, a baker's dozen works of fiction: eleven novels and two collections of short stories.)

Suppose—still trying for some broad basis of approach at the outset of our short visit—we imagine that this unclassifiable author has confronted the human condition as squarely as possible in order to earn the right to ask the ultimate question. Take life at its lowest levels, its most dilapidated, unbuttoned, ineffectual, unmanageable, or plainly revolting circumstances, then enquire: is it worth what it costs, this unequal struggle, this endless chronicle of suffering? The answer he gives us is firmly yes, but not before we have reviewed the evidence, which he steadily refuses to edit or cosmetize. Not unsimilarly, he asks, or implies through his practice, questions about fictional form, as Jack Lindsay reminds us:

White forces us to reconsider the nature of the novel, its relation to social process and individual experience, its ways of exploring new dimensions of consciousness; and this involves in turn a reconsideration of the nature of man himself and of just what is happening to people in the modern world—what are the forces to which they are subjected, how they are changing, and in what direction.[53]

The novels at the beginning of his career (preceded by inconsequential feints at poetry and drama) do stand somewhat apart so far as quality is concerned: *Happy Valley* (1939) and *The Living and the Dead* (1941). The first of these is set in a small town, ironically christened, in outback New South Wales. The plot, hung on the sharp corners of two love triangles, involves chiefly a doctor, Oliver Holliday, who functions mostly as a spokesman for the individualistic point of view. The second, set in England, contains only one triangle but takes a family chronicle from the beginning of the century to the 1930s. Critics see it as stylistically somewhat dependent upon the reigning figures in British fiction of the thirties: Joyce, Lawrence, and Woolf. Both of these novels are generally regarded as apprenticework, but it should be observed that *Happy Valley* clearly served notice on Australians as to what they might prepare themselves to expect. Thus White set the stage himself for a long period of controversy and critical coolness, which it may be well to look at before proceeding to his major works.

With a good many Australians still rather paper-skinned about their nationality, quite a bit like early Americans when Charles Dickens broke their hearts with *American Notes,* such comments from White as this one (in an essay, "The Prodigal Son," 1958) would never endear him:

> In all directions stretched the Great Australian Emptiness, in which the mind is the least of possessions, in which the rich man is the important man, in which the schoolmaster and the journalist rule what intellectual roost there is, in which beautiful youths and girls stare at life through blind blue eyes, in which human teeth fall like autumn leaves, the buttocks of cars grow hourly glassier, food means cake and steak, muscles prevail, and the march of material ugliness does not raise a quiver from the average nerves.[54]

Except for the reference to automobiles, virtually all of what is said here might have been taken from Dickens's book of the mid-nineteenth century. It should be added that an increasing minority of Australians would agree, substantially, with these strictures.

In the same essay, drawing nearer to the problem of being a literary artist in the Great Australian Emptiness, White says, of undertaking *The Tree of Man,* that

> It was the exaltation of the "average" that made me panic most, and in this frame of mind, in spite of myself, I began to conceive another novel. Because the void I had to fill was so immense, I wanted to try to suggest in this book every possible aspect of life, through the lives of an ordinary man and woman. But at the same time I wanted to discover the extraordinary behind the ordinary, the mystery and the poetry which alone could make bearable the lives of such people, and incidentally, my own life since my return.[55]

White also said, in another context, that in writing *Voss* he was "above all, determined to prove that the Australian novel is not the dreary, dun-coloured offspring of journalistic realism" (quoted in the *Penguin Book of Australian Short Stories,* p. 11).

Scholars are now inclined to deny, or at least play down, some of the impression of a massive Australian hostility to White's work. Alan Lawson, for example, writing in *Meanjin* not long after the Nobel Prize award, surveyed White's critical reception both in Australia and elsewhere, concluding that his treatment "has not been worse in Australia than elsewhere: it has indeed been much better in many respects."[56] He did have to face, however, the uncompromising disapproval of critics like A. D. Hope who thundered out of dark Olympian clouds (from the heights of Canberra) in such language as "he knows too much, he tells too much and he talks too much" with the unhappy result that (*The Tree of Man* is here being stormed at) his work is "pretentious and illiterate verbal sludge."[57] In his essay "Standards in Australian Literature" (1956), Hope speaks in less extreme terms, though still disapprovingly, and includes *Voss* in a list of "successful Australian novels written since the turn of the century" which "create a picture of the country through the medium of fiction."[58]

Alongside such less than generous treatment it is satisfying to record that in Australia there could be found a critic as evenhanded and at the same time perceptive of high potential in a writer as Edwin Muir had been in his early review of *The Living and the Dead*. Marjorie Barnard's 1956 review article in *Meanjin*, "The Four Novels of Patrick White," relatively early on the Australian scene (or indeed virtually any scene, at that time), describes White's prose as

. . . not the traditional Australian discursiveness, like a yarn told at the campfire. White is an artist who knows how to use his material and is sometimes too skillful for verisimilitude. He uses various styles to achieve his ends . . . stream-of-consciousness . . . broken sentence . . . Joycean idiom. . . . at moments it is almost in the vein of Gertrude Stein.[59]

In summary, Barnard (a distinguished historian-novelist, already encountered as part of the collaborative team M. Barnard Eldershaw) finds *The Tree of Man* "done with great patience, insight and art, and . . . deeply moving,"[60] a work in which, despite "always the burden of pain, . . . the goal of man's long, inarticulate searching is glimpsed."

It is the ineffable moment. It has no substance, it is of the creative spirit, it comes and it goes; but that it should come, even once in a lifetime, is a positive gain, an apotheosis. It is the troubling of the waters at Bethesda. It does not touch the loneliness for it is a personal, private and detached revelation. Each man's life is a mystery between himself and God. . . .

Poetry, music, religion are the paths that the soul, imprisoned in flesh, may take, "the paths out of sleep." Life is an illusion, pain a certainty but the capacity to feel pain is the mask of the human being. And pain is its own reward.[61]

Another critic, Vincent Buckley, in seeing White fundamentally, irrecoverably removed from the campfire tradition, makes an interesting observation on White and Furphy (who along with Lawson virtually *is* the campfire tradition):

White is an impressive mixture of the sophisticated and the naive; but he is not some queer hybrid phenomenon. He is, in some sense, in the line of Joseph Furphy: not the Furphy whom our nostalgic critics love to idolize, the whimsical raconteur beneath the bullock-dray, but the Furphy whose unillusioned, ironic and sophisticated attitude to the human predicament was pleasantly new in his own day, as it is still. But I think White is bigger than Furphy.[62]

Having explored this far in the continually growing commentary on White, we turn now to a brief examination of his novels and stories from 1948 through 1976.

The Aunt's Story (1948) gives us in Theodora ("loved of God") Goodman the first in White's company of mystics and fool-saints. Largely new, as well, are shifts in style and content from the earlier two novels: a sharply increased use of symbols and symbolic language, together with multiple layers of meaning. It takes Theodora, following the death of her mother (to whom she has been a kind of bond-slave), away from Australia first to the French Riviera and at length to the American Midwest. We see her withdrawing more and more into herself—"going to pieces," as we are accustomed to say, and yet her physical and social disintegration seems to offer her compensations within herself; she is subtly ennobled by the experience of release.

Theodora's rejection of the world of persons is forced upon her not simply by the inadequacy—judged by narrowly rational standards—of her own nature, but by that nature's sense of the selfishness, uncreativeness and philistinism of the world she moves in. Her withdrawal is not merely a psychological but a moral revulsion.[63]

We shall see, as we progress through the novels, that White's choice of a woman as protagonist is not a mere caprice but a constant, a correlative to life. It is instructive to note, as well, that Australian women writers before White had explored in considerable depth the theme of suffering and its excruciating consequences to all concerned. Barbara Baynton, Henry Handel Richardson, Eleanor Dark, and

Christina Stead are all distinguished figures in this special context, and there are numerous others.

The Tree of Man (1955) is a much roomier novel than *The Aunt's Story* both in its time framework and in the number of characters it employs. It is a family chronicle, with noticeable differences from the genre as used by, say, Richardson, Palmer, or Barnard Eldershaw: the story of Stan and Amy Parker, pioneers in the bush who live the kind of lives that many thousands of Australian couples lived from the end of the nineteenth century into the mid-twentieth. The work is structured in quasi-symphonic fashion using several groups or sequences of four: the seasons, the classical four elements, and—marking the stages in a continuing search for stability in a slippery world—four movements that the Swedish critic Björkstén describes as innocence, experience, death, and reconciliation. "Experience" includes events well-known throughout Australian fiction: bush work, flood, fire, departure to a foreign war. As in *The Aunt's Story,* there is a final epiphany, this time for a male, Stan, whose slow but cumulative progress toward self-realization demonstrates that common life *can* be enough. "I would not be here if I was not stubborn," Stan the old man tells a prying young evangelist concerned for the state of his soul. Amy does not achieve the kind of final peace passing understanding that Stan does, but we see her at full length as a frontier-type wife with equal ranking alongside her husband as a unit of work. "The acknowledgement that wives of Australian workmen and women in the bush have souls and feelings of their own," says Björkstén, "may be regarded as one of the contributions White has made to the literature of his country."[64] This is only partly correct, since similar revelations go all the way back to Henry Lawson, but it is still only too largely true that the "average" Australian male would have to be persuaded by more than ordinarily forcible means before he would pay it any heed.

White's firm devotion to religious experience is apparent in *The Tree of Man* as it was in *The Aunt's Story*. His brand of Christianity, which he would hardly even define as such, is what might be termed simple grass-roots or outback or perhaps more accurately "farback" Christianity, a species old enough, primitive enough, to embrace a sort of Erasmian divine madness or folly and perhaps other irrational elements—which, let us add, are highly useful to narrative. "*God* in White," says Björkstén, "represents rather what his characters have learnt through tradition to call the object of their striving for totality than the traditional God."[65] It may be useful as well, at this point, to note the extensive impact of Carl Jung upon White: Jungians will find plenty of archetypal figures and situations in *The Tree of Man*. Björkstén, again, is a very helpful critic in assessing what he sees as Jung's "decisive importance":

> White's "elect," those who have the possibility of achieving clarity of vision concerning their destiny, or just strive to do so, do not exist only in the world of consciousness; they also have free communication with the unconscious. Their longing for freedom and reconciliation of the spirit—"the transcending function of the psyche" as Jung calls it—is the force that urges them on. They can be recognized by their well-developed powers of perception, thought, feeling, and foresight. These qualities, called by Jung "the four means by which the consciousness finds its bearing," are what set them as a class apart in an insensitive and dehumanized world.
>
> In other words, what Patrick White brings clearly to the fore in his "elect" is self-fulfilment: what Jung calls the process of individuation. It is not until a person frees his individual personality through this self-fulfilment that he attains the highest aim of his existence. Then he has realized what Jung regards as the collective purpose of man: to function harmoniously in a social setting while retaining a specifically determined individuality.[66]

Australian criticism, which over the years has tended in religious and metaphysical matters toward firm-set orthodoxy or else insular agnosticism, has not been equipped to deal with such dimensions as well as the criticism in, say, Canada where Jung has had a larger and more sympathetic audience.

With *Voss* (1957), White's professional fortunes took a turn quite definitely upward, both at home and abroad (the novel was a bookclub choice in the United States, for example), when he was awarded his first important prizes: the Miles Franklin Award in Australia and the W. H. Smith Prize in London, both for *Voss*. The story of Voss, White tells us in "The Prodigal Son," was possibly conceived during the early days of the German bombing of London, when he "sat reading Eyre's *Journal* in a London bed-sitting room."

> Nourished by months spent traipsing backwards and forwards across the Egyptian and Cyrenaican deserts, influenced by the arch-megalomaniac of the day, the idea finally matured after reading contemporary accounts of Leichhardt's expeditions and A. H. Chisholm's *Strange New World* on returning to Australia.[67]

This massive excursion into the unknown sets one hell against another, physical and social; it is a double response to the worst that Australia has to offer, with physical death in the desert as one level, "death by torture in the country of the mind" (Laura's view at the end) as another, but "true knowledge" nevertheless the prize, and death swallowed up in victory. We encounter resonances from Schopenhauer, Nietzsche, and Dostoevsky; and in the spiritual pairing of Voss in the desert, Laura in already effete and sterile Sydney, resonances from Christianity and Jungian mythology. In Jungian terms, Laura is Voss's anima, he is her animus; in Christian terms, Laura is grace and Voss is pride. Measured against the tradition of hubris in British literature, Voss as hero is in Walsh's term "Marlovian"; from American literature the figure most clearly comparable is Melville's Captain Ahab. By his own terms, he is quite right about the country: it is the only thing fit to be challenged by his will. At the same time, it becomes clear that the country and its aboriginal inhabitants are counterweights to rationality and will—fleeting, unpredictable, impossible to localize and deal with summarily. Through Voss, White seems to be telling us that only through the portal of suffering can humanity ever expect real illumination, redemption, transcendence of its own evil ways—through a sort of Keatsian "negative capability" of empathy, never easy for Prometheans to achieve.

Voss is the purest example of the explorer's psychology, but he is saved from unconvincing super-humanity by a grubby stain of backsliding man. There is a touch of malignancy, of Hitler, in the way he treats his companions. This, paradoxically, makes his illumination—conversion is too revivalist a word—which is religious in its source and derived from the acceptance which is part of his love for Laura, possible, and when it takes place, convincing. Only the sinful man can become the redeemed man.[68]

Not only did White begin winning prizes with *Voss;* he began seeing some of his critical countrymen swinging over to his side. James McAuley thought of the novel as a dramatic poem, a viewpoint later agreed with by Brian Kiernan:

It is only by approaching [White's] novels as, in a sense, poems that we are likely to respond to them fully. They are "poems" in the sense that they are extremely complex, ambiguous and ironic linguistic structures. . . . White's complex, dramatic and finally untranslatable awareness of our being has something Shakespearian about it, even to such patterns of imagery as the use of clothing and nakedness in *Voss* to suggest with rich ambiguity the stripping away of defences.[69]

The four principal characters, the "riders," of *Riders in the Chariot* (1961) are to be found at the opposite extreme from the high-aspiring, will-driven Voss. All of them are outwardly unpretentious people, brought together from widely divergent origins to be united in their devotion to the inner life. Miss Mary Hare, to all appearances a decayed Australian gentlewoman at last gone mad, has her closest affinities with nature, in contrast with Mrs. Ruth Godbold from East Anglia, who seems predestined to do as much as she can to minister to a suffering humanity. Mordecai Himmelfarb, a German refugee from the Nazi concentration camps, the most intellectual of the group, personifies religion by becoming the Christ-figure of a mock crucifixion and as the object of persecution is linked with Alf Dubbo, who represents "that most miserable of human beings, the artist." All four are "chosen" ones, chosen most especially to suffer and to endure in a blending of Old and New Testament types of suffering and endurance. With reference to Himmelfarb and Dubbo, Swedish and Australian styles of egalitarianism confront one another in Björkstén's comment:

What White portrays in Himmelfarb and in the fourth chosen figure, the Aboriginal Alf Dubbo, is the deadly mechanism of exclusion that is wielded by a conformist society, in his own particular case Australian society. Every society that does not tolerate its odder members has the mechanism of the German solution of the Jewish "problem" built into its system; in *Riders in the Chariot* Patrick White shows how easily it is set into operation.[70]

Consciously or not, White adapts a famous Swiftian metaphor *(Tale of a Tub)* to describe Himmelfarb's attitude toward formal religion, which, "like a winter overcoat, grew oppressive and superfluous as spring developed into summer, and the natural sources of warmth were gradually revealed." But at the same time, "there was no mistaking the love and respect the young man kept for the enduring qualities of his old, discarded coat." In the climactic episode, Himmelfarb, employed in an Australian factory, is crucified in a jacaranda tree as an Easter prank by some of his fellow blue-collar associates. Unexpectedly, it kills him, and his friend, the artist Dubbo, does not long survive the shock of the event. And yet the shop foreman, sympathetic as he is with Himmelfarb, is ready to laugh it all off in the easygoing Australian assumption that "she'll be right." "Remember," he says, glibly,

". . . we have a sense of humour, and when the boys start to horse around, it is that that is gettin' the better of 'em. They can't resist a joke. Even when a man is full of beer, you will find the old sense of humour at work underneath. It has to play a joke. See? No offence can be taken where a joke is intended."[71]

Writing in 1971, Geoffrey Dutton concluded that *Riders in the Chariot* showed "the greatest range of sympathy of all his novels,"[72] a judgment with which some readers, perhaps even a good many, would still agree.

The Solid Mandala (1966) develops, once more, the contrast between living and dead lives through a pair of twins, Arthur and Waldo Brown. Of these, Arthur is the outgoing, compassionate, and intuitive one, but thought to be rather more feeble-minded than not. Waldo, who has literary pretensions and makes his living as a librarian, is a narrow-gauge Voss, the man of intellect and will, desperately introverted. The title derives from four glass marbles which Arthur as a boy chooses as mandalas for Waldo, himself, and two women, Dulcie Feinstein and Mrs. Poulter, both motivated by love. By comparison with its predecessors, this novel is brief, but concentrated, a parable on the manner in which loneliness and isolation can destroy people.

The Vivisector (1970) returns to the theme of the artist and society, this time with minimal sympathy for the artist (which will be encountered again in the portrait of the actor Basil Hunter in *The Eye of the Storm*). Hurtle Duffield, the artist-to-be, is born in a semislum of Sydney but reared by rich pastoralist foster parents who literally buy him. Having enlisted in World War I at age sixteen, he studies art in Paris before returning to Sydney to live with a prostitute and paint. This life-style is repeated with other women of various classes, all of whom are finally sacrificed to Duffield's ambition. Clement Semmler calls the book "genius fabricating genius," remarking on its expression of White's abiding interest in painting and offering the opinion that White has now reached a point where "any international novelist writing in English that could be named cannot possibly be any more than his peer."[73] Geoffrey Dutton thought the novel "perilously close to a final condemnation of human beings for their cruelty and indifference."[74] Walsh also finds it strong medicine, whereby

Duffield's relationship with his first woman, Nance Lightfoot, "suggests intermittently that the sex is being looked at with an observer's disgust at the antics of caged monkeys."[75] Looking only, or chiefly, at the dismal side of this and some of White's other novels, one might almost construct a Hardian paraphrase and say that in White's view, decency is but the occasional episode in a general drama of filth. But there is much more than that.

The Eye of the Storm (1973) is a peak among White's later novels comparable with *Voss* or *The Tree of Man* among the earlier ones. Having learned to expect from White, long since, an amalgam of bitterness, strangeness, and compassion, we are here on familiar ground. The plot is a simple one, but quite adequate to the purpose of developing the grand-dame figure of Elizabeth Hunter, dominant even in senility and very close to death. Her son and daughter, both expatriates, return to visit their mother, far less to comfort her last days than to duel with one another over the disposition of the property. Taking care of her are four nurses whose attitudes range from complete devotion to brassy demi-indifference. As in the quartet of *Riders in the Chariot,* these four are drawn temporarily together from diverse origins. One of the strongest passages of a good many is Elizabeth's recollection of the tropical storm that broke into her competition with her daughter for the attentions of a Norwegian scientist. On the comic side, there is an episode bringing together the aristocratic Hunter children, now Sir Basil and the Princesse de Lascabanes, with the Macrory family, who are Australian bush to the hilt.

In this novel, by contrast with some earlier ones, White is less severe both upon the erstwhile Australian gentry and upon the parents to be encountered among them. Most of the other mothers come off less handsomely than Elizabeth does, and Alfred Hunter, the recalled father, is shown to have had good qualities which Elizabeth realizes too late. Nonverbal communication is still strongly emphasized (Sir Basil's triumphs on the stage notwithstanding): there is more than a lingering suspicion of words, perhaps even of language itself, which one might think of as the Whitean Paradox. The Nobel Prize citation spoke of "a wrestling with the language in order to extract all its power and all its nuances, to the verge of the unattainable"; yet there appears every now and then in his work a downgrading of verbal expression in favor of paint, music, or the ineffable visions in a state of altered consciousness. Not much impressed by White's disclaimers, Björkstén observes:

This theme has become less and less convincing in White. If one analyses it in the light of his works one has to state that it is rather an *idée fixe* than anything so universally applicable as his continual return to it would have it. But his writing points to the opposite conclusion. What in fact he gives expression to is more his own pains of creative composition than a general truth; when he has finished with them Patrick White's words are filled with the sense he has impregnated them with. His scepticism towards words as carriers of meaning reflects his own difficulties while working with them.[76]

A Fringe of Leaves (1976) makes somewhat the same use of historical materials that *Voss* did of explorers' journals. The story of the heroine, Mrs. Ellen Roxburgh, is based on the shipwreck and subsequent experiences of Mrs. Eliza Fraser in 1836. Ellen, a Cornish farm girl married to a cold, exacting, semi-invalid husband, has an affair with her husband's brother in Tasmania after which she and her husband set sail for England in the *Bristol Maid,* which is wrecked. There is a harrowing journey in lifeboats, including a miscarriage, and then an attack and general slaughter by the aborigines, with Ellen made a captive slave to the tribe. She meets an escaped convict, Jack Chase, whom she genuinely loves and he her, but they part when they reach Moreton Bay and she returns to civilization, having interceded with officialdom for Jack. She is last seen aboard ship, being given close attention by a well-to-do widower, Mr. Jevons.

As this synopsis suggests, *A Fringe of Leaves* is easier reading than most White novels. There are vivid bush scenes as well as those at sea, with a generally sympathetic portrait of Ellen Roxburgh. For example, not long after her capture and enslavement, a sick child placed in her charge dies. As an elderly medicine man performs rites over the body, Ellen breaks in to exclaim (in the Cornish accent to which she reverts under stress), "Can't 'ee see she is gone? She's dead!"

It sounded the more terrifying for being unintelligible to her audience, just as her emotion, her bursting into tears, must have seemed disproportionate to those who had not shared her sufferings.

While Ellen Roxburgh wept for her own experience of life, the pseudo physician, to judge by his excited jabber, appeared to be holding her responsible for his failure. He did not succeed, however, in rousing an opposition. For the first time since the meeting on the beach, the captive and her masters, especially the women, were united in a common humanity.[77]

In this novel, Veronica Brady believes, White has at last "overcome what Cleanth Brooks once suggested was the great danger facing the contemporary writer, the hubris of 'the assumption that the solutions to the problems of mankind . . . can be obtained through one's privileged insights or that one's own psychic disturbances are somehow continuous with the disturbances of society at large.' "[78]

The bond of suffering, expressed in *A Fringe of Leaves* with great sympathy and clarity, is one of the leading areas of exploration in White's novels and in his short stories as well, one collection of which he called *The Burnt Ones* (1964)—a name applicable to many of his more extensively realized characters, all the way from Theodora Goodman onward. A second collection, *The Cockatoos*, appeared in 1974. Life is no easier or more explicable in the stories than in the novels, but there is a variety in the settings embracing a number of European as well as Australian places. Such variety appears, as well, in his latest novel, *The Twyborn Affair* (1979). Setting, plot, and character all are plural: Australia, the Mediterranean, and Britain; warfare, pastoralism, and brothel keeping; with Eddie Twyborn, the central figure, as both male and female in three separate incarnations. With this much complexity, it is not surprising that critics have found the novel invading surrealism, at times excessively tense (even for White), and not readily invoking suspension of disbelief.

Commenting on the Australian landscape as the source of White's imagery, Elizabeth Salter quotes a passage quickly sketching the atmosphere of a store veranda where some men are loafing, and observes, "The reader could be looking at a Drysdale painting of an outback town."[79] This observation might easily be extended to portraiture. White has been criticized more than once for the severity with which he draws his people, but his technique with words may be fairly set alongside that with paint as used by modern Australian painters like Boyd, Dobell, Drysdale, or Nolan.

What does White think of his own work? Reams and whole volumes of personal estimates on the man continue to accumulate, out of which many impressions are available. This one, from Max Harris, who has known White for a long time, may serve as a kind of trial balance:

> Over coffee and brandy, conversation does not turn on any analysis of White's past creations, nor gratuitous details of his present projects. There is no literary egotism about the man, although he will freely discuss the trials and tribulations of the writing profession. But the hellishness of the

writing process itself is rigidly demarcated from the relaxation of normal civilised social intercourse.

Patrick White sweats his novels out, and he sweats them out under the additional burden of uncertain health; he suffers chronic and recurrent bouts of asthma. I have never known him to talk over the immediate substance of his literary preoccupations, to articulate about the pessimistic, often wayward, and yet ultimately humane vision of human affairs which provides the nucleonic centre of everything he writes.

Patrick White, on the surface of life, is the ordinary man—admirable, civilised, likeable, testy, angry, acid, clear and high-minded in his critical judgments, but not predictable in those judgments. He finds his own opal patch wherever he finds it.

His Achilles heel is the hypersensitivity which is common to most intensively creative people. Ignorant, misinformed, inferior criticism from people with inferior critical resources gnaws at his vitals. . . .

It is another, and completely positive thing, that he loathes the conformist dehumanisation of urban life. The world we have come to inhabit provides good reasons for hate and some occasions for love.[80]

Summary and Prospects

What we have encountered in Australian fiction is the emergence from an intentionally unpromising cultural matrix of a very substantial body of fiction both long and short. This, during the past fifty years, has gradually cohered into what critics can now speak of with confidence as a tradition. Until 1900 and indeed for some time afterward, thematic concerns were heavily retrospective. Colonial handicaps—political, social, and environmental—were not quickly to be overcome, as the fiction clearly reveals. Violence, both legal and contralegal, was long the rule, not the exception, in Australian life. What began as a slow-developing if not exactly leisurely pastoral pattern was abruptly transformed by the gold rushes of mid-century, which hastened urbanization. The aborigines to be found in Australian stories play quite different roles from those of the Maoris in New Zealand, the Zulus and other tribes in Africa, or the Amerindians; and for the better part of a century, various Pacific Islanders together with a few Asiatics have, at times, been present. Emphasis upon a difficult past naturally produces historical fiction, including the family or generational chronicle, a mode that has proved quite successful and durable in Australian hands. A twentieth-century counterpart to the pell-mell influx of gold seekers has been the massive immigration following World War II, introducing new cultural situations to be explored and new explorers as writers. Experimentation, most recently, has received a better hearing than it would have, say, thirty years ago.

Were one required to name the "big ten" Australian writers of fiction, he would find himself quickly protesting so drastic a limitation and lamenting his exclusions so strongly that all he could comfortably propose would be to offer a list three or four times as long and let the reader choose his own first team. Even then there would be disagreements and objections to omissions, but at a venture here are somewhat over forty formidable names: Astley, Barnard Eldershaw, Baynton, Becke, Boldrewood, Boyd, Casey, Clarke, Cowan, Cusack, Dark, Davison, Drake-Brockman, Durack, Franklin, Furphy, Harrower, Hay, Herbert, Johnston, Keneally, Kingsley, Lawson, Lindsay, Marshall, Martin, Mathers, Morrison, Palmer, Porter, Praed, Prichard, Richardson, Spence, Stead, Stivens, Stone, Stow, Stuart, Tennant, Upfield, West, Warung, and White.

And the future? D. R. Burns, at the end of his study, *The Directions of Australian Fiction 1920–1974,* is pessimistic about the possibility of "much further development of fiction along the way of refinement"—that is, "an interest in private and special states of feeling and being" of the kind to be found, for instance, in the novels of Martin Boyd. This is

. . . quite out of favour for the present as public spectacle is what is sought after. Australians want to see the newer larrikins acting up in the way of the old. Novelists, dramatists and film directors have made a common decision. It is for togetherness.[81]

At the time Burns was writing it was easy enough to be discouraged and/or alarmed, not only in Australia but pretty well everywhere else; "refinement" simply is not part of any society in the 1970s and 1980s, and the same tendencies that Burns deplores are to be found in the fiction of Canada, for example, or Britain or Africa. A different aspect troubles another critic, Chris Wallace-Crabbe, who feels that the "single most discouraging thing for the man of letters in Australia" will still be "a nagging sense that new ideas are being worried into shape elsewhere and are only slowly filtering through to here."

The physical distance to North America and Europe is still considerable; the surface mails are still slow, and eminent visitors relatively few. He is apt to have a sense of things happening in slow motion at times: he reads in the press some allusion to a new book by Konrad Lorenz, or Levi-Strauss, or Trilling, or Christopher Hill; a week or two later he sees the book reviewed in an airmail copy of some overseas magazine; he orders the book, and receives it two months later; even when he has read it, he has nobody to compare notes with, for none of his friends or colleagues has seen it yet. Under the circumstances, it is hard to repress a feeling of isolation.[82]

But when these possible difficulties have been pointed out, and when the Australianness of Australian fiction has been emphasized (as in the present volume we hope it has been at proper times), there is more to be said; and seldom has the world vision of literature been so eloquently expressed as in Professor C. D. Narasimhaiah's preface to *An Introduction to Australian Literature:*

> It is because these Australian writers have striven to preserve and promote the criterion of what "human wholeness" is they have a claim to our attention. Besides, . . . there is today no English or American literature; literature is one and indivisible, for great literature, to whatever country it belongs, shall be studied by all. It is like the study of history today: History has ceased to be the history of any one country and you can't study the history of your own country except in the perspective of the whole world. So too literature: whichever literature consoles, inspires and sustains man in his illness and old age, broadens his sympathies, enlarges his vision, and strengthens his imagination belongs to the entire human family. For we are heirs to all that man has thought and felt and done.[83]

What Professor Narasimhaiah is saying here was anticipated also in Australia, over a hundred years before him, by Frederick Sinnett. How long it does take an idea for its time to come! But the time is now obviously here, and the idea cannot much longer be ignored. Australian fiction clearly belongs to the entire human family.

Notes and References

Chapter One

1. Oliver Goldsmith, "The Deserted Village" (1770), lines 341–58. The "matted woods where birds forget to sing"—apparently Georgia, where in fact the mockingbird performs particularly well—were to appear later in Australia, far down into the next century: a hundred years after Goldsmith, the immigrant poet Adam Lindsay Gordon penned a much-resented libel on Australian nature: ". . . lands where bright blossoms are scentless,/And songless bright birds."

2. Geoffrey Serle, *From Deserts the Prophets Come: The Creative Spirit in Australia 1788–1972* (Melbourne, 1973), p. 119.

3. *Australian Book Review,* February 1963, p. 70.

4. Cecil Hadgraft, *Australian Literature: A Critical Account to 1955* (London, 1961), p. 12.

5. Brian Elliott, *Marcus Clarke* (Oxford, 1958), p. 148.

6. John Barnes, "Australian Fiction to 1920," in *The Literature of Australia,* ed. Geoffrey Dutton (Harmondsworth, 1976), p. 161.

7. H. M. Green, *A History of Australian Literature,* 2 vols. (Sydney, 1961), 1:89.

8. Hadgraft, *Australian Literature,* p. 18.

9. W. S. Ramson, ed., *The Australian Experience: Critical Essays on Australian Novels* (Canberra, 1974), p. 18.

Chapter Two

Epigraph: From Bill Wannan, *Dictionary of Australian Humorous Quotations and Anecdotes* (Melbourne: Macmillan, 1974).

1. John Barnes, ed., *The Writer in Australia: A Collection of Literary Documents 1855–1964* (Melbourne, 1969), p. 47.

2. John Barnes, *Henry Kingsley and Colonial Fiction* (Melbourne: Oxford, 1971), p. 37. Henry David Thoreau received his ideas about behavior on the goldfields, castigated in "Life without Principle," from an American edition of Howitt's *Land, Labour and Gold* (1855).

3. *Squatter,* it must be remembered, meant "large landholder"—the proprietor of a sheep run stocking thousands—rather than "small farmer" (later "selector," the counterpart in some ways of the American homesteader). He squatted in the sense that usually he leased his vast acreage rather than actually owning it, though part of a run might be freehold.

4. *The Portable Marcus Clarke,* ed. Michael Wilding (St. Lucia, 1976), pp. 106–7.

5. Coral Lansbury, *Arcady in Australia: The Evocation of Australia in Nineteenth-Century English Literature* (Melbourne: Melbourne University Press, 1970), pp. 131–32.

6. Ibid., p. 134.

7. Rolf Boldrewood, *Robbery under Arms* (London: Macmillan's Colonial Library, 1898), p. 2.

8. Ibid., pp. 392–93.

9. Itinerant.

10. A. W. Jose, *The Romantic Nineties* (Sydney: Angus & Robertson, 1933), p. 10.

11. Rolf Boldrewood, *The Miner's Right* (London: Macmillan, 1927), p. 160.

12. Ibid., p. 379.

13. Alan Brissenden, *Rolf Boldrewood* (Melbourne, 1972), pp. 42–43.

14. Michael Wilding, "The Short Stories of Marcus Clarke," in *Bards, Bohemians, & Bookmen,* ed. Leon Cantrell (St. Lucia, 1976), p. 73.

15. A. J. Boyd, *Old Colonials* (Sydney: Sydney University Press, 1974), pp. 248–49.

16. Barry Andrews, *Price Warung* (Boston, 1976), p. 159.

17. T. Inglis Moore, *Social Patterns in Australian Literature* (Sydney, 1971), pp. 27–28.

18. Arthur A. Phillips, *Henry Lawson* (New York, 1970), p. 36.

19. Ibid., p. 143.

20. Barnes, ed., *The Writer in Australia,* p. 200.

21. Lorna Ollif, *Andrew Barton Paterson* (New York, 1971), p. 108.

22. Ibid., p. 108.

23. George Nadel, *Australia's Colonial Culture* (Melbourne, 1957), p. 109.

24. A. Grove Day, *Louis Becke* (New York, 1966), p. 156.

25. Steele Rudd, *On Our Selection, Our New Selection, Sandy's Selection, Back at Our Selection* (Melbourne, 1973), p. 82.

26. E. D. Davis, *The Life and Times of Steele Rudd* (Melbourne, 1976), p. 222.

27. Catherine Helen Spence, *Clara Morison* (Adelaide: Rigby, 1971), p. 402.

28. Barnes, ed., *The Writer in Australia,* pp. 19–20.

29. Quoted in Colin Roderick, *The Australian Novel* (Sydney: William Brooks, 1945), p. 79.

30. Hadgraft, *Australian Literature,* p. 91.

31. Mrs. Campbell Praed, *My Australian Girlhood* (London: T. F. Unwin, 1902), pp. 158–59.

32. Hadgraft, *Australian Literature,* p. 87.

Chapter Three

Epigraph: From Barnes, ed., *The Writer in Australia,* pp. 201–2.
1. Walter Murdoch and Alfred Deakin, *Books and Men: Letters and Comments 1900–1918,* ed. J. A. LaNauze and Elizabeth Nurser (Melbourne, 1974), p. 93.
2. Quoted in Wannan, *Dictionary of Australian Humorous Quotations.*
3. Ibid.
4. Moore, *Social Patterns,* p. 77.
5. Miles Franklin, *My Brilliant Career* (Sydney: Angus & Robertson, 1966), p. 231.
6. Miles Franklin, *Prelude to Waking* (Sydney: Angus & Robertson, 1950), p. 189.
7. Cecil Hadgraft, "Literature," in *The Pattern of Australian Culture,* ed. A. McLeod (Ithaca: Cornell University Press, 1963), p. 71.
8. Marjorie Barnard, *Miles Franklin* (New York, 1967), p. 178.
9. Thomas Hobbes, *Leviathan* (1651).
10. Barbara Baynton, *Bush Studies* (Sydney: Angus & Robertson, 1965), p. 33.
11. Hadgraft, *Australian Literature,* p. 95.
12. Baynton, *Bush Studies,* pp. 135–36.
13. Joseph Furphy, *Such Is Life* (Sydney: Angus & Robertson, 1944), pp. 271–72.
14. Douglas Killam, "Notes on Adaptation and Variation in the Use of English by Haliburton, Furphy, Achebe, Narayan and Naipaul," in *The Commonwealth Writer Overseas,* ed. Alastair Niven (Brussels, 1976), p. 128.
15. Barnes, ed., *The Writer in Australia,* p. 129.
16. Arthur A. Phillips, *The Australian Tradition: Studies in a Colonial Culture* (Melbourne: Cheshire, 1958), pp. 89–90.
17. Ibid., p. 38.
18. Hadgraft, *Australian Literature,* p. 156.
19. Louis Stone, *Jonah* (Sydney: Angus & Robertson, 1965), p. xii.
20. H. J. Oliver, *Louis Stone* (Melbourne, 1968), p. 32.
21. Serle, *From Deserts,* p. 134.
22. G. A. Wilkes, *Australian Literature: A Conspectus* (Sydney: Angus & Robertson, 1969), p. 67.
23. Vance Palmer, *The Big Fellow* (Sydney, 1959), p. 161.
24. John Barnes, "Fiction Chronicle," *Meanjin,* no. 1 (1960), p. 100.
25. Frank Dalby Davison, "Vance Palmer and His Writings," *Meanjin,* no. 1 (1948), p. 12.
26. Ibid., p. 18.
27. Green, *History of Australian Literature,* pp. 1106–7.
28. Ibid., p. 1106.
29. See W. and J. E. Hiener, "Literary Composition on Board a Convict

Ship: The 'Pestonjee Bomajnee Journal,' " *Australian Literary Studies* 4, no. 2 (October 1969):164–69.

30. Fayette Gosse, *William Gosse Hay* (Melbourne, 1965), p. 19.

31. Ibid., p. 25.

32. William Gosse Hay, *The Escape of the Notorious Sir William Heans* (Melbourne, 1955), p. 123.

33. Ibid., p. xix.

34. Frank Dalby Davison, *Man-Shy* (Sydney, 1931), p. 31.

35. Walter Murdoch, *Moreover* (Sydney: Angus & Robertson, 1932), p. 61.

36. John Hetherington, *Norman Lindsay* (Melbourne, 1969), p. 11.

37. Norman Lindsay, *Saturdee* (Sydney, 1961), p. 35.

38. Thelma Forshaw, Review of *Saturdee, Australian Book Review,* December 1961, p. 29.

39. *The Best of Lennie Lower* (Melbourne, 1963), p. 25.

40. Green, *History of Australian Literature,* p. 643.

41. Louise E. Rorabacher, ed., *Aliens in Their Land: The Aborigine in the Australian Short Story* (Melbourne: Cheshire, 1968), p. 17.

42. Geoffrey Dutton, ed., *The Literature of Australia* (Harmondsworth, 1964), p. 161.

43. James Hackston, *Father Clears Out* (Sydney, 1966), p. xiii.

Chapter Four

Epigraph: Story by Lesley Rowlands in *Two Ways Meet: Stories of Migrants in Australia,* ed. Louise E. Rorabacher (Melbourne, 1963), p. 169.

1. F. H. Mares, *"The Fortunes of Richard Mahony:* A Reconsideration," *Meanjin,* no. 1 (1962), p. 70.

2. Henry Handel Richardson, *The Fortunes of Richard Mahony* (London: Heinemann, 1931), p. 3.

3. Ibid., p. 983.

4. Leonie Kramer, "Henry Handel Richardson," in *Literature of Australia,* ed. Dutton (1976), p. 375.

5. William D. Elliott, *Henry Handel Richardson* (Boston, 1975), p. 140.

6. Katharine S. Prichard, *Working Bullocks* (London: Cape, 1926), p. 225.

7. Katharine S. Prichard, *Coonardoo* (Sydney: Angus & Robertson, 1956), p. 227.

8. J. J. Healy, *Literature and the Aborigine in Australia 1770–1975* (St. Lucia, 1978), p. 136.

9. Jack Lindsay, "The Novels of Katharine Susannah Prichard," *Meanjin,* no. 4 (1961), p. 386.

10. Serle, *From Deserts,* p. 123.

11. M. Barnard Eldershaw, *A House Is Built* (Melbourne, 1972), p. 359.

12. Louise E. Rorabacher, *Marjorie Barnard and M. Barnard Eldershaw* (New York, 1973), p. 177.

13. L. J. Blake, *Australian Writers* (Adelaide, 1968), p. 88.

14. Keven Margery, review, *Australian Book Review,* March 1964, p. 110.

15. Hadgraft, *Australian Literature,* p. 240.

16. A. Grove Day, *Eleanor Dark* (Boston, 1976), pp. 89–90. If the reader of American fiction finds this passage reminiscent of the openings of James A. Michener's *Hawaii* or *Centennial,* the reason is that Michener was much impressed with *The Timeless Land,* as Day's book reveals, pp. 93–94.

17. Green, *History of Australian Literature,* p. 1078.

18. Rex Ingamells, *Of Us Now Living, a Novel of Australia* (Melbourne, 1952), p. 358.

19. Vincent Buckley, *"Capricornia,"* Grahame Johnston, ed. *Australian Literary Criticism* (Melbourne, 1962), p. 169.

20. Ibid., p. 186.

21. Hadgraft, *Australian Literature,* p. 256.

22. Laurie Clancy, *"Poor Fellow My Country:* Herbert's Masterpiece?" *Southerly* 37, no. 2 (June 1974):163, 175. For another view, see Healy, *Literature and the Aborigine,* pp. 263–88.

23. Blake, *Australian Writers,* p. 137.

24. Martin Boyd, *Lucinda Brayford* (Melbourne, 1969), p. 113.

25. Dorothy Green, "Martin Boyd," in *Literature of Australia,* ed. Dutton (1976), pp. 523–24.

26. Brenda Niall, *Martin Boyd* (Melbourne, 1974), p. 29.

27. Vance Palmer, review, *Meanjin,* no. 4 (1958), p. 433.

28. Norman Ashbolt, review, *Australian Book Review,* February 1963, p. 58.

29. Brian Elliott, "Martin Boyd: An Appreciation," *Meanjin,* no. 1 (1957), pp. 15, 22. Another generally favorable estimate appears in Anthony Bradley's "The Structure of Ideas Underlying Martin Boyd's Fiction," *Meanjin,* no. 2 (1969), pp. 177–83.

30. William H. New, *Among Worlds* (Erin, Ont.: Press Porcepic, 1975), p. 174.

31. Quoted in *The Australian Experience,* ed. Ramson, p. 135.

32. Stephen Murray-Smith, "The Manning Revival," *Australian Book Review,* October 1964, p. 229.

33. Green, *History of Australian Literature,* pp. 1131–32.

34. Alan Marshall, *How Beautiful Are Thy Feet* (Melbourne, 1949), p. 51.

35. Green, *History of Australian Literature,* p. 1141.

36. Eric Lambert, review, *Meanjin,* no. 4 (1952), p. 415.

37. Beatrice Davis, ed., *Short Stories of Australia: The Moderns* (Sydney, 1967), p. viii.

38. Ibid., p. 241.

39. Ibid., pp. 73–74.

40. Ibid., p. 295.

41. Ibid., p. 162.

42. Ibid., pp. 227–28.

43. Ibid., p. 83.

Chapter Five

Epigraph: From Barnes, ed., *Writer in Australia*, p. 331.

1. Barry Ovenden, ed., *The Australian & New Zealand Writers Handbook* (Sydney and Wellington, 1975), pp. 31–32.

2. Prichard, *Coonardoo*, pp. 117–18.

3. Marjorie Barnard, in *Meanjin*, no. 4 (1960), p. 442.

4. Mary Durack, "Pilgrimage," in *Aliens in Their Own Land*, ed. Rorabacher, pp. 64–65.

5. Tom Ronan, *Vision Splendid* (Melbourne: O'Neil, 1972), p. 95.

6. Ibid., p. 331.

7. F. B. Vickers, *No Man Is Himself* (Sydney: Australasian, 1969), pp. 143–44.

8. F. B. Vickers, *Without Map or Compass* (Sydney, 1974), p. 202.

9. John Barnes, "Fiction Chronicle," *Meanjin*, no. 1 (1960), p. 111.

10. Donald Stuart, *Prince of My Country* (Melbourne, 1974), pp. 232–33.

11. Nancy Cato and V. R. Ellis, *Queen Trucanini* (London, 1976), p. 250.

12. Arthur Upfield, *Man of Two Tribes* (London: Heinemann, 1969), pp. 174–75.

13. Colin Johnson, *Wild Cat Falling* (Harmondsworth: Penguin, 1966), pp. 18–19.

14. Ibid., p. 19.

15. Derek Whitelock, review, *Australian Book Review*, May 1965, p. 127.

16. Louise E. Rorabacher, ed., *Two Ways Meet: Stories of Migrants in Australia* (London: Angus & Robertson, 1963), p. 13.

17. Herz Bergner, *Light and Shadow*, trans. Alec Braizblatt (London, 1963), pp. 124–25.

18. H. P. Heseltine, "Fiction Chronicle," *Meanjin*, no. 4 (1961), p. 482.

19. Colin Thiele, *Labourers in the Vineyard* (Adelaide, 1970), p. 6.

20. Blake, *Australian Writers*, pp. 166–67.

21. Iris Milutinovic, *Talk English Carn't Ya* (Melbourne, 1978), p. 1.

22. Ibid., preface.

23. Martha Leeming in *Australian Book Review*, August 1969, p. 220.

24. Eric Lambert, review, *Meanjin*, no. 4 (1951), pp. 415–16.

25. Dymphna Cusack, *The Sun Is Not Enough* (London: Heinemann, 1967), p. 201.

26. Barnes, "Fiction Chronicle," pp. 106–7.

27. Flora Eldershaw, "Bastardry, Bastardry, Bastardry," *Meanjin*, no. 3 (1950), pp. 222–25.

28. Frank Hardy, *The Four-Legged Lottery* (Melbourne, 1972), p. 219.

29. H. P. Heseltine in *Australian Encyclopedia* (Sydney: Grolier Society of Australia, 1977) 4:38.

30. C. Semmler and D. Whitelock, eds., *Literary Australia* (Melbourne: Cheshire, 1966), pp. 69–80.

31. Moore, *Social Patterns*, p. 281.

32. John Iggulden, *The Clouded Sky* (London: Macdonald, 1965), p. 130.

33. Geoffrey Dutton, *Tamara* (London, 1970), p. 78.

34. Eve Langley, *The Pea-Pickers* (Sydney, 1942), p. 141.

35. R. G. Geering, *Recent Fiction* (Melbourne: Oxford, 1973), p. 47.

36. Dorothy Auchterlonie, "The Novels of Kylie Tennant," *Meanjin,* no. 4 (1953), p. 400.

37. Kylie Tennant, *The Honey Flow* (London, 1956), pp. 126–27.

38. Frank Dalby Davison, review, *Meanjin,* no. 2 (1956), p. 216.

39. David Malouf, *An Imaginary Life* (New York: Braziller, 1978), pp. 149–50.

40. Donald Horne, *But What If There Are No Pelicans?* (Sydney, 1971), p. 12.

Chapter Six

Epigraph: Peter Mathers, *The Wort Papers* (Melbourne, 1972), pp. 2 3.

1. Serle, *From Deserts,* p. 221. Serle does not name his half dozen novelists; among them, perhaps, might appear such names as Heney, Koch, Langley, and McCallum.

2. John Barnes, ed., *An Australian Selection: Short Stories by Lawson, Palmer, Porter, White, Cowan* (Sydney, 1974), p. xiii; Leonie Kramer, ed., *Hal Porter: Selected Stories* (Sydney: Angus & Robertson, 1971), p. xiv.

3. G. A. Wilkes, *Australian Literature: a Conspectus* (Sydney, 1969), pp. 98–99; Mary Lord, *Hal Porter* (Melbourne, 1973), p. 25.

4. Harry Heseltine, ed., *Penguin Book of Australian Short Stories* (Harmondsworth, 1976), introduction.

5. Heseltine, "Fiction Chronicle," p. 491.

6. Hal Porter, *The Tilted Cross* (London, 1961), p. 179.

7. Brian Kiernan, *Images of Society and Nature: Seven Essays on Australian Novels* (Melbourne, 1971), p. 80.

8. Christina Stead, *Seven Poor Men of Sydney* (London: P. Davis, 1934), pp. 154–55.

9. R. G. Geering, *Christina Stead* (New York, 1969), p. 162.

10. Clement Semmler, "The Novels of Christina Stead," in *Literature of Australia,* ed. Dutton (1976), p. 498.

11. Blake, *Australian Writers,* p. 174.

12. George Johnston, *A Cartload of Clay* (Sydney, 1971), pp. 47–48.

13. J. M. Couper, "The Novels of Thea Astley," *Meanjin,* no. 3 (1967), p. 336.

14. Thea Astley, *The Acolyte* (Sydney, 1972), p. 93.

15. Thea Astley, *A Kindness Cup* (Melbourne, 1974), p. 152.

16. Heseltine, "Fiction Chronicle," p. 489.

17. Geering, *Recent Fiction*, pp. 39, 48.

18. Max Harris in *Australian Book Review*, July 1964, p. 168.

19. Kiernan, *Images of Society and Nature*, p. 158.

20. Frances McInherny, "*Bring Larks and Heroes:* The Moral and the Dream," *Southerly* 37, no. 1 (March 1977):75.

21. Thomas Keneally, *The Chant of Jimmy Blacksmith* (Sydney, 1972), p. 82.

22. Thomas Keneally, *A Victim of the Aurora* (Sydney, 1977), p. 191.

23. David Martin, review, *Meanjin*, no. 1 (1957), pp. 88–89.

24. Randolph Stow, *To the Islands* (London: Macdonald, 1958), p. 192.

25. Ibid., pp. 203–4.

26. Randolph Stow, *Tourmaline* (London, 1963), p. 8.

27. Ray Willbanks, *Randolph Stow* (Boston, 1978), p. 142.

28. David Malouf, *Johnno* (St. Lucia, 1975), pp. 47–48.

29. H. P. Heseltine, *Australian Encyclopedia*, 4:37.

30. Serle, *From Deserts*, p. 185.

31. *The Naked Country*, published by Heinemann in 1960 as by Michael East, was republished as by West in the New English Library format in 1967. It is a story of a cattleman pursued by aboriginal trackers through the northwest cattle country because he has witnessed an aboriginal ritual murder.

32. Aldridge's *My Brother Tom* (London, 1966) takes place in a small town on the Murray River in the 1930s. It portrays a Romeo-Juliet romance between Tom Quayle (who hopes to be a writer) and Peggy MacGibbon, whose families are locked into a Catholic-Protestant embroilment.

33. Colleen McCullough, *Tim* (New York: Harper & Row, 1974), pp. 48–49.

34. Colleen McCullough, *The Thorn Birds* (New York, 1977), pp. 390–91.

35. Suzanne Edgar in *Australian Book Review*, December/January 1967–68, p. 46.

36. Space permits no more than a selective list of authors and titles (arranged chronologically), which the reader might find of interest to explore for himself. Styles range from the poetic to the supersordid, agglomeratively realistic; most of the characters are young, either loners or in collective pads; the plots may involve events as large as an international war or as small as a domestic quarrel: Christopher Koch, *The Boys in the Island,* 1958 (revised ed., 1974); Criena Rohan, *The Delinquents,* 1962; Mungo McCallum, *Son of Mars,* 1963; Suzanne Holly Jones, *Harry's Child,* 1964; William Dick, *A Bunch of Ratbags,* 1965; Christopher Koch, *Across the Sea Wall,* 1965; John Rowe, *Count Your Dead: A Novel of Vietnam,* 1968; David Daye, *The Austra-*

lian, 1970; Richard Beilby, *No Medals for Aphrodite*, 1970; John P. Gilders, *Man Alone*, 1971; Craig McGregor, *Don't Talk to Me about Love*, 1971; Lola Irish, *Time of the Dolphins*, 1972; David M. Foster, *North South West* and *The Pure Land*, 1973; Barbara Hanrahan, *The Scent of Eucalyptus*, 1973; David Richards, *Peanuts in Penang*, 1973; Suzanne Holly Jones, *Crying in the Garden*, 1974; Geoff Dike, *Henry Golightly*, 1974; John Duigan, *Badge*, 1975; David Malouf, *Johnno*, 1975; Louis Nowra, *The Misery of Beauty*, 1976; Ronald McKie, *The Crushing*, 1977; Helen Garner, *Monkey Grip*, 1978; Michael Wilding, *The Phallic Forest*, 1978; Michael F. Page, *A Nasty Little War*, 1979; Laurie Clancy, *The Wife Specialist*, 1979; and Frank Moorhouse, *The Everlasting Secret Family and Other Secrets*, 1980.

37. Derek Whitelock, review, *Australian Book Review*, April 1965, p. 101.

38. Dan Reidy, *It's This Way* (London, 1964), p. 166.

39. Keith Leopold, *My Brow Is Wet* (Sydney: Angus & Robertson, 1970), p. 103.

40. Jack Lindsay, "The Stories of Patrick White," *Meanjin*, no. 4 (1964), p. 373.

41. Derek Whitelock in *Australian Book Review*, June 1966, p. 153.

42. L. J. Clancy, "Trap for Young Players: Peter Mathers' Novel," *Meanjin*, no. 4 (1966), p. 485.

43. Peter Mathers, *The Wort Papers*, p. 232.

44. Barry Oakley, *A Salute to the Great McCarthy* (Melbourne, 1970), p. 77.

45. Barry Oakley, *Let's Hear It for Prendergast* (Melbourne, 1970), p. 27.

46. David Ireland, *The Unknown Industrial Prisoner* (Sydney, 1971), p. 10.

47. Ibid., pp. 13–14.

48. David Ireland, *The Flesheaters* (Sydney, 1972), p. 133.

49. Frank Moorhouse, *Futility and Other Animals* (Sydney, 1969), flyleaf.

50. Rod McConchie, in *Overland* 60 (1975):83, reviewing works by Adamson-Hanford, Carey, Viidikas, and Wilding.

51. Fay Zwicky, in *Overland* 63 (1975):55, reviewing works by Astley, Bail, Hall, Kefala, and Wilding.

52. Brian Kiernan, *Cunning Exiles* (Sydney: Angus & Robertson, 1974), p. 102.

53. Lindsay, "Stories of Patrick White," pp. 372–73.

54. Quoted in Ingmar Björkstén, *Patrick White: A General Introduction* (St. Lucia, 1976), p. 11.

55. Ibid., p. 50.

56. Alan Lawson, "Unmerciful Dingoes? The Critical Reception of Patrick White," *Meanjin*, no. 4 (1973), pp. 379–92.

57. A. D. Hope, *Native Companions* (Sydney: Angus & Robertson, 1974), pp. 77, 79.

58. A. D. Hope, "Standards in Australian Literature," in *Australian Literary Criticism,* ed. Grahame Johnston (Melbourne, 1962), p. 7.

59. Marjorie Barnard, "The Four Novels of Patrick White," *Meanjin,* no. 2 (1956), p. 159.

60. Ibid., p. 166.

61. Ibid., p. 170.

62. Vincent Buckley in *Australian Literary Criticism,* ed. Johnston, p. 197.

63. William Walsh, *Patrick White's Fiction* (Sydney, 1977), p. 25.

64. Björkstén, *Patrick White,* pp. 53–54.

65. Ibid., p. 23.

66. Ibid., pp. 23–24.

67. Ibid., p. 57.

68. Walsh, *Patrick White's Fiction,* p. 47.

69. Kiernan, *Images of Society and Nature,* p. 147. Compare Ian Turner's "The Parable of Voss," in *An Overland Muster* (Brisbane: Jacaranda, 1965), pp. 71–75. Turner feels that although Australians "speak continually (and usually sardonically) of men's imperfections" they are still optimists. That "is why Patrick White has not succeeded for Australians": he constructs "a mad world—one in which all the familiar signposts are standing, but are all pointing in the wrong directions, towards no land of experience that we can recognise as our own. And that is why, in the end (although reluctantly, because there is power in White's writing, if not conviction) my vote is with the local majority."

70. Björkstén, *Patrick White,* pp. 70–71.

71. Quoted in Walsh, *Patrick White's Fiction,* p. 58.

72. Geoffrey Dutton, *Patrick White* (Melbourne, 1971), p. 31.

73. Clement Semmler, review, *Australian Book Review,* October 1970, pp. 331–32.

74. Dutton, *Patrick White,* p. 44.

75. Walsh, *Patrick White's Fiction,* p. 101.

76. Björkstén, *Patrick White,* p. 113.

77. Patrick White, *A Fringe of Leaves* (London, 1976), p. 261.

78. Veronica Brady, "A Fringe of Leaves: Civilization by the Skin of Our Own Teeth," *Southerly* 37, no. 2 (June 1977):140.

79. Elizabeth Salter, "The Australianism of Patrick White," in *The Commonwealth Writer Overseas,* ed. Niven, p. 240.

80. Max Harris, *The Angry Eye* (Sydney: Pergamon, 1973), pp. 252–53.

81. D. R. Burns, *The Directions of Australian Fiction 1920–1974* (Melbourne, 1975), p. 266.

82. Chris Wallace-Crabbe, *Melbourne or the Bush: Essays on Australian Literature and Society* (Sydney, 1974), p. 55.

83. C. D. Narasimhaiah, *An Introduction to Australian Literature,* whole number of *The Literary Criterion* (Mysore: 1964), p. xiii.

Selected Bibliography

GENERAL REFERENCE

Gibbs, Malcolm, ed. *The Australian Character as Evinced in Quotations*. Sydney: Collins, 1968.

Hubble, Gregory V., comp. *The Australian Novel: A Title Checklist 1900–1970*. Perth: Privately printed, 1970. Upwards of 2,500 titles.

Johnston, Grahame, ed. *Annals of Australian Literature*. Melbourne: Oxford, 1970. Covers 1789 to 1968, on the model of the Oxford *Annals of English Literature*.

King, Bruce, ed. *Literatures of the World in English*. London: Routledge & Kegan Paul, 1974. Australia, pp. 23–41.

Lock, Fred, and Lawson, Alan, eds. *Australian Literature—A Reference Guide*. Melbourne: Oxford, 1977. Two chapters on bibliography and reference sources, a third on authors (forty names), others on library resources (fifteen Australian libraries), literary studies.

Myers, Robin, ed. *A Dictionary of Literature in the English Language*. 2 vols. Oxford: Pergamon, 1970. Coverage to 1940 only, but useful for earlier figures; vol. 2 is an index to titles and authors.

Ovenden, Barrie, ed. *The Australian & New Zealand Writers Handbook*. Sydney and Wellington: Reed, 1975. Chapters on practicalities: copyrights, marketing, handling manuscript and proof, writing for radio/ TV; useful directories listing literary organizations, awards and prizes, major magazines and journals, publishers.

Stone, Graham, comp. *Australian Science Fiction Index, 1925–1967*. Canberra: Australian Science Fiction Association, 1968. Includes magazines, series, and separate books.

Vinson, James, ed. *Contemporary Novelists*. 2d ed. London: St. James Press, 1976. About six hundred names, based on recommendations from an extensive panel of advisers; world coverage.

Wannan, Bill, comp. *Dictionary of Australian Humorous Quotations and Anecdotes*. Melbourne: Macmillan, 1974.

HISTORICAL AND SOCIAL BACKGROUND

Baker, Sidney J. *The Australian Language*. 2d ed. Sydney: Currawong, 1966. Divided into social categories, each with extensive vocabulary analysis; large comprehensive word list at end.

Barnard, Marjorie. *A History of Australia.* Sydney: Angus & Robertson, 1962.

Blainey, Geoffrey, *The Tyranny of Distance.* Melbourne: Sun Books, 1967.

Durack, Mary. *Kings in Grass Castles.* London: Corgi, 1967 [1959]. Classic account of early station life on marginal land.

Grattan, C. Hartley. *The Southwest Pacific Since 1900.* Ann Arbor: University of Michigan Press, 1963. Comprehensive, including literary discussion along with historical, economic, political aspects.

Horne, Donald. *The Lucky Country: Australia in the Sixties.* Rev. ed. Sydney: Angus & Robertson, 1966.

————. *The Next Australia.* Sydney: Angus & Robertson, 1971. A social view.

Ingleton, Geoffrey. *True Patriots All.* Sydney: Angus & Robertson, 1952. Colonial broadside literature.

Moorehead, Alan. *The Fatal Impact.* London: H. Hamilton, 1966. Disastrous effects of overexploitation in the Southwest Pacific, early nineteenth century.

Mountford, Charles P. *Brown Men and Red Sand: Wanderings in Wild Australia.* Melbourne: Robertson & Mullens, 1948. Memorable encounters with aborigines.

Nadel, George. *Australia's Colonial Culture.* Melbourne: Cheshire, 1957.

Pike, Douglas. *Australia: The Quiet Continent.* 2d ed. Cambridge: Cambridge University Press, 1970.

Rienits, Rex and Thea. *A Pictorial History of Australia.* London: Paul Hamlyn, 1969.

Smith, Bernard. *Australian Painting, 1788–1960.* London: Oxford, 1962.

————. *European Vision and the South Pacific.* Oxford: Clarendon Press, 1960.

Tatz, Colin, and McConnochie, Keith, eds. *Black Viewpoints: The Aboriginal Experience.* Sydney: Australian and New Zealand Book Col., 1975. Biracial authorship; some nineteen topics (well cross-indexed) discussed by the same number of authors.

Turner, G. W. *The English Language in Australia and New Zealand.* London: Longmans, 1966. Systematic topical treatment, with bibliography, word and phrase index.

Unstead, R. J., and Henderson, W. F. *Pioneer Home Life in Australia.* London: A. & C. Black, 1971.

Ward, Russel. *The Australian Legend.* Melbourne: Oxford, 1962 [1958].

————. *The History of Australia: The Twentieth Century.* New York: Harper & Row, 1977.

LITERARY HISTORY AND CRITICISM

Note: Special attention is directed to the entries "Periodicals" and "Series" in the following list. Biographical and critical studies of single authors appear at the end of various author references in Authors of Fiction, the final section.

Anderson, D., and Knight, S., eds. *Cunning Exiles: Studies on Modern Prose Writers.* Sydney: Angus & Robertson, 1974. Christina Stead and Patrick White share critical attention with such other moderns as Borges, Lowry, Mailer, and Sillitoe in a study by nine writers all associated with Sydney University.

Argyle, Barry. *An Introduction to the Australian Novel, 1830–1930.* London: Oxford, 1972. Uneven treatment, especially of nineteenth-century works.

Barnes, John, ed. *The Writer in Australia: A Collection of Literary Documents 1855–1964.* Melbourne: Oxford, 1969. Well-chosen selections, with commentaries by the editor.

Beilby, Raymond, and Hadgraft, Cecil. *Ada Cambridge, Tasma, and Rosa Praed.* Melbourne: Oxford, 1979.

Bettison, Margaret, and Summers, Anne, comps. *Her Story: Australian Women in Print 1788–1975.* Sydney: Hale & Iremonger, 1980. Contains, as part of a comprehensive guide, bibliographical entries about women writers and a useful section on individual biographies.

Blake, L. J. *Australian Writers.* Adelaide: Rigby, 1968. Concrete summary accounts with brief critical estimates.

Brisbane, Katharine, Brissenden, R. F., and Malouf, David. *New Currents in Australian Writing.* Sydney: Angus & Robertson, 1978. Discussions of novels, stories, and sketches, covering a wide range of authors.

Burns, D. R. *The Directions of Australian Fiction, 1920–1974.* Melbourne: Cassell, 1975. Seventeen chapters, many dealing with pairs, e.g., Herbert/Stead, Stow/Keneally, Porter/Astley; summaries of novels and story collections; reading list.

Cantrell, Leon, ed. *Bards, Bohemians, & Bookmen: Essays in Australian Literature.* St. Lucia: University of Queensland Press, 1976. Previously unpublished criticism by twenty contributors on Clarke, Furphy, Hay, Lawson, Lindsay, White.

Day, A. Grove, ed. *Modern Australian Prose, 1901–1975: A Guide to Information Sources.* Detroit: Gale Research Co., 1980. Covers fiction, nonfiction prose, and drama, with main emphasis upon fiction; some fifty or more writers of fiction receive special attention.

Docker, John. *Australian Cultural Elites.* Sydney: Angus & Robertson, 1974. Contrasting analyses of intellectual traditions in Sydney and Melbourne.

Dutton, Geoffrey, ed. *The Literature of Australia.* Rev. ed. Harmondsworth: Penguin, 1976. A much-revised version of a work first published in 1964; both editions will remain useful for some time to come.

Green, H. M. *A History of Australian Literature.* 2 vols. Sydney: Angus & Robertson, 1961. The standard work, with extensive coverage to 1950.

Hadgraft, Cecil. *Australian Literature: A Critical Account to 1955.* London: Heinemann, 1961. Readable; not reluctant to state opinions positively.

Healy, J. J. *Literature and the Aborigine in Australia 1770–1975*. St. Lucia: University of Queensland Press, 1978. Twelve chapters, with some twenty or more principal writers discussed in detail.

Hetherington, John. *Forty-Two Faces*. Melbourne: Cheshire, 1962. Profiles of Australian literary personalities originally published in the Melbourne *Age;* well illustrated.

Ingamells, Rex. *Conditional Culture*. Adelaide: F. W. Preece, 1938. The Jindyworobak manifesto, with heavy stress upon environmentalism; included in *The Writer in Australia,* ed. J. Barnes.

Johnston, Grahame, ed. *Australian Literary Criticism*. Melbourne: Oxford, 1962. Selected essays.

Jones, Joseph. "Provincial to International: Southwest Pacific Literature in English since the 1920s." In *Australia, New Zealand, and the Pacific Islands since the First World War*. Edited by William S. Livingston and William Roger Louis. Austin: University of Texas Press, 1979, pp. 125–47. Summary survey.

————. *Radical Cousins: Nineteenth Century American & Australian Writers*. St. Lucia: University of Queensland Press, 1976. Major emphasis on poetry, with some attention to fiction.

Keesing, Nancy, ed. *Australian Postwar Novelists: Selected Critical Essays*. Brisbane: Jacaranda, 1975.

Kiernan, Brian. *Images of Society and Nature: Seven Essays on Australian Novels*. Melbourne: Oxford, 1971. On Furphy, Richardson, Stead, Herbert, White, and Keneally, followed by a general essay.

Kramer, Leonie, ed. *The Oxford History of Australian Literature*. Melbourne: Oxford, 1981. A sizable reference volume, well annotated and indexed. The section on fiction, pp. 27–172, is rather more idiosyncratic than comprehensive.

Lock, Fred, and Lawson, Alan, eds. *Australian Literature—a Reference Guide*. Melbourne: Oxford, 1977.

Modern Fiction Studies (special issue). *Modern New Zealand and Australian Fiction*. West Lafayette, Ind.: Purdue University, 1981. A dozen articles, several of the survey type, together with useful bibliographies.

Moore, T. Inglis. *Social Patterns in Australian Literature*. Sydney: Angus & Robertson, 1971. Maintains a good critical distance; written out of abundant personal knowledge.

Murdoch, Walter, and Deakin, Alfred. *Books and Men: Letters and Comments 1900–1918*. Edited by J. A. LaNauze and Elizabeth Nurser. Melbourne: Melbourne University Press, 1974.

Narasimhaiah, C. D. *An Introduction to Australian Literature*. Mysore: Mysore University, 1964. Especially useful for Asian and other comparative perspectives.

Narasimhaiah, C. D., and Nagarajan, S., eds. *Studies in Australian and Indian Literature*. New Delhi: Indian Council for Cultural Relations,

1971. Minimal attention to fiction; publication grew out of a seminar in India, January 1970.

New, William H. *Among Worlds: An Introduction to Modern Commonwealth and South African Fiction.* Erin, Ont.: Press Porcepic, 1975. The Australian chapter, emphasizing responses to "a new old land," is particularly good on modern women writers; cites parallels with other Commonwealth novelists.

―――― , comp. *Critical Writings on Commonwealth Literatures: A Selective Bibliography to 1970.* University Park: Pennsylvania State University Press, 1975. Listings by country; includes research aids, general references, single authors.

Niven, Alastair, ed. *The Commonwealth Writer Overseas.* Brussels: Didier, 1976. Essays on Caroline Leakey, Patrick White; references to Furphy in an essay on language.

Palmer, Vance. *Intimate Portraits and Other Pieces.* Melbourne: Cheshire, 1969. Sections on "The Community of Letters," "Writers I Remember," and "The Spirit of Prose" especially useful.

――――. *The Legend of the Nineties.* Melbourne: Melbourne University Press, 1966 [1954]. Essays by a distinguished inheritor of the Lawson tradition.

Periodicals

Australian Book Review, monthly, Kensington Park, 1961–73
Australian Literary Studies, semiannual, St. Lucia, Qld., 1963 +
Journal of Commonwealth Literature, London, 1965 +
Kovave [Papua New Guinea lit.], semiannual, Brisbane, 1969 +
Meanjin, quarterly, Melbourne, 1941 +
Overland, quarterly, Melbourne, 1954 +
Southerly, quarterly, Sydney, 1939 +
Southern Review, 3 issues yearly, Adelaide, 1963 +
Westerly, quarterly, Nedlands. W.A., 1956 +
WLWE, semiannual (Austin and Arlington, Texas, 1962–79), Guelph, Ont., 1979 +

Phillips, Arthur A. *The Australian Tradition: Studies in a Colonial Culture,* 2d rev. ed. Melbourne: Melbourne University Press, 1966 [1958]. Stresses the need for a more cosmopolitan outlook in Australian writing.

Ramson, W. S., ed. *The Australian Experience: Critical Essays on Australian Novels.* Canberra: ANU Press, 1974. Seventeen essays by leading Australian scholars and critics.

Reid, Ian. *Fiction and the Great Depression: Australia and New Zealand, 1930– 1950.* Melbourne: E. Arnold, 1979. Surveys a crucial period in both countries.

Series

A & R Classics. Sydney: Angus & Robertson.
Australian Classics. Melbourne: O'Neil.

Australian Writers and Their Work. Melbourne: Oxford.

Paperback Prose. St. Lucia: University of Queensland Press (also in "library edition").

Twayne's World Authors Series. Boston: Twayne Publishers.

Serle, Geoffrey. *From Deserts the Prophets Come: The Creative Spirit in Australia 1788–1972*. Melbourne: Heinemann, 1973. Many astute insights from an experienced cultural historian.

Sinnett, Frederick. *The Fiction Fields of Australia*. Edited by Cecil Hadgraft. St. Lucia: University of Queensland Press, 1966 [1856]. One of the best early estimates; included in *The Writer in Australia*, ed. J. Barnes.

Smith, Graeme Kinross. *Australia's Writers*. Melbourne: Nelson, 1980. Brief sketches of fifty-four writers, with portraits and other illustrations.

Stephens, A. G. *Selected Writings*. Edited by Leon Cantrell. Sydney: Angus & Robertson, 1978. Early criticism, often of high quality and always interesting.

Stephenson, P. R. *The Foundations of Culture in Australia*. Sydney: W. J. Miles, 1936. Subtitled "An Essay towards National Self-Respect"; included in *The Writer in Australia*, ed. J. Barnes.

Stewart, Douglas. *The Broad Stream*. Sydney: Angus & Robertson, 1975. By one of Australia's best-known writer-editors.

————— . *Writers of the Bulletin*. Sydney: Australian Broadcasting Commission, 1977. Brief but wide-ranging.

Walker, David. *Dream and Disillusion: A Search for Australian Cultural Identity*. Canberra: ANU Press, 1976. Uses four literary figures (Vance Palmer is the one novelist of the group) to study Australian literary nationalism.

Wallace-Crabbe, Chris, ed. *The Australian Nationalists: Modern Critical Essays*. Melbourne: Oxford, 1971. Emphasis on Lawson and Furphy, with attention also to Baynton, Rudd, and Stone.

————— . *Melbourne or the Bush: Essays on Australian Literature and Society*. Sydney: Angus & Robertson, 1974. Novelists treated: Boyd, Furphy, Lawson.

ANTHOLOGIES

Barnes, John, ed. *An Australian Selection: Short Stories by Lawson, Palmer, Porter, White, Cowan*. Sydney: Angus & Robertson, 1974.

Beier, Ulli, ed. *Black Writing from New Guinea*. St. Lucia: University of Queensland Press, 1973.

Bennett, Bruce, ed. *New Country: A Selection of Western Australian Short Stories*. Fremantle: Fremantle Arts Centre Press, 1976.

Coast to Coast: Australian Stories. Sydney: Angus & Robertson, annually 1941–61.

The Cool Man and Other Contemporary Stories. Sydney: Angus & Robertson, 1973.

Cusack, Frank, ed. *Australian Ghost Stories.* Melbourne: Heinemann, 1967.

Davis, Beatrice, ed. *Short Stories of Australia: The Moderns.* Sydney: Angus & Robertson, 1967.

Dugan, Michael, and Jenkins, John, eds. *The Outback Reader.* Melbourne: Outback Press, 1975.

Friederich, Werner P. *Australia in Western Imaginative Prose Writings: An Anthology and a History of Literature.* Chapel Hill: University of North Carolina Press, 1967.

Hadgraft, Cecil, and Wilson, Richard, eds. *A Century of Australian Short Stories.* London: Heinemann, 1963.

Heseltine, Harry, ed. *The Penguin Book of Australian Short Stories.* Harmondsworth: Penguin, 1976.

Hewett, Dorothy, ed. *Sandgropers, a Western Australian Anthology.* Perth: University of Western Australia Press, 1973.

Higham, Charles, ed. *Australian Writing Today.* Harmondsworth, Penguin, 1968.

Ingram, Anne Bower, ed. *Shudders and Shakes: Ghostly Tales from Australia.* Sydney: Collins, 1972.

―――――. *Too True: Australian Tall Tales.* Sydney: Collins, 1974.

Keesing, Nancy, comp. *Shalom: A Collection of Australian Jewish Stories.* Sydney: Collins, 1978.

Kiernan, Brian, ed. *The Most Beautiful Lies.* Sydney: Angus & Robertson, 1977.

Lord, Mary, ed. *Modern Australian Short Stories.* London: Edward Arnold, 1971.

Mayman, Ted, ed. *View from Kalgoorlie.* Perth: Landfall Press, 1969.

Munro, Craig, ed. *UQP Story Anthology.* St. Lucia: University of Queensland Press, 1981.

The Night Warrior and Other Stories from Papua New Guinea. Brisbane: Jacaranda, 1972.

Osborne, Charles, ed. *Australian Short Stories of Today.* London: Faber, 1961.

Porter, Hal, ed. *It Could Be You.* Adelaide: Rigby, 1972.

Rorabacher, Louise E., ed. *Aliens in Their Land: The Aborigine in the Australian Short Story.* Melbourne: Longman Cheshire, 1977 [1963].

―――――. *Two Ways Meet: Stories of Migrants in Australia.* Melbourne: Cheshire, 1963.

Stewart, Douglas, ed. *Short Stories of Australia: The Lawson Tradition.* Sydney: Angus & Robertson, 1967.

Stewart, Douglas, and Davis, Beatrice, eds. *Best Australian Short Stories.* Melbourne: O'Neil, 1971.

Tiffin, Chris and Helen, eds. *South Pacific Stories.* St. Lucia: SPACLALS, 1980.

Wannan, Bill, ed. *Modern Australian Humor.* Melbourne: Lansdowne, 1962.
Waten, Judah, and Murray-Smith, Stephen, eds. *Classic Australian Short Stories.* Melbourne: Wren, 1974.
Zurbo, S., ed. *Stories of Her Life: An Anthology of Short Stories by Australian Women.* Melbourne: Outback Press, 1979.

AUTHORS OF FICTION
(Arranged alphabetically)

Note: Authors' life-dates, when known, are given after their names, and biographical studies are noted after each author's book titles. The lists are selective; only the more important titles are given for most authors: for complete information, the reader should consult the biographical studies or other bibliographical guides. When a work has been republished some years after its original appearance, the later edition is usually cited and the date of first publication appears in brackets at the end of the entry.

Abdullah, Mena (b. 1930) and Mathew, Ray (b. 1929). *The Time of the Peacock* (stories). Sydney: Angus & Robertson, 1965.
Adams, Francis (1862–92). *John Webb's End; Australian Bush Life.* London: Eden, Remington & Co., 1891.
––––––. *The Melbournians, a Novel.* London and Sydney: Eden, Remington & Co., 1892.
Aitken, D. A. *The Second Chair.* Sydney: Angus & Robertson, 1977.
Aldridge, James (b. 1918). *The Diplomat.* London: Bodley Head, 1949.
––––––. *Goodbye Un-America.* London: M. Joseph, 1979.
––––––. *Heroes of the Empty View.* New York: Knopf, 1954.
––––––. *My Brother Tom.* London: H. Hamilton, 1966.
––––––. *Signed with Their Honor.* London: M. Joseph, 1942. [Eric Partridge, "Man of Action, Words in Action: The Novels of James Aldridge," *Meanjin,* no. 3 (1961), pp. 256–63.]
Amos, Peter. *The Silver Kings.* London: Harrap, 1970.
Anderson, Ethel (1883–1958). *The Best of Ethel Anderson: Tales of Parramatta and of India.* Edited by John Douglas Pringle. Sydney: Angus & Robertson, 1973.
Anderson, Jessica. *The Impersonators.* Melbourne: Macmillan, 1980.
––––––. *Tirra Lirra by the River.* Melbourne: Macmillan, 1978.
Astley, Thea (b. 1925). *The Acolyte.* Sydney: Angus & Robertson, 1972.
––––––. *A Boatload of Home Folk.* Sydney: Angus & Robertson, 1968.
––––––. *Descant for Gossips.* Sydney: Angus & Robertson, 1960.
––––––. *Girl with a Monkey.* Sydney: Angus & Robertson, 1958.
––––––. *Hunting the Wild Pineapple, and Other Related Stories.* Melbourne: Nelson, 1979.

————. *A Kindness Cup.* Melbourne: Nelson, 1974.

————. *The Slow Natives.* Sydney: Angus & Robertson, 1965.

————. *The Well Dressed Explorer.* Sydney: Angus & Robertson, 1962.

Astley, William [Price Warung] (1855–1911). *Half-Crown Bob and Tales of the Riverine.* Melbourne: G. Robertson, 1892.

————. *Tales of the Convict System.* Sydney: Bulletin, 1892.

————. *Tales of the Convict System.* Edited by B. G. Andrews. St. Lucia: University of Queensland Press, 1975. Contains seventeen stories, an introduction, and notes. [Barry Andrews, *Price Warung* (Boston: Twayne Publishers, 1976).]

Atkinson, Hugh (b. 1925). *The Games.* London: World Books, 1968.

————. *Low Company.* Melbourne: Cheshire, 1961.

————. *The Manipulators.* Sydney: Angus & Robertson, 1978.

————. *The Pink and the Brown.* London: V. Gollancz, 1957.

————. *The Reckoning.* London: Bodley Head, 1965.

Bail, Murray (b. 1941). *Contemporary Portraits and Other Stories.* St. Lucia: University of Queensland Press, 1975.

————. *Homesickness.* Melbourne: Macmillan, 1980.

————. *Ian Fairweather.* Sydney: Bay Books, 1981. [Interview, *Meanjin,* no. 2 (1982), pp. 264–76.]

Bailey, John (b. 1944). *The Wire Classroom.* Sydney: Angus & Robertson, 1972.

Banjo. See Paterson, A. B.

Barnard, Marjorie (b. 1897). *The Persimmon Tree and Other Stories.* Sydney: Clarendon, 1943.

Barnard-Eldershaw. See Eldershaw.

Baylebridge, William. See Blocksidge, William.

Baynton, Barbara (1862–1929). *Bush Studies.* Introduction by A. A. Phillips. Sydney: Angus & Robertson, 1980 [1902].

————. *Human Toll.* London: Duckworth, 1907.

————. *The Portable Barbara Baynton.* Edited by Sally Krimmer and Alan Lawson. St. Lucia: University of Queensland Press, 1980.

Becke, Louis (1855–1913). *By Reef and Palm.* Freeport, N.Y.: Books for Libraries Press, 1970 [1894].

————. (with W. J. Jeffery). *A First Fleet Family.* London: Unwin, 1896.

————. *Notes from My South Sea Log.* London: Laurie, 1905.

————. *Pacific Tales.* Freeport, N.Y.: Books for Libraries Press, 1969 [1897].

————. *Under Tropic Skies.* Freeport, N.Y.: Books for Libraries Press, 1970 [1904]. [A. Grove Day, *Louis Becke* (New York: Twayne, 1966).]

Beilby, Richard (b. 1918). *The Bitter Lotus.* Sydney: Angus & Robertson, 1978.

————. *The Brown Land Crying.* Sydney: Angus & Robertson, 1976.

————. *No Medals for Aphrodite.* Sydney: Angus & Robertson, 1970.

Bergner, Herz (b. 1907). *Between Sky and Sea.* Translated by J. L. Waten. Melbourne: Dolphin, 1946.

———. *Light and Shadow.* Translated by Alec Braizblatt. Foreword by Alan Marshall. London: Angus & Robertson, 1963.

Blocksidge, William [William Baylebridge] (1887–1942). *An Anzac Muster* (stories). Sydney: Privately printed, 1921.

Boldrewood, Rolfe. See Browne, Thomas Alexander.

Boyd, A. J. (1842–1928). *Old Colonials.* Introduction by G. A. Wilkes. Sydney: Sydney University Press, 1974 [1882].

Boyd, Martin (1893–1972). *The Cardboard Crown.* London: Cresset, 1952.

———. *A Difficult Young Man.* London: Cresset, 1955.

———. *Lucinda Brayford.* Melbourne: Lansdowne, 1969 [1946].

———. *The Montforts.* Adelaide: Rigby, 1963 [1928].

———. *Outbreak of Love.* London: Murray, 1957.

———. *The Teatime of Love.* London: Bles, 1969.

———. *When Blackbirds Sing.* London and New York: Abelard-Schuman, 1962. [Brenda Niall, *Martin Boyd* (Melbourne: Oxford, 1974).]

Broinowsky, Alison. *Take One Ambassador.* Melbourne: Macmillan, 1973.

Brown, Max. *The Jimberi Track.* Sydney: Australasian, 1966.

Browne, Thomas Alexander [Rolfe Boldrewood] (1826–1915). *A Colonial Reformer.* London: Macmillan, 1890.

———. *In Bad Company and Other Stories.* London: Macmillan, 1901.

———. *The Miner's Right.* London: Macmillan, 1890.

———. *Robbery under Arms.* Sydney: Angus & Robertson, 1980 [1888].

———. *A Sydney-Side Saxon.* London: Macmillan, 1891. [Alan Brissenden, *Rolfe Boldrewood* (Melbourne: Oxford, 1972).]

Burke, David (b. 1927). *Monday at McMurdo.* Wellington: Reed, 1967.

Butler, Richard (b. 1925). *The Blood-Red Sun at Noon.* Sydney: Collins, 1980.

———. *The Man That God Forgot.* London: Hutchinson, 1975.

———. *The Sullivans.* Melbourne: Unicorn, 1980.

Caddie (pseud.). *Caddie, a Sydney Barmaid; an Autobiography.* Introduction by Dymphna Cusack. London: Constable, 1953.

Calthorpe, Mena (b. 1905). *The Defectors.* Sydney: Australasian, 1969.

———. *The Dyehouse.* Sydney: Ure Smith, 1961.

Cambridge, Ada (Cross, Ada, or Mrs. G. F. Cross, 1844–1926). *Fidelis.* London: Hutchinson, 1895.

———. *A Humble Enterprise.* London: Ward, Lock, 1896.

———. *A Marked Man.* London: Heinemann, 1890.

———. *A Marriage Contract.* New York: Appleton, 1894. [*See* Beilby, under Literary History and Criticism.]

Campbell, David (1915–79). *Evening under Lamplight* (stories). Sydney: Angus & Robertson, 1959.

———— . *Flame and Shadow: Selected Short Stories*. St. Lucia: University of Queensland Press, 1976.

Carey, Peter (b. 1943). *Bliss*. St. Lucia: University of Queensland Press, 1981.

———— . *The Fat Man in History* (stories). London: Faber, 1980 [1974].

———— . *War Crimes: Short Stories*. St. Lucia: University of Queensland Press, 1979.

Casey, Gavin S. (1907–64). *Amid the Plenty*. Sydney: Australasian, 1962.

———— . *City of Men*. London: Peter Davies, 1950.

———— . *Downhill Is Easier*. Sydney: Angus & Robertson, 1945.

———— . *It's Harder for Girls, and Other Stories*. Sydney: Angus & Robertson, 1942. (Republished, 1973, as *Short Shrift and Other Stories*.)

———— . *Snowball*. Sydney: Angus & Robertson, 1958.

———— . *The Wits Are Out*. Sydney: Angus & Robertson, 1947.

Cato, Nancy (b. 1917). *All the Rivers Run*. London: New English Library, 1978 [1958].

———— . *Brown Sugar*. London: Heinemann, 1974.

———— . *The Sea Ants and Other Stories*. London: Heinemann, 1964.

———— and Ellis, V. R. *Queen Truuanini*. London: Heinemann, 1976.

Charlwood, D. E. *All the Green Year*. Sydney: Angus & Robertson, 1980 [1965].

Clancy, Laurie (b. 1942). *A Collapsible Man*. New York: St. Martin's Press, 1977.

———— . *The Wife Specialist* (stories). Melbourne: Hyland House, 1979.

Clark, Manning (b. 1915). *Disquiet and Other Stories*. Sydney: Angus & Robertson, 1969.

Clarke, Marcus (1846–81). *His Natural Life*. Edited by S. Murray-Smith. Baltimore: Penguin, 1970 [1870–72]. Other eds., as *For the Term of His Natural Life*.

———— . *The Portable Marcus Clarke*. Edited by Michael Wilding. St. Lucia: University of Queensland Press, 1976. (See this and other references for extensive listings.) [Brian Elliott, *Marcus Clarke* (Oxford: Clarendon Press, 1958); Michael Wilding, *Marcus Clarke* (New York: Oxford, 1977).]

Cleary, Jon (b. 1917). *The Country of Marriage*. London: Collins, 1962.

———— . *The Safe House*. New York: Morrow, 1975.

———— . *The Sundowners*. London: Laurie, 1952.

Cobb, Chester Francis (1899–1943). *Days of Disillusion*. London: G. Allen & Unwin, 1926.

———— . *Mr. Moffatt*. London: G. Allen & Unwin, 1925.

Collins, Betty. *The Copper Crucible*. Brisbane: Jacaranda, 1966.

———— . *The Second Step*. Sydney: Australasian, 1972.

Cook, Kenneth (b. 1929). *Bloodhouse*. London: Heinemann, 1974.

———— . *Pig.* Melbourne: Schwartz, 1980.

———— . *Play, Little Victim.* Sydney: Pergamon, 1978.

———— . *Stormalong.* London: M. Joseph, 1963.

———— . *Tuna.* Melbourne: Sun Books, 1978 [1972].

———— . *Wake in Fright.* Sydney: Angus & Robertson, 1981 [1961].

Cornish, Richard (b. 1942). *The Woman Lilith.* Melbourne: Macmillan, 1975.

Couvreur, Jessie C. [Tasma] (1848–97). *A Sydney Sovereign and Other Tales.* London: Trubner, 1890.

———— . *Uncle Piper of Piper's Hill.* London: Trubner, 1889. (See also Beilby under Critical Works.)

Cowan, Peter (b. 1914). *Drift* (stories). Adelaide: Reed & Harris, 1944.

———— . *The Empty Street* (stories). Sydney: Angus & Robertson, 1965.

———— . *Mobiles and Other Stories.* Fremantle: Fremantle Arts Centre Press, 1979.

———— . *Summer.* Sydney: Angus & Robertson, 1964.

———— . *The Tins and Other Stories.* St. Lucia: Univ. of Queensland Press, 1973.

———— . *The Unploughed Land* (stories). Sydney: Angus & Robertson, 1958.

Crick, Donald (b. 1916). *Martin Place.* Sydney: Australasian, 1964.

———— . *Period of Adjustment.* Sydney: Australasian, 1966.

Cusack, Dymphna (b. 1902). *A Bough in Hell.* London: Heinemann, 1971.

———— . *The Half-burnt Tree.* London: Mayflower, 1969.

———— . *Picnic Races.* Melbourne: Hutchinson, 1978 [1962].

———— . *Say No to Death.* London: Heinemann, 1951.

———— . *Southern Steel.* Melbourne: Marlin Books, 1977 [1953].

———— . *The Sun in Exile.* Melbourne: Marlin Books, 1977 [1955].

———— and James, Florence. *Come in Spinner!* London: Heinemann, 1951. [Norman Freehill, *Dymphna Cusack* (Melbourne: Nelson, 1975).]

D'Alpuget, Blanche (b. 1944). *Monkeys in the Dark.* Sydney: Aurora Press, 1980.

———— . *Turtle Beach.* Melbourne: Penguin, 1981.

Dark, Eleanor (b. 1901). *Lantana Lane.* London: Collins, 1959.

———— . *The Little Company.* New York: Macmillan, 1945.

———— . *No Barrier.* Sydney: Angus & Robertson, 1980 [1953].

———— . *Prelude to Christopher.* Sydney: P. R. Stephensen, 1934.

———— . *Return to Coolami.* Sydney: Angus & Robertson, 1981 [1936].

———— . *Slow Dawning.* London: John Long, 1932.

———— . *Storm of Time.* Sydney: Angus & Robertson, 1980 [1949].

———— . *Sun Across the Sky.* London: Collins, 1937.

———— . *The Timeless Land.* Sydney: Angus & Robertson, 1980 [1941].

———— . *Waterway.* Sydney: Angus & Robertson, 1979 [1938]. [A. Grove Day, *Eleanor Dark* (Boston: Twayne Publishers, 1976).]

Davies, Alan (b. 1924). *A Sunday Kind of Love and Other Stories*. Melbourne: Cheshire, 1961.

Davis, A. H. [Steele Rudd] (1868–1935). *On Our Selection, Our New Selection, Sandy's Selection, Back at Our Selection*. Melbourne: O'Neil, 1973 [1899, 1903, 1904]. [E. D. Davis, *The Life and Times of Steele Rudd* (Melbourne: Lansdowne, 1976).]

Davison, Frank Dalby (1893–1970). *Children of the Dark People*. Sydney: Angus & Robertson, 1936.

————. *Dusty*. Sydney: Angus & Robertson, 1946.

————. *Forever Morning*. Sydney: Angus & Robertson, 1931.

————. *Man-Shy*. Sydney: Angus & Robertson, 1931.

————. *The Road to Yesterday* (stories). Sydney: Angus & Robertson, 1964.

————. *The Wells of Beersheba*. Sydney: Angus & Robertson, 1933.

————. *The White Thorn Tree*. Melbourne: National Press, 1968.

————. *The Woman at the Mill* (stories). Sydney: Angus & Robertson, 1940. [Hume Dow, *Frank Dalby Davison* (Melbourne: Oxford, 1971); Louise E. Rorabacher, *Frank Dalby Davison* (Boston: Twayne Publishers, 1979).]

Denton, Kit. *The Breaker*. Sydney: Angus & Robertson, 1979 [1973].

Devanny, Jean (Crooks) (b. 1894). *The Butcher Shop*. London: Duckworth, 1926.

————. *Old Savage, and Other Stories*. London: Duckworth, 1927.

————. *Sugar Heaven*. Sydney: Modern Publishing Co., 1936.

Dick, William Charles (b. 1937). *A Bunch of Ratbags*. London: Collins, 1965.

————. *Naked Prodigal*. Melbourne: Hutchinson, 1969.

Downs, Ian (b. 1915). *The Stolen Land*. Brisbane: Jacaranda, 1970.

Drake-Brockman, Henrietta (1901–68). *The Fatal Days*. Sydney: Angus & Robertson, 1947.

————. *Sheba Lane*. Sydney: Angus & Robertson, 1936.

————. *Sydney or the Bush* (stories). Sydney: Angus & Robertson, 1948.

————. *The Wicked and the Fair*. Sydney: Angus & Robertson, 1957.

Drewe, Robert (b. 1943). *A Cry in the Jungle Bar*. Sydney: Collins, 1979.

————. *The Savage Crows*. Sydney: Collins, 1976.

Duigan, John (b. 1949). *Badge*. Melbourne: Macmillan, 1975.

Durack, Mary (b. 1913). *Keep Him, My Country*. London: Constable, 1955.

Dutton, Geoffrey (b. 1922). *Andy*. London: Collins, 1968.

————. *The Eye Opener*. St. Lucia: University of Queensland Press, 1982.

————. *Tamara*. London: Collins, 1970.

————. *The Wedge-Tailed Eagle* (stories). Melbourne: Macmillan, 1980.

Dyson, Edward G. (1865–1931). *"Fact'ry 'Ands."* Melbourne: G. Robertson, 1906.

————. *The Golden Shanty* (stories). Sydney: Cornstalk, 1929.

Eldershaw, Flora (1897–1956), and Barnard, Marjorie (b. 1897) [M. Barnard Eldershaw]. *The Glasshouse.* London: Harrap, 1936.

_____ . *Green Memory.* London: Harrap, 1931.

_____ . *A House Is Built.* Melbourne: O'Neil, 1972 [1929].

_____ . *Plaque with Laurel.* London: Harrap, 1937.

_____ . *Tomorrow and Tomorrow.* Melbourne: Hutchinson, 1978 [1947]. [Louise E. Rorabacher, *Marjorie Barnard and M. Barnard Eldershaw* (New York: Twayne Publishers, 1973).]

Eldershaw, M. Barnard. See Eldershaw, Flora and Barnard, Marjorie.

Elliott, Brian (b. 1910). *Leviathan's Inch.* Sydney: Angus & Robertson, 1946.

Ellis, Havelock (1859–1939). *Kanga Creek.* Introduction by John Heuzenroeder. Melbourne: Nelson, 1970 [1922].

Emery, John. *Summer Ends Now.* St. Lucia: University of Queensland Press, 1980.

Eri, Vincent (b. 1936). *The Crocodile.* Brisbane: Jacaranda, 1971.

Ewers, John K. (1904–78). *For Heroes to Live In.* Melbourne: Georgian House, 1948.

_____ . *Harvest, and Other Stories.* Sydney: Angus & Robertson, 1949.

_____ . *Men against the Earth.* Melbourne: Georgian House, 1946.

_____ . *Money Street.* London: Hodder & Stoughton, 1933.

_____ . *Who Rides on the River.* Sydney: Angus & Robertson, 1956.

Ford, John (b. 1912). *The Blue Comedian.* London: Angus & Robertson, 1968.

_____ . *The Tokyo Contract.* Sydney: Angus & Robertson, 1972.

Forrest, David (b. 1924). *The Hollow Woodheap.* Brisbane: Jacaranda, 1962.

_____ . *The Last Blue Sea.* London: Heinemann, 1959.

Forshaw, Thelma (b. 1923). *An Affair of Clowns.* Sydney: Angus & Robertson, 1967.

Foster, David Manning (b. 1944). *Escape to Reality* (stories). Melbourne: Macmillan, 1977.

_____ . *Moonlite.* Melbourne: Macmillan, 1981.

_____ . *North, South, West: Three Novellas.* Melbourne: Macmillan, 1973.

_____ . *The Pure Land.* London: Macmillan, 1974.

Franklin, Miles (1879–1954). *All That Swagger.* Sydney: Angus & Robertson, 1979 [1936].

_____ . *Back to Bool Bool.* Edinburgh: Blackwood, 1931.

_____ . *Bring the Monkey.* Sydney: Endeavour Press, 1933.

_____ . *Cockatoos.* Sydney: Angus & Robertson, 1954.

_____ . *Gentlemen at Gyang Gyang.* Sydney: Angus & Robertson, 1956.

_____ . *My Brilliant Career.* Sydney: Angus & Robertson, 1979 [1901].

_____ . *My Career Goes Bung.* London: Virago Press, 1981 [1946].

_____ . *Old Blastus of Bandicoot.* London: C. Palmer, 1931.

————. *Some Everyday Folk and Dawn*. Edinburgh: Blackwood, 1909.

————. *Ten Creeks Run*. Edinburgh: Blackwood, 1928.

————. *Up the Country*. Edinburgh: Blackwood, 1931.

———— and Cusack, Dymphna. *Pioneers on Parade*. Sydney: Angus & Robertson, 1939. [Marjorie Barnard, *Miles Franklin* (New York: Twayne Publishers, 1967); Miles Franklin, *Laughter, Not for a Cage: Notes on Australian Writing, with Biographical Emphasis on the Struggle, Function, and Achievement of the Novel in Three Half Centuries* (Sydney: Angus & Robertson, 1956); Ray Mathew, *Miles Franklin* (Melbourne: Oxford, 1963).]

Free, Colin (b. 1925). *Carbon Copy*. London: Heinemann, 1972.

Furphy, Joseph (1843–1912). *The Buln-Buln and the Brolga*. Sydney: Angus & Robertson, 1948.

————. *The Portable Furphy*. Edited by John Barnes. St. Lucia: University of Queensland Press, 1981.

————. *Rigby's Romance*. Sydney: Angus & Robertson, 1946 [1905–6].

————. *Such Is Life*. Sydney: Angus & Robertson, 1962 [1903]. [John Barnes, *Joseph Furphy* (Melbourne: Oxford, 1963).]

Gare, Nene (b. 1919). *Bend to the Wind* (stories). Melbourne: Macmillan, 1978.

————. *The Fringe-Dwellers*. Melbourne: Sun Books, 1966.

————. *A House with Verandahs*. Melbourne: Macmillan, 1980.

————. *An Island Away*. Melbourne: Macmillan, 1981.

Garner, Helen. *Honour & Other People's Children*. Melbourne: McPhee Gribble, 1980.

————. *Monkey Grip*. Melbourne: Penguin, 1978.

Garvey, Keith (b. 1922). *Shout for the Adder and Other Bush Yarns* (stories). Melbourne: Hutchinson, 1980.

Gilders, John P. *Man Alone*. Sydney: Australasian, 1971.

Glaskin, G. M. (b. 1923). *The Beach of Passionate Love*. London: Barrie & Rockliff, 1961.

————. *A Change of Mind*. London: Barrie & Rockliff, 1959.

————. *Flight to Landfall*. New York: St. Martin's Press, 1980 [1963].

————. *Lion in the Sun*. London: Barrie & Rockliff, 1960.

————. *A Minor Portrait*. London: Barrie, 1957.

————. *A Small Selection of Short Stories*. London: Barrie & Rockliff, 1962.

Glassop, Lawson (1913–66). *The Rats in New Guinea*. London: Horwitz, 1963.

————. *We Were the Rats*. Sydney: Angus & Robertson, 1944.

Hackston, James (1888–1967). *Father Clears Out* (stories). Sydney: Angus & Robertson, 1966.

Hall, Rodney (b. 1935). *A Place among People*. St. Lucia: University of Queensland Press, 1975.

_____. *The Ship on the Coin*. St. Lucia: University of Queensland Press, 1972.

Halls, Geraldine. *The Felling of Thawle*. London: Constable, 1979.

_____. *The Last Summer of the Men Shortage*. Melbourne: Hutchinson, 1977.

_____. *The Voice of the Crab*. London: Constable, 1974.

Hanrahan, Barbara (b. 1939). *The Albatross Muff*. London: Chatto & Windus, 1977.

_____. *The Frangipani Gardens*. St. Lucia: University of Queensland Press, 1980.

_____. *The Peach Groves*. St. Lucia: University of Queensland Press, 1979.

_____. *The Scent of Eucalyptus*. Sydney: Fontana, 1980 [1973].

_____. *Sea-Green*. Sydney: Fontana, 1980 [1973].

_____. *Where the Queens All Strayed*. St. Lucia: University of Queensland Press, 1978.

Harcourt, John (b. 1902). *Upsurge*. London: John Long, 1934.

Hardy, Frank (b. 1917). *But the Dead Are Many*. London: Bodley Head, 1975.

_____. *The Four-Legged Lottery*. Melbourne: Gold Star, 1972 [1958].

_____. *It's Moments Like These* (stories). Melbourne: Gold Star, 1972.

_____. *Power without Glory*. Melbourne: O'Neil, 1972 [1950].

_____. *Who Shot John Kirkland?* Melbourne: E. Arnold, 1981.

Harris, Alexander (1805–74). *The Emigrant Family*. London: Smith, Elder, 1849.

_____. *Settlers and Convicts*. Melbourne: Melbourne University Press, 1953 [1847]. [John Barnes, *Henry Kingsley and Colonial Fiction* (Melbourne: Oxford, 1971).]

Harris, Max (b. 1921). *The Vegetative Eye*. Melbourne: National Press, 1943.

Harrower, Elizabeth (b. 1928). *The Catherine Wheel*. Sydney: Angus & Robertson, 1979 [1960].

_____. *Down in the City*. London: Cassell, 1957.

_____. *The Long Prospect*. Sydney: Angus & Robertson, 1979 [1958].

_____. *The Watch Tower*. Sydney: Angus & Robertson, 1977 [1966]. [R. G. Geering, *Recent Fiction* (Melbourne: Oxford, 1973).]

Hay, William Gosse (1875–1945). *Captain Quadring*. London: Unwin, 1912.

_____. *The Escape of the Notorious Sir William Heans*. Melbourne: Melbourne University Press, 1955 [1918].

_____. *Herridge of Reality Swamp*. London: Unwin, 1907.

_____. *The Mystery of Alfred Doubt*. London: G. Allen & Unwin, 1937.

_____. *Stifled Laughter*. London: John Macqueen, 1901.

———. *Strabane of the Mulberry Hills*. London: G. Allen & Unwin, 1929. [Fayette Gosse, *William Gosse Hay* (Melbourne: Oxford, 1965).]

Hazzard, Shirley (b. 1931). *The Bay of Noon* (stories). Boston and London: Macmillan, 1970.

———. *Cliffs of Fall and Other Stories*. New York and London: Macmillan, 1963.

———. *The Evening of the Holiday*. New York and London: Macmillan, 1966.

———. *People in Glass Houses*. New York and London: Macmillan, 1967.

———. *The Transit of Venus*. New York: Viking, 1980. [R. G. Geering, *Recent Fiction* (Melbourne: Oxford, 1973).]

Heney, Helen (b. 1907). *The Chinese Camellia*. London: Collins, 1950.

———. *Dark Moon*. Sydney: Angus & Robertson, 1953.

———. *The Proud Lady*. London: Collins, 1951.

Herbert, Xavier (b. 1901). *Capricornia*. Sydney: Angus & Robertson, 1977 [1938].

———. *Dream Road*. Sydney: Collins, 1977.

———. *Larger Than Life* (stories). Sydney: Angus & Robertson, 1963.

———. *Poor Fellow My Country*. Sydney: Collins, 1975.

———. *Seven Emus*. Sydney: Angus & Robertson, 1959.

———. *Soldiers' Women*. Sydney: Angus & Robertson, 1961. [Laurie Clancy, *Xavier Herbert* (Boston: Twayne Publishers, 1981); Harry Heseltine, *Xavier Herbert* (Melbourne: Oxford, 1973).]

Hewett, Dorothy (b. 1923). *Bobbin Up*. Melbourne: Australasian, 1959.

Hill, Barry. *Near the Refinery*. Melbourne: McPhee Gribble, 1980.

———. *A Rim of Blue* (stories). Melbourne: Penguin, 1980 [1978].

Hill, Ernestine (1899–1972). *My Love Must Wait*. Sydney: Angus & Robertson, 1981 [1942].

Horne, Donald (b. 1921). *But What If There Are No Pelicans?* Sydney: Angus & Robertson, 1971.

Howitt, William (1792–1879). *Tallangetta, the Squatter's Home: A Story of Australian Life*. London: Longman, 1857. [John Barnes, *Henry Kingsley and Colonial Fiction* (Melbourne: Oxford, 1971).]

Hungerford, T. A. G. (b. 1915). *The Ridge and the River*. Sydney: Angus & Robertson, 1978 [1952].

———. *Riverslake*. Sydney: Angus & Robertson, 1953.

———. *Sowers of the Wind, a Novel of the Occupation of Japan*. Sydney: Angus & Robertson, 1954.

Iggulden, John M. (b. 1917). *Breakthrough*. London: Chapman & Hall, 1960.

———. *The Clouded Sky*. New York: Macmillan, 1964.

———. *Dark Stranger*. New York: McGraw-Hill, 1965.

———— . *The Storms of Summer.* London: Chapman & Hall, 1960.

Ingamells, Rex (1913–55). *Of Us Now Living, a Novel of Australia.* Melbourne: Hallcraft, 1952.

Ireland, David (b. 1927). *Burn.* Sydney: Angus & Robertson, 1974.

———— . *The Chantic Bird.* London: Heinemann, 1968.

———— . *City of Women.* Melbourne: Allen Lane, 1981.

———— . *The Flesheaters.* Sydney: Angus & Robertson, 1972.

———— . *The Glass Canoe.* Melbourne: Penguin, 1981 [1976].

———— . *The Unknown Industrial Prisoner.* Sydney: Angus & Robertson, 1978 [1971].

———— . *A Woman of the Future.* Melbourne: Allen Lane, 1979.

James, Brian. See Tierney, John.

Jefferis, Barbara (b. 1917). *Beloved Lady.* London: Dent, 1956.

———— . *Half Angel.* London: Dent, 1960.

———— . *One Black Summer.* London: Hart-Davis, 1967.

———— . *Solo for Several Players.* New York: W. Sloan Associates, 1961.

———— . *The Tall One.* London: V. Gollancz, 1977.

———— . *Time of the Unicorn.* Melbourne: Marlin Books, 1977 [1974].

Johnson, Colin (b. 1938). *Long Live Sandawarra.* Melbourne: Quartet, 1979.

———— . *Wild Cat Falling.* Foreword by Mary Durack. Sydney: Angus & Robertson, 1979 [1965].

Johnson, Joseph (b. 1914). *A Low Breed.* Melbourne: Nelson, 1976.

Johnston, George (1912–70). *A Cartload of Clay.* Sydney: Collins, 1971. Trilogy.

———— . *Clean Straw for Nothing.* London: Collins, 1969. Trilogy.

———— . *Closer to the Sun.* London: Collins, 1960.

———— . *The Darkness Outside.* London: Collins, 1959.

———— . *The Far Face of the Moon.* London: Collins, 1964.

———— . *The Far Road.* London: Collins, 1962.

———— . *My Brother Jack.* London: Collins, 1964. Trilogy.

Jolly, Elizabeth. *The Travelling Entertainer* (stories). Fremantle: Fremantle Arts Centre Press, 1979.

Jones, Suzanne Holly (b. 1944). *Crying in the Garden.* Melbourne: Outback Press, 1974.

———— . *Harry's Child.* Brisbane: Jacaranda, 1964.

Kaye, David (b. 1938). *The Australian.* London: Calder & Boyars, 1970.

Kellaway, Frank (b. 1922). *A Straight Furrow.* London: Cassell, 1960.

Keneally, Thomas (b. 1935). *Blood Red, Sister Rose.* New York: Viking, 1974.

———— . *Bring Larks and Heroes.* Melbourne: Cassell, 1967.

———— . *The Chant of Jimmy Blacksmith.* Sydney: Angus & Robertson, 1972.

————. *Confederates.* Sydney: Collins, 1979.

————. *A Dutiful Daughter.* Sydney: Angus & Robertson, 1971.

————. *The Fear.* Melbourne: Cassell, 1965.

————. *Gossip from the Forest.* Sydney: Collins, 1975.

————. *Passenger.* London: Collins, 1979.

————. *The Place at Whitton.* London: Cassell, 1964.

————. *Schindler's List.* New York: Simon & Schuster, 1982.

————. *Season in Purgatory.* Sydney: Collins, 1976.

————. *The Survivor.* Sydney: Angus & Robertson, 1969.

————. *Three Cheers for the Paraclete.* Sydney: Angus & Robertson, 1968.

————. *A Victim of the Aurora.* Sydney: Collins, 1977. [R. G. Geering, *Recent Fiction* (Melbourne: Oxford, 1975).]

Kingsley, Henry (1830–76). *The Hillyars and the Burtons.* London: Macmillan, 1865.

————. *The Portable Henry Kingsley.* Edited by J. S. D. Mellick. St. Lucia: University of Queensland Press, 1982.

————. *The Recollections of Geoffrey Hamlyn.* Melbourne: O'Neil, 1970 [1859]. [John Barnes, *Henry Kingsley and Colonial Fiction* (Melbourne: Oxford, 1971).]

Koch, Christopher (b. 1932). *Across the Sea Wall.* Sydney: Angus & Robertson, 1982 [1965].

————. *The Boys in the Island.* Sydney: Angus & Robertson, 1979 [1958].

————. *The Year of Living Dangerously.* London: M. Joseph, 1978.

Kodak. See O'Ferrall, Ernest.

Lambert, Eric (1921–66). *Dolphin.* London: F. Muller, 1963.

————. *The Five Bright Stars.* Melbourne: Australasian, 1954.

————. *Kelly.* London: F. Muller, 1964.

————. *The Veterans.* London: Shakespeare Head, 1954.

————. *Watermen.* London: F. Muller, 1956. [Zoë O'Leary, *The Desolate Market: A Biography of Eric Lambert* (Sydney: Edwards & Shaw, 1974).]

Lamond, Henry George (1885–1969). *Big Red.* Melbourne: Sun Books, 1978 [1953].

————. *Dingo.* Melbourne: Sun Books, 1978 [1957].

————. *Tooth and Talon.* Sydney: Angus & Robertson, 1934.

Lancaster, G. B. See Lyttleton, Edith Joan.

Lane, William (1861–1917). *The Workingman's Paradise: An Australian Labour Novel.* Sydney: Sydney University Press, 1980 [1892].

Langley, Eve (1908–74). *The Pea-Pickers.* Sydney: Angus & Robertson, 1942.

Lawrence, David Henry (1885–1930). *Kangaroo.* London: Martin Secker, 1923.

———— with Mary L. Skinner. *The Boy in the Bush.* London: Martin Secker, 1924.

Lawson, Henry (1867–1922). *Henry Lawson's Best Stories.* Edited by Cecil Mann. Sydney: Angus & Robertson, 1966.

—————. *Joe Wilson and His Mates.* Edinburgh: Blackwood, 1901.

—————. *On the Track and Over the Sliprails.* Sydney: Angus & Robertson, 1900.

—————. *The Portable Henry Lawson.* Edited by Brian Kiernan. St. Lucia: University of Queensland Press, 1976.

—————. *The Stories of Henry Lawson.* Edited by Cecil Mann. 3 vols. Sydney: Angus & Robertson, 1964.

—————. *Stories in Prose and Verse.* Sydney: [Louisa Lawson], 1894.

—————. *While the Billy Boils.* Sydney: Angus & Robertson, 1896.

—————. *The World of Henry Lawson.* Edited by W. Stone. Sydney: Lansdowne, 1980 [1974]. [Manning Clark, *In Search of Henry Lawson* (Melbourne: Macmillan, 1978); Stephen Murray-Smith, *Henry Lawson* (Melbourne: Oxford, 1975); W. H. Pearson, *Henry Lawson among Maoris* (Canberra: ANU Press, 1968); A. A. Philips, *Henry Lawson* (New York: Twayne, 1970); Denton Prout, *Henry Lawson: the Grey Dreamer* (Adelaide: Rigby, 1963).]

Leakey, Caroline (1827–81). *The Broad Arrow, Being Passages from the History of Maida Gwynnham, a "Lifer."* London: Bentley, 1859. [John Barnes, *Henry Kingsley and Colonial Fiction* (Melbourne: Oxford, 1971).]

Lee, Gerard. *Pieces for a Glass Piano* (stories). St. Lucia: University of Queensland Press, 1978.

Lehmann, Geoffrey (b. 1940). *A Spring Day in Autumn.* Melbourne: Nelson, 1974.

Lindsay, Jack (b. 1900). *Choice of Times.* London: F. Muller, 1964.

—————. *Hannibal Takes a Hand.* London: Dakers, 1941.

—————. *Rome for Sale.* London: E. Mathews & Marrot, 1934.

—————. *1649; a Novel of a Year.* London: Methuen, 1938.

Lindsay, Joan. *Picnic at Hanging Rock.* Adelaide: Rigby, 1975 [1967].

Lindsay, Norman (1879–1969). *Age of Consent.* New York: Farrar & Rinehart, 1938.

—————. *The Cautious Amorist.* New York: Farrar & Rinehart, 1932.

—————. *The Magic Pudding.* Sydney: Angus & Robertson, 1918.

—————. *Redheap.* Sydney: Angus & Robertson, 1979 [1930].

—————. *Rooms and Houses.* Sydney: Ure Smith, 1968.

—————. *Saturdee.* Sydney: Ure Smith, 1961 [1934]. [John Hetherington, *Norman Lindsay* (Melbourne: Oxford, 1969).]

Lindsay, Philip (1906–58). *An Artist in Love.* New York: Roy Publishers, 1954.

—————. *The Heart of a King.* London: H. Baker, 1968.

—————. *London Bridge Is Falling.* London: Nicholson & Watson, 1934.

—————. *The Loves of My Lord Admiral.* London: Hutchinson, 1949.

Loukakis, Angelo (b. 1951). *For the Patriarch* (stories). St. Lucia: University of Queensland Press, 1981.

Lower, Lennie (1903–47). *The Best of Lennie Lower.* Presented by Cyril Pearl and WEP. Melbourne: Lansdowne, 1963.

Lurie, Morris (b. 1938). *Dirty Friends: Stories.* Melbourne: Penguin, 1981.

_____ . *Flying Home.* Melbourne: Outback Press, 1978.

_____ . *Happy Times* (stories). London: Hodder & Stoughton, 1969.

_____ . *Inside the Wardrobe* (stories). Melbourne: Outback Press, 1976.

_____ . *The London Jungle Adventures of Charlie Hope.* London: Hodder & Stoughton, 1968.

_____ . *Rappaport.* London: Hodder & Stoughton, 1966.

_____ . *Rappaport's Revenge.* London: Angus & Robertson, 1973.

_____ . *Running Nicely and Other Stories.* Melbourne: Nelson, 1979.

Luscombe, Tom. *A Village on the Yarra.* Melbourne: Nelson, 1974.

Lyttleton, Edith Joan [G. B. Lancaster] (1874–1945). *Pageant.* Sydney: Endeavour Press, 1933.

_____ . *Promenade.* Sydney: Angus & Robertson, 1938.

McCallum, Mungo (b. 1913). *Son of Mars.* Sydney: Ure Smith, 1963.

_____ . *A Voyage in Love.* Adelaide: Rigby, 1960.

McCullough, Colleen (b. 1937). *An Indecent Obsession.* New York: Harper & Row, 1981.

_____ . *The Thorn Birds.* New York: Harper & Row, 1977.

_____ . *Tim.* London: Angus & Robertson, 1975.

McDonald, Roger. *1915.* St. Lucia: University of Queensland Press, 1979.

McGarrity, John. *Once a Jolly Black Man.* Melbourne: Wren, 1973.

MacKenzie, Kenneth [Seaforth] (1913–54). *Chosen People.* London: Cape, 1938.

_____ . *Dead Men Rising.* New York: Harper, 1951.

_____ . *The Refuge.* London: Cape, 1954.

_____ . *The Young Desire It.* London: Cape, 1937. [Evan Jones, *Kenneth Mackenzie* (Melbourne: Oxford, 1969).]

McKie, Ronald (b. 1909). *Bitter Bread.* Sydney: Collins, 1978.

_____ . *The Crushing.* Sydney: Collins, 1977.

_____ . *The Mango Tree.* Sydney: Collins, 1974.

McLean, Don (b. 1905). *No Man Is An Island.* London: Heinemann, 1955.

McNamara, Barbara W. [Elizabeth O'Conner]. *The Chinese Bird.* Sydney: Ure Smith, 1966.

_____ . *Find a Woman.* Sydney: Angus & Robertson, 1963.

_____ . *The Irishman.* Sydney: Angus & Robertson, 1960.

_____ . *The Sprit Man.* Sydney: Angus & Robertson, 1980.

Malouf, David (b. 1934). *An Imaginary Life.* Sydney: Pan, 1980 [1978].

_____ . *Johnno.* St. Lucia: University of Queensland Press, 1975.

Mann, Cecil (b. 1896). *The River and Other Stories.* Sydney: Dymock's, 1945.

Mann, Leonard (b. 1895). *Andrea Caslin.* London: Cape, 1959.

_____ . *Flesh in Armour.* Melbourne: Phaedrus, 1932.

_____ . *The Go-Getter.* Sydney: Angus & Robertson, 1942.

————. *Venus Half-Caste.* London: Hodder & Stoughton, 1963.

Manning, Fredric (1882–1935). *The Middle Parts of Fortune.* New York: St. Martin's Press, 1977 [1930, originally titled *Her Privates, We*].

Marshall, Alan (b. 1902). *The Complete Stories of Alan Marshall.* Melbourne: Nelson, L. O'Neil, 1977.

————. *Fight for Life.* Melbourne: Cassell, 1972.

————. *How Beautiful Are Thy Feet.* Melbourne: Chesterhill Press, 1949.

Martin, David (b. 1915). *Foreigners* (stories). Adelaide: Rigby, 1981.

————. *Frank and Francesca.* Melbourne: Nelson, 1972.

————. *The Hero of Too.* Sydney: Angus & Robertson, 1979 [1965].

————. *Hughie.* Melbourne: Nelson, 1971.

————. *The King Between.* Melbourne: Cassell, 1966.

————. *Many a Mile.* Melbourne: Nelson, 1976.

————. *Where a Man Belongs.* London: Cassell, 1969.

————. *The Young Wife.* London: Macmillan, 1962.

Matane, Paulias. *Aimbe the Pastor.* Hicksville, N.Y.: Exposition Press, 1979.

Mathers, Peter (b. 1931). *Trap.* Melbourne: Cassell, 1966.

————. *The Wort Papers.* Melbourne: Cassell, 1972.

Mathew, Ray (b. 1929). *The Joys of Possession.* London: Chapman & Hall, 1967.

Milutinovic, Iris (b. 1908). *Talk English Carn't Ya.* Melbourne: Hyland House, 1978.

Minchin, Devon (b. 1919). *The Money Movers.* Sydney: Angus & Robertson, 1972.

Mitchell, Elyne (b. 1913). *Flow River, Blow Wind.* London: Harrap, 1953.

Moore, T. Inglis (1901–78). *The Half Way Sun; a Tale of the Philippine Islands.* Sydney: Angus & Robertson, 1935.

Moorhouse, Frank (b. 1938). *The Americans, Baby.* Sydney: Angus & Robertson, 1972.

————. *Conference-ville.* Sydney: Angus & Robertson, 1976.

————. *The Electrical Experience.* Sydney: Angus & Robertson, 1974.

————. *The Everlasting Secret Family and Other Secrets.* Sydney: Angus & Robertson, 1980.

————. *Futility and Other Animals.* Sydney: Angus & Robertson, 1973 [1969].

————. *Tales of Mystery and Romance.* Sydney: Angus & Robertson, 1977. [Interview in *Meanjin* 36, no. 2 (July 1977):156–71.]

Morphett, Tony (b. 1938). *Dynasty.* Brisbane: Jacaranda, 1967.

————. *Mayor's Nest.* Brisbane: Jacaranda, 1964.

————. *Thorskald.* Melbourne: O'Neil, 1969.

Morrison, John (b. 1904). *Australian by Choice* (stories). Adelaide: Rigby, 1973.

————— . *The Creeping City*. Melbourne: Cassell, 1949.

————— . *Port of Call*. Melbourne: Cassell, 1950.

————— . *Selected Stories*. Introduction by Ian Reid. Adelaide: Rigby, 1972.

————— . *Twenty Three* (stories). Sydney: Australasian, 1962.

Nicholls, R. A. *Almost Like Talking*. Melbourne: Macmillan, 1978.

————— . *Hemlock*. Melbourne: Macmillan, 1979.

Niland, D'Arcy (1917–1967). *The Big Smoke*. Melbourne: Penguin, 1978 [1952].

————— . *Call Me When the Cross Turns Over*. Melbourne: Penguin, 1978 [1952].

————— . *Dead Men Running*. London: M. Joseph, 1969.

————— . *The Shiralee*. Sydney: Angus & Robertson, 1980 [1955].

Nixon, Christopher W. (b. 1946). *The Tour*. Sydney: Reed, 1973.

Norway, Nevil Shute [Nevil Shute] (1899–1960). *The Far Country*. London: Heinemann, 1964 [1952].

————— . *On the Beach*. London: Heinemann, 1957.

————— . *A Town Like Alice*. Sydney: Pan Books and Heinemann, 1981 [1950].

Nowra, Louis (b. 1950). *The Misery of Beauty: The Loves of Frogman*. Sydney: Angus & Robertson, 1976. [Interview in *Meanjin* 39, no. 4 (December 1980):479–95.]

Oakley, Barry (b. 1931). *Let's Hear It for Prendergast*. Melbourne: Heinemann, 1970.

————— . *A Salute to the Great McCarthy*. Melbourne: Heinemann, 1970.

————— . *Walking through Tigerland* (stories). St. Lucia: University of Queensland Press, 1977.

————— . *A Wild Ass of a Man*. Melbourne: Cheshire, 1967.

O'Conner, Elizabeth. See McNamara, Barbara W.

O'Donnell, G. C. C. *Time Expired*. Sydney: Published by the author, 1967.

O'Ferrall, Ernest [Kodak] (1881–1925). *Stories by "Kodak,"* Sydney: Endeavour Press, 1933.

O'Grady, Desmond (b. 1929). *Deschooling Kevin Carew*. Melbourne: Wren, 1974.

————— . *A Long Way from Home* (stories). Melbourne: Cheshire, 1966.

————— . *Valid for All Countries*. St. Lucia: University of Queensland Press, 1979.

O'Reilly, John Boyle (1844–90). *Moondyne: A Story from the Under-World*. Boston: Pilot Publishing Co., 1879.

Page, Michael F. (b. 1922). *A Nasty Little War*. Adelaide: Rigby, 1979.

Palmer, Vance (1885–1959). *The Big Fellow*. Sydney: Angus & Robertson, 1959. Trilogy.

————— . *Golconda*. Sydney: Angus & Robertson, 1948. Trilogy.

————— . *Legend for Sanderson*. Sydney: Angus & Robertson, 1937.

————— . *Let the Birds Fly* (stories). Sydney: Angus & Robertson, 1955.

————— . *The Passage*. London: S. Paul, 1930.

————— . *Sea and Spinifex* (stories). Sydney: Shakespeare Head, 1934.

————— . *Seedtime*. Sydney: Angus & Robertson, 1957. Trilogy.

————— . *The Swayne Family*. Sydney: Angus & Robertson, 1934.

————— . *The World of Men* (stories). London: Euston Press, 1915. [H. P. Heseltine, *Vance Palmer* (St. Lucia: University of Queensland Press, 1970); Vivian Smith, *Vance Palmer* (Melbourne: Oxford, 1971); Vivian Smith, *Vance and Nettie Palmer* (Boston: Twayne Publishers, 1975).]

Park, Ruth (b. 1923). *The Harp in the South*. Sydney: Angus & Robertson, 1980 [1948].

————— . *Pink Flannel*. Sydney: Angus & Robertson, 1955.

————— . *Poor Man's Orange*. London: Angus & Robertson, 1980 [1949].

————— . *Swords and Crowns and Rings*. Melbourne: Nelson, 1977.

————— . *The Witch's Thorn*. Melbourne: Penguin, 1979 [1952].

Paterson, A. B. [Banjo] (1864–1941). *The Best of Banjo Paterson*. Edited by W. Stone. Sydney: Lansdowne, 1977.

————— . *An Outback Marriage*. Sydney: Angus & Robertson, 1906.

————— . *The Shearer's Colt*. Sydney: Angus & Robertson, 1936.

————— . *Three Elephant Power and Short Stories*. Sydney: Lansdowne, 1980 [1917]. [Lorna Ollif, *Andrew Barton Paterson* (New York: Twayne Publishers, 1971); Clement Semmler, *A. B. Paterson*. 2d ed. Melbourne: Oxford, 1972).]

Patrick, John. *Inapatua*. Melbourne: Cassell, 1966.

Penton, Brian (b. 1904). *The Inheritors*. Sydney: Angus & Robertson, 1936.

————— . *Landtakers*. New York: Farrar & Rinehart, 1935.

Phelan, Nancy (b. 1913). *Serpents in Paradise*. Melbourne: Macmillan, 1967.

Pike, Geoff (b. 1929). *Golightly Adrift*. Sydney: Angus & Robertson, 1977.

————— . *Henry Golightly: A Novel of the Sea*. Sydney: Angus & Robertson, 1974.

Pinney, Peter (b. 1922). *Ride the Volcano*. Sydney: Angus & Robertson, 1960.

————— . *Road into the Wilderness*. Melbourne: Australasian, 1952.

————— , and Runcie, E. *Too Many Spears*. Sydney: Angus & Robertson, 1978.

Porteous, Richard [Standby] (1897–1963). *Little Known of These Waters*. Sydney: Dymock's, 1945.

————— . *Sailing Orders*. Sydney: Dymock's, 1949.

Porter, Hal (b. 1911). *A Bachelor's Children* (stories). Sydney: Angus & Robertson, 1962.

————— . *The Cats of Venice* (stories). Sydney: Angus & Robertson, 1965.

————— . *Fredo Fuss Love Life* (stories). Sydney: Angus & Robertson, 1974.

———. *A Handful of Pennies.* Sydney: Angus & Robertson, 1958.

———. *Mr. Butterfry and Other Tales of New Japan.* Sydney: Angus & Robertson, 1970.

———. *The Portable Hal Porter.* Edited by Mary Lord. St. Lucia: University of Queensland Press, 1980.

———. *The Right Thing.* Adelaide: Rigby, 1971.

———. *The Tilted Cross.* London: Faber, 1961. [Mary Lord, *Hal Porter* (Melbourne: Oxford, 1973); Hal Porter, *The Paper Chase* (St. Lucia: University of Queensland Press, 1980 [1966]).]

Praed, Mrs. Rosa Campbell (1851–1935). *An Australian Heroine.* London: Chapman & Hall, 1880.

———. *Fugitive Anne.* London: John Long, 1902.

———. *The Head Station.* London: Chapman & Hall, 1885.

———. *Mrs. Tregaskiss.* New York: Appleton, 1895.

———. *Outlaw and Lawmaker.* London: Chatto & Windus, 1893.

———. *Policy and Passion.* London: R. Bentley, 1881.

———. *The Romance of a Station.* London: Trischler & Co., 1889. [Colin Roderick, *In Mortal Bondage: the Strange Life of Rosa Praed* (Sydney: Angus & Robertson, 1948); see also Beilby, under Literary History and Criticism.]

Prichard, Katharine S. (1883–1969). *The Black Opal.* London: Heinemann, 1921.

———. *Coonardoo.* Sydney: Angus & Robertson, 1961 [1929].

———. *Golden Miles.* London: Cape, 1948. Trilogy.

———. *Happiness* (selected stories). Sydney: Angus & Robertson, 1967.

———. *Haxby's Circus.* Sydney: Angus & Robertson, 1979 [1930].

———. *Potch and Colour* (stories). Sydney: Angus & Robertson, 1944.

———. *The Roaring Nineties.* London: Cape, 1946. Trilogy.

———. *Subtle Flame.* Sydney: Australasian, 1967.

———. *Winged Seeds.* London: Cape, 1950. Trilogy.

———. *Working Bullocks.* Sydney: Angus & Robertson, 1980 [1926]. [Jack Beasley, *The Rage for Life: the Work of Katharine Susannah Prichard* (Sydney: Current Book Distributors, 1964); Henrietta Drake-Brockman, *Katharine Susannah Prichard* (Melbourne: Oxford, 1967); Ric Throssell, *Wild Weeds and Wind Flowers: The Life and Letters of Katharine Susannah Prichard* (Sydney: Angus & Robertson, 1975).]

Reidy, Dan (b. 1928). *It's This Way.* London: Heinemann, 1964.

Richards, David (b. 1954). *Peanuts in Penang.* St. Lucia: University of Queensland Press, 1973.

Rienits, Rex (1909–1971). *Stormy Petrel.* London: F. Muller, 1963.

Riley, E. *All That False Instruction.* Sydney: Angus & Robertson, 1975.

Robertson, Mrs. Ethel F. [Henry Handel Richardson] (1870–1946). *The End of a Childhood and Other Stories.* London: Heinemann, 1934.

————— . *The Fortunes of Richard Mahony.* 3 vols. Melbourne: Penguin, 1978 [1917].

————— . *The Getting of Wisdom.* London: Virago Press, 1981 [1910].

————— . *Maurice Guest.* London: Virago Press, 1981 [1908].

————— . *The Young Cosima.* London: Heinemann, 1934. [Vincent Buckley, *Henry Handel Richardson* (Melbourne: Oxford, 1970); William D. Elliott, *Henry Handel Richardson* (Boston: Twayne Publishers, 1975); Dorothy Green, *Ulysses Bound: Henry Handel Richardson and Her Fiction* (Canberra: Australian National University Press, 1973); Leonie Kramer, *Henry Handel Richardson* (Melbourne: Oxford, 1967).]

Robinson, Roland (b. 1912). *Black-Feller White-Feller* (stories, tales). Sydney: Angus & Robertson, 1958.

Rohan, Criena (1928–1963). *The Delinquents.* London: V. Gollancz, 1962.

————— . *Down by the Dockside.* London: V. Gollancz, 1963.

Rolleston, Juliet (b. 1942). *In My Lady's Chamber.* Sydney: Angus & Robertson, 1962.

Ronan, Tom (b. 1907). *Moleskin Midas.* London: Cassell, 1956.

————— . *Once There Was a Bagman.* Melbourne: Cassell, 1966.

————— . *The Pearling Master.* Sydney: Angus & Robertson, 1967.

————— . *Vision Splendid.* London: Cassell, 1964 [1954].

Rose, Lyndon. *Country of the Dead.* Sydney: Angus & Robertson, 1959.

Rowcroft, Charles (fl. 1840s). *The Bushranger of Van Diemen's Land.* London: Smith, Elder, 1846.

————— . *Tales of the Colonies.* London: Saunders & Otley, 1843.

Rowe, John (b. 1936). *The Chocolate Crucifix.* Melbourne: Wren, 1972.

————— . *Count Your Dead: A Novel of Vietnam.* Sydney: Angus & Robertson, 1968.

————— . *The Jewish Solution.* Sydney: Holt, Rinehart, Winston, 1980.

Rowlands, Lesley (b. 1925). *A Bird in the Hand.* Sydney: Ure Smith, 1965.

————— . *On Top of the World.* Sydney: Ure Smith, 1961.

Roy, Thomas Albert. *The Curse of the Turtle.* London: Bodley Head, 1977.

Rudd, Steele. See Davis, A. H.

Ruhen, Olaf (b. 1911). *The Flockmaster.* London: Macdonald, 1963.

————— . *Land of Dahori: Tales of New Guinea.* Philadelphia: Lippincott, 1957.

————— . *Naked under Capricorn.* London: Macdonald, 1958.

————— . *Scan the Dark Coast.* London: Hodder & Stoughton, 1969.

————— . *White Man's Shoes.* London: Macdonald, 1960.

Savery, Henry (fl. 1830). *Quintus Servinton.* Hobart: H. Melville, 1830–31.

Schlunke, E. O. (1906–60). *The Man in the Silo* (stories). Sydney: Angus & Robertson, 1955.

————— . *Stories of the Riverina.* Sydney: Angus & Robertson, 1966.

Seaforth. See Mackenzie, Kenneth.

Shute, Nevil. See Norway, Nevil Shute.

Sidney, Neilma (b. 1922). *Saturday Afternoon* (stories). Melbourne: Cheshire, 1959.

Simons, Kosti (b. 1934). *Not with a Kiss.* Sydney: Author, 1962.

Simpson, Helen (1897–1940). *Boomerang.* London: Heinemann, 1932.

————. *Under Capricorn.* London: Heinemann, 1937.

————. *The Woman on the Beast.* London: Heinemann, 1933.

Skinner, Mary L. See Lawrence, D. H.

Spence, Catherine Helen (1825–1910). *The Author's Daughter.* London: R. Bentley, 1868.

————. *Clara Morison.* Adelaide: Rigby, 1971 [1854].

————. *Gathered In.* Sydney: Sydney University Press, 1977 [1881–82].

————. *Mr. Hogarth's Will.* London: Bentley, 1865.

————. *Tender and True.* London: Smith, Elder, 1856. [John Barnes, *Henry Kingsley and Colonial Fiction* (Melbourne: Oxford, 1971); Janet Cooper, *Catherine Spence* (Melbourne: Collins, 1972).]

Stead, Christina (b. 1902). *The Beauties and the Furies.* New York: Appleton-Century, 1936.

————. *Cotters' England* [*Dark Places of the Heart*]. London: Virago Press, 1980 [1966].

————. *Dark Places of the Heart.* New York: Holt, Rinehart, & Winston, 1966.

————. *For Love Alone.* New York: Harcourt, Brace, 1941.

————. *House of All Nations.* New York: Simon & Schuster, 1938.

————. *Letty Fox: Her Luck.* New York: Harcourt, Brace, 1946.

————. *The Little Hotel.* Sydney: Angus & Robertson, 1973.

————. *A Little Tea, A Little Chat.* New York: Harcourt, Brace, 1948.

————. *The Man Who Loved Children.* Sydney: Angus & Robertson, 1978 [1940].

————. *Miss Herbert (the Suburban Wife).* New York: Random House, 1976.

————. *The People with the Dogs.* London: Virago Press, 1981.

————. *The Puzzleheaded Girl* (stories). New York: Holt, Rinehart & Winston, 1967.

————. *The Salzburg Tales.* London: P. Davies, 1934.

————. *Seven Poor Men of Sydney.* Sydney: Angus & Robertson, 1981 [1934]. [R. G. Geering, *Christina Stead* (Melbourne: Oxford, 1969); R. G. Geering, *Christina Stead* (New York: Twayne Publishers, 1969).]

Stewart, Douglas (b. 1913). *A Girl with Red Hair and Other Stories.* Sydney: Angus & Robertson, 1944. [Nancy Keesing, *Douglas Stewart* (Melbourne: Oxford, 1965); Clement Semmler, *Douglas Stewart* (New York: Twayne Publishers, 1975).]

Stivens, Dal (b. 1911). *The Courtship of Uncle Henry.* Melbourne: Reed & Harris, 1946.

———. *The Demon Bowler and Other Cricket Stories.* Melbourne: Outback Press, 1979.

———. *Jimmy Brockett.* Sydney: Australasian, 1966 [1951].

———. *A Horse of Air.* Melbourne: Nelson, 1978 [1970].

———. *Selected Stories, 1936–1968.* Introduction by H. P. Heseltine. Sydney: Angus & Robertson, 1969.

———. *The Unicorn and Other Tales.* Sydney: Wild & Woolley, 1976.

Stone, Louis (1871–1935). *Betty Wayside.* London: Hodder & Stoughton, 1915.

———. *Jonah.* Sydney: Angus & Robertson, 1981 [1911]. [H. J. Oliver, *Louis Stone* (Melbourne: Oxford, 1968).]

Stow, Randolph (b. 1935). *The Bystander.* London: Macdonald, 1957.

———. *The Green Girl as Elderflower.* London: Secker & Warburg, 1980.

———. *A Haunted Land.* London: Macdonald, 1956.

———. *The Merry-Go-Round in the Sea.* London: Macdonald, 1965.

———. *Midnite: The Story of a Wild Colonial Boy.* Melbourne: Cheshire, 1967.

———. *To the Islands.* Harmondsworth: Penguin, 1962 [1958].

———. *Tourmaline.* London: Macdonald, 1963.

———. *Visitants.* London: Secker & Warburg, 1979. [R. G. Geering, *Recent Fiction* (Melbourne: Oxford, 1973); Ray Willbanks, *Randolph Stow* (Boston: Twayne Publishers, 1978).]

Stuart, Donald (b. 1913). *The Driven.* London: M. Joseph, 1961.

———. *I Think I'll Live.* Melbourne: Georgian House, 1981.

———. *Ilbarana.* Melbourne: Georgian House, 1971.

———. *Morning Star Evening Star: Tales of Outback Australia.* Melbourne: Georgian House, 1973.

———. *Prince of My Country.* Melbourne: Georgian House, 1974. (First in a tetralogy, succeeded by *Walk, Trot, Canter and Die,* 1976, *Drought Foal,* 1977, and *Crank Back on Roller,* 1979.)

———. *Yandy.* Adelaide: Rigby, 1978 [1959].

———. *Yaralie.* London: M. Joseph, 1962.

Szymanski, Lesek (b. 1933). *On the Wallaby Track.* London: Poets' & Painters' Publishers, 1967.

Tasma. See Couvreur, Jessie C.

Tennant, Kylie (b. 1912). *The Battlers.* London: V. Gollancz, 1941.

———. *Foveaux.* Sydney: Angus & Robertson, 1981 [1939].

———. *The Honey Flow.* London: Macmillan, 1956.

———. *Lost Haven.* London: Macmillan, 1947.

———. *Ma Jones and the Little White Cannibals* (stories). London: Macmillan, 1967.

————. *Ride on, Stranger*. Sydney: Angus & Robertson, 1980 [1943].

————. *Speak You So Gently*. London: V. Gollancz, 1959.

————. *Tell Morning This*. Sydney: Angus & Robertson 1981 [1967].

————. *Tiburon*. Sydney: Angus & Robertson, 1981 [1935].

————. *Time Enough Later*. London: Macmillan, 1945. [M. Dick, *The Novels of Kylie Tennant* (Adelaide: Rigby, 1966).]

Thiele, Colin (b. 1920). *The Best of Colin Thiele*. Adelaide: Rigby, 1980.

————. *Labourers in the Vineyard*. Adelaide: Rigby, 1970.

————. *The Sun on the Stubble*. Adelaide: Rigby, 1962.

Thomas, Keith. *Idlers in the Land*. Melbourne: Hutchinson, 1978.

————. *There Was a Man of Our Town*. Sydney: Alpha Books, 1968.

Tierney, John [Brian James] (b. 1892). *The Advancement of Spencer Button*. Sydney: Angus & Robertson, 1974 [1950].

————. *The Big Burn* (stories). Sydney: Angus & Robertson, 1965.

————. *Hopeton High*. Sydney: Angus & Robertson, 1963.

Timms, E. V. (1895–1960). *The Big Country*. Sydney: Angus & Robertson, 1962.

————. *Conflict*. Sydney: Angus & Robertson, 1934.

————. *The Falcon*. Sydney: Angus & Robertson, 1956.

————. *The Fury*. Sydney: Angus & Robertson, 1955.

————. *Maelstrom*. Sydney: Angus & Robertson, 1938.

————. *The Scarlet Frontier*. Sydney: Angus & Robertson, 1954.

Tomasetti, Glen (b. 1929). *Man of Letters*. Melbourne: McPhee Gribble, 1981.

————. *Thoroughly Decent People*. Melbourne: McPhee Gribble, 1976.

Townsend, Christine Elizabeth. *Travels with Myself*. Sydney: Wild & Woolley, 1976.

Trist, Margaret (b. 1914). *Daddy*. Sydney: Angus & Robertson, 1947.

————. *Morning in Queensland*. Sydney: Angus & Robertson, 1979 [1958].

————. *What Else Is There?* (stories). Sydney: Angus & Robertson, 1946.

Trollope, Anthony (1815–82). *Harry Heathcote of Gangoil*. London: Angus & Robertson, 1963 [1873].

————. *John Caldigate*. London: Oxford, 1946 [1879].

Tucker, James (fl. 1825–44). *Ralph Rashleigh, or, The Life of an Exile*. Edited by Colin Roderick. Sydney: Angus & Robertson, 1952.

Turner, George R. (b. 1916). *The Lame Dog Man*. Melbourne: Cassell, 1971.

————. *Transit of Cassidy*. Melbourne: Nelson, 1978.

Upfield, Arthur (1888–1964). *The Bone Is Pointed*. Sydney: Angus & Robertson, 1966 [1938].

————. *Death of a Swagman*. Sydney: Angus & Robertson, 1980 [1962].

————. *Man of Two Tribes*. London: Heinemann, 1956.

————. *The Widows of Broome*. London: Heinemann, 1967.

————. *Wings above the Diamantina.* Baltimore: Penguin, 1965 [1936].

Vickers, F. B. (b. 1903). *First Place to the Stranger.* London: Constable, 1956.

————. *The Mirage.* Berlin: Seven Seas, 1958.

————. *A Stranger No Longer.* Sydney: Australasian, 1977.

————. *Without Map or Compass.* Sydney: Australasian, 1974.

Vidal, Mary Theresa (1815–69). *Bengala, or Some Time Ago.* London: Parker, 1860.

————. *Cabramatta and Woodleigh Farm.* London: Rivington, 1849.

————. *Tales for the Bush.* Sydney: D. L. Welch, 1845.

Viidikas, Vicki (b. 1948). *Wrappings* (stories). Sydney: Wild & Woolley, 1974.

Walker, Joe (b. 1910). *No Sunlight Singing.* London: Hutchinson, 1960.

Warung, Price. See Astley, William.

Waten, Judah L. (b. 1911) *Alien Son* (stories). Sydney: Angus & Robertson, 1952.

————. *Distant Land.* Melbourne: Cheshire, 1964.

————. *Love and Rebellion* (stories). Melbourne: Macmillan, 1978.

————. *Season of Youth.* Melbourne: Cheshire, 1966.

————. *Shares in Murder.* Melbourne: Australasian, 1957.

————. *So Far No Further.* Melbourne: Wren, 1971.

————. *The Unbending.* Melbourne: Australasian, 1954.

West, Morris (b. 1916). *Backlash.* New York: Morrow, 1958.

————. *The Clowns of God.* Sydney: Hodder & Stoughton, 1981.

————. *The Concubine.* London: New English Library, 1969 [1958].

————. *The Devil's Advocate.* London: Heinemann, 1959.

————. *The Naked Country.* London: New English Library, 1960.

————. *The Salamander.* London: Heinemann, 1973.

————. *The Shoes of the Fisherman.* New York: Morrow, 1963.

————. *The Tower of Babel.* London: World Books, 1969.

White, Patrick (b. 1912). *The Aunt's Story.* London: Routledge & Kegan Paul, 1948.

————. *The Burnt Ones* (stories). London: Eyre & Spottiswoode, 1964.

————. *Cockatoos* (stories). London: Cape, 1974.

————. *The Eye of the Storm.* London: Cape, 1973.

————. *A Fringe of Leaves.* London: Cape, 1976.

————. *Happy Valley.* London: Harrap, 1939.

————. *The Living and the Dead.* London: G. Routledge & Sons, 1941.

————. *Riders in the Chariot.* London: Eyre & Spottiswoode, 1961.

————. *The Solid Mandala.* London: Eyre & Spottiswoode, 1966.

————. *The Tree of Man.* New York: Viking, 1955.

————. *The Twyborn Affair.* Sydney: Cape, 1979.

————. *The Vivisector.* London: Cape, 1970.

_____. *Voss*. New York: Viking, 1957. [Ingmar Björkstén, *Patrick White: A General Introduction* (St. Lucia: University of Queensland Press, 1976); Geoffrey Dutton, *Patrick White* (Melbourne: Oxford, 1971); Alan Lawson, comp., *Patrick White* (bibliography) (Melbourne: Oxford, 1974); William Walsh, *Patrick White's Fiction* (Sydney: G. Allen & Unwin, 1977); John A. Weigel, *Patrick White* (Boston: Twayne Publishers, 1983); Patrick White, *Flaws in the Glass: A Self-Portrait* (London: Cape, 1981).]

Wilding, Michael (b. 1942). *Aspects of the Dying Process* (stories). St. Lucia: University of Queensland Press, 1972.

_____. *Living Together*. St. Lucia: University of Queensland Press, 1974.

_____. *The Phallic Forest* (stories). Sydney: Wild & Woolley, 1978.

_____. *Scenic Drive*. Sydney: Wild & Woolley, 1976.

_____. *The Short Story Embassy*. Sydney: Wild & Woolley, 1975.

_____. *The West Midland Underground*. St. Lucia: University of Queensland Press, 1974.

Williams, Maslyn (b. 1911). *The Benefactors*. Melbourne: Penguin, 1978 [1971].

_____. *The Far Side of the Sky*. London: Angus & Robertson, 1967.

Wilson, Helen. *The Skedule and Other Australian Short Stories*. Sydney: Angus & Robertson, 1979.

Wongar, Birimbir. *The Track to Bralgue* (stories). Boston: Little, Brown, 1978.

_____. *The Trackers*. Melbourne: Outback Press, 1975.

Wright, Judith (b. 1915). *The Nature of Love* (stories). Melbourne: Sun Books, 1966.

Wyatt, Geoff (b. 1937). *The Tidal Forest*. St. Lucia: University of Queensland Press, 1974.

Index

Abbott, J.H.M., 50
Aborigines, 4, 42, 47–48, 52, 53–54, 61, 64–66, 77, 79, 80, 81, 86, 93, 106, 119, 120, 123, 125
Adams, Francis, 20, 21, 29, 34
Adelaide, 34
Aesop, 110
Africa, 82, 126
Aitken, D.A., 104
Aldridge, James, 101
Amerindians, 125
Andrews, Barry, 17
Animal stories, 38–39
Antarctica, 96–97
Archibald, J.F., 42
Ashbolt, Norman, 56
Asia (Southeast), 82
Astley, Thea, 93–94, 100, 104, 126
Astley, William: Price Warung, 15, 16–17, 37, 42, 126
Atkinson, Caroline Louisa, 22
Atkinson, Hugh, 73
Auchterlonie, Dorothy, 83
Austen, Jane, 1
Australasian Critic, 8
Australia Council, 34
Australian and New Zealand Writers Handbook, 64
Australian Book Review, 56
"Australian Cultural Cringe," 32
Australian Literary Studies, 111
Austria, 76
Authorship (problems of, in Australia). See *Bulletin*, Censorship, Commonwealth Literary Fund, Expatriation, Market, Novel,

Popular Fiction, Psychology, Publishing

Bail, Murray, 82, 111
Bailey, John, 72
Barker, Jimmie, 64
Barnard, Marjorie, 28, 49, 65, 115
Barnard Eldershaw. *See* Eldershaw, Flora
Barnes, John, 5, 35, 42, 68, 88
Baylebridge, William. *See* Blocksidge, William
Baynton, Barbara, 28–29, 42, 51, 116, 126
Becke, Louis, 7, 19–20, 42, 72, 126
Beckett, Samuel, 110
Beilby, Richard, 70, 82
Bellamy, Edward, 29
Bergner, Herz, 73–74
Bergson, Henri, 105
Björkstén, Ingmar, 117, 118, 120, 122
Black comedy, 41
"Blackbirding," 72, 76
Blake, William, 104
Blocksidge, William: William Baylebridge, 43
Boldrewood, Rolf. *See* Browne, T.A.
Bookfellow, The, 13
Boomerang, The, 20
Botany Bay, 7
Boyd, A.J., 16
Boyd, Arthur, 124
Boyd, Martin, 54–57, 88, 126
Brady, Veronica, 124
Bridges, Roy, 50

Brisbane, 32, 34
Brissenden, Alan, 14–15
Broken Hill, 50
Brontë family, 24
Brooks, Cleanth, 124
Brown, Max, 69
Browne, Thomas Alexander: Rolf
    Boldrewood, 9, 10, 12–15, 19,
    80, 126
Buckley, Vincent, 46, 53, 116
Budapest, 73
Buddhism. *See* Zen Buddhism
Bulletin, The, 15–20, 26, 30, 41,
    42–43, 64, 80
Bunyan, John, 32
Burney, Frances, 1
Burns, D.R., 126
Burns, Robert, 26, 32, 71
Bush (special significance in Aus-
    tralia), 17–18, 26, 27, 48, 74
Bushranger(s), 3, 4, 9, 13, 14

Calthorp, Mena, 77, 80, 103
Cambridge, Ada, 22–23, 26, 42
Cambridge, England, 56
Campbell, David, 61
Campbell, Jean, 49
Canada, 1, 22, 110, 118, 126
Canberra, 50, 106, 107, 115
Candide (Voltaire), 86
Carey, Peter, 111
Cargo cult, 71, 72
Casey, Gavin, 41, 61, 77, 80, 126
Cather, Willa, 76
Cato, Nancy, 50, 69, 72
Censorship (Australian), 40, 109
Cervantes, Miguel de, 30
Change (as fictional theme), 79–86
Charlwood, D.E., 40–41
Chicago, 79
Childhood, (in A. fiction), 40,
    85–86, 98
China, 92
Chisholm, A.H., 118

Chisholm, Caroline, 9
Christianity, 57, 89, 117–18, 119,
    120
Chronicle fiction, 44–54, 113
City (as setting), 90
Civil War, American, 82
Clancy, Laurie J., 54, 106
Clare, John, 71
Clarke, Marcus, 3, 9, 10–11, 15,
    34, 37, 41, 126
Cleary, Jon, 100, 101
Clift, Charmian, 92
Climate, Australian, 3
Cobb, Chester, 54
Cobbett, William, 39
Coleman, Terry, 52
Collins, Betty, 77
Colmer, John, 83
Commonwealth, British, 63
Commonwealth (of Australia) Liter-
    ary Fund, 34
Conrad, Joseph, 19
Convict fiction, 3–5, 10–11,
    36–38, 89, 95
Cooper, James Fenimore, 1, 4
Couvrer, Jessie: Tasma, 24, 26, 34,
    42
Cowan, Peter, 61, 126
Crick, D.H., 103
Culotta, Nino. *See* O'Grady, John
    Patrick
Curnow, Tim, 64
Cusack, Dymphna, 49, 77–78, 80,
    103, 126

D'Alpuget, Blanche, 82
Dante, Alighieri, 29
Dark, Eleanor, 7, 49, 51–52, 88,
    116, 126
Darwin, Charles, 51
Davis, Arthur H.: Steele Rudd,
    20–21, 41, 42
Davis, Beatrice, 60
Davis, E.D., 20–21

Davison, Frank Dalby, 36, 38–39, 61, 85, 126
Day, A. Grove, 12, 52
Deakin, Alfred, 25
DeCock, Paul, 22
Defoe, Daniel, 8
de la Roche, Mazo, 51
Dennis, C.J., 33
Depression (1930s), 54, 73, 101
Devaney, James, 50
Devanny, John, 39
Dickens, Charles, 1, 9, 30, 53, 100, 113–14
Dictionary of Austral English, 63
Dobell, William, 124
Donnelly, Ignatius, 29
Dostoevsky, Feodor J., 119
Downs, Ian, 72
Drake-Brockman, Henrietta, 49, 50, 126
Drewe, Robert, 69
Drysdale, Russell, 124
Dugan, Michael, 111
Dunkirk, 55
Durack, Mary, 66, 70–71, 126
Dutton, Geoffrey, 81, 82, 121
Dyson, Edward G., 42, 103

Eldershaw, Flora and Barnard, Marjorie: M. Barnard Eldershaw, 49–50, 51, 117, 126
Eliot, George, 83
Elliott, Brian, 5, 56
Ellis, Vivienne Rae, 69
England, 45, 59, 63, 82, 113
English language, Australian variety, 7, 31–32, 63
English novel, 1, 2–3
Eri, Vincent, 72
Euphrates River, 92
Eureka Stockade, 76
Expatriation (and exile), 44, 54–55, 63, 79, 92
Eyre, Edward J., 118

Faulkner, William, 51
Fielding, Henry, 1, 30, 52
Film(s), 13, 28
"First Fleet" (convict ships), 1, 37, 51
Flinders, Matthew, 50
Football (as Autralian big business), 107
Forshaw, Thelma, 40, 61, 62
Foster, David M., 110
France, 116
Franklin, Miles (also Brent of Bin Bin), 26–28, 49, 126. *See also* Miles Franklin Award
Fraser, Mrs. Eliza, 123
Free, Colin, 107
Furphy Joseph (also Tom Collins), 29–32, 41, 42, 95, 116, 126

Galsworthy, John, 51
Gare, Nene, 69
Garland, Hamlin, 76
Garner, Helen, 110
Gaskell, Mrs. Elizabeth C., 24
Gaskin, Catherine, 50
Gay, John, 8
Geering, R.G., 83, 91, 94
Genet, Jean, 110
George, Henry, 29
Germans, in Australia, 74, 77–78
Gippsland, 83
Glaskin, G.M., 81–82
Glassop, Lawson, 72
Gold (and goldfields), 8, 12, 14–15, 21, 45, 46, 49, 77, 80, 125
Goldsmith, Oliver, 1
Gosse, Fayette, 37
Graham, T.M.A., 103
Grant Watson, E.L., 48
Greece, 92
Green, Dorothy, 56
Green, H.M., 6, 42, 52, 58–59, 60

Grove, F.P., 51, 76
Gunn, Mrs. Aeneas, 42

Hackston, James, 43
Hadgraft, Cecil, 4, 7, 23, 27, 28, 51, 53
Halls, Geraldine, 72
Harcourt, John, 39
Hardy, Frank, 33, 78–79
Hardy, Thomas, 70, 122
Harris, Alexander, 3, 7
Harris, Max, 54–55, 95, 124–25
Harrower, Elizabeth, 94, 126
Harte, Bret, 26
Hay, William Gosse, 36–38, 126
Haylen, Leslie, 39
Hazzard, Shirley, 83
Healy, J.J., 48, 71
Hemingway, Ernest, 58, 109
Herbert, Xavier, 53–54, 64, 65, 106, 126
Heseltine, H.P., 89, 100
Hewett, Dorothy, 77, 78, 80, 103
Hill, Ernestine, 50
Hitler, Adolf, 119
Hobart, 3
Hobbes, Thomas, 28, 51
Hope, A.D., 115
Hope (vs. exile, as fictional theme), 80
Horne, Donald, 86
Howarth, R.G., 38
Howitt, William, 9
Humor, 40–41, 43, 83
Hungerford, T.A.G., 60, 72
Hyde, Robin, 92

Idriess, Ion L., 50
Iggulden, John, 81
Immigration (in A. fiction), 72–76, 77
India, 73
Indonesia, 71, 82, 101
Ingamells, Rex, 52–53, 64, 66

Ireland, David, 69, 107–109
Ireland, 62
Irish, Lola, 94
Irving, Washington, 1
Italy, 83, 100

Japan, 89
Jefferis, Barbara, 101
Jeffery, W.J., 19
Jenkins, John, 111
Jewish fiction (in A.), 73, 74, 75
Jindyworobak movement, 65–66
Johnson, Colin, 70–71
Johnston, George, 92–93, 126
Journal of Australasia, 22
Joyce, James, 105, 113, 115
Jung, Carl, 118

Kalgoorlie, 77
Kanakas, 76
Keats, John, 119
Kellaway, Frank, 69
Kelly, Ned, 13, 73
Keneally, Thomas, 7, 82, 87, 94–97, 126
Kiernan, Brian, 90, 95, 96, 111, 112, 119
Killam, Douglas, 31
Kinglake, Edward, 8
Kingsley, Henry, 9, 10, 27, 126
Kipling, Rudyard, 26
Klein, A.M., 76
Koch, Christopher, 82
Kramer, Leonie, 46, 89
Kreisel, Henry, 76

Labor (issues in A. fiction), 76, 77
Lambert, Eric, 76, 77
Lamond, Henry G., 39
Lancaster, G.B. *See* Lyttleton, Edith Joan
Lane, William, 20, 21, 29
Lang, John, 4, 41
Langley, Eve, 49, 83

Lansbury, Coral, 12
Larrikins (young hoodlums), 17
Lawrence, D.H., 36, 113
Lawson, Alan, 114
Lawson, Henry, 15, 17–19, 25,
    26, 29, 32, 39, 40, 41, 42, 60,
    116, 117, 126
Leakey, Caroline W., 5
Lee, John A., 39
Leichardt, Ludwig, 118
Leopold, Keith, 104
Lindall, Edward, 72
Lindsay, Jack, 48, 105, 113
Lindsay, Joan, 28
Lindsay, Norman, 40, 126
London, Jack, 19
London, England, 14, 54, 55, 63,
    64, 81, 89, 90, 92, 94, 102,
    106, 118
Lower, Lennie, 33, 41
Lurie, Morris, 106, 111
Lyttleton, Edith Joan: G.B. Lancas-
    ter, 50

Malaysia, 81
Malley, Ern (poetic hoax), 55, 107
Malouf, David, 85–86, 99–100
Mander, Jane, 92
Mann, Cecil, 61, 63
Mann, Leonard, 39, 57, 58–59
Manning, Frederic, 57–58
Mansfield, Katharine, 43, 92
Maoris, 125
Mares, F.H., 45
Margery, Keven, 51
Market (literary, in SW Pacific), 64
Marquand, John P., 51
Marshall, Alan, 41, 59, 61, 65,
    103, 126
Martin, David, 73, 97, 126
Marxism, 29, 48
Matane, Paulias, 72
Mathers, Peter, 87, 106, 126

Matthews, Harley, 43
McAuley, James, 119
McCrae, Hugh, 42
McCullough, Colleen, 101–102
McGarrity, John, 69
McInherny, Frances, 96
McLean, Donald, 50
McQuaig, Ronald, 33
Macquarie, Gov. Lachlan, 50, 51
Meanjin, 105, 114
Melbourne, 34, 45, 56, 55, 59,
    73, 74, 75, 79, 92, 106, 107
Melville, Herman, 19, 20, 32, 119
Middle East, 92, 101
Midwest, American, 116
Miles Franklin Award (for A. fic-
    tion), 92, 118
Mill, J.S., 22
Milutinovic, Iris, 75–76
Mining. *See* Gold
Mitchell, Mary, 49, 50
Mobility (as fictional theme),
    81–85
Moodie, Susanna, 76
Moore, T. Inglis, 18, 26, 60, 80
Moorhouse, Frank, 109–110, 111
Morant, "Breaker," 28
Morphett, Tony, 41, 103–104
Morrison, John, 61, 62, 126
Motherwell, Phil, 41
Muir, Edwin, 115
Murdoch, Walter, 39
Murray-Smith, Stephen, 58

Nadel, George, 19
Narasimhaiah, C.D., 127
New, W.H., 57
New Australia (socialist colony,
    Paraguay), 20
"New Australians," 44, 72–76
New Guinea. *See* Papua New
    Guinea
New Holland (early name of A.), 1,
    3

New South Wales, 3, 7, 8, 30, 34, 40, 50, 83, 84, 95, 96, 102, 109, 113
New York (N.Y.), 64, 82
New Zealand, 39, 51, 54, 55, 59, 72
Newcastle (N.S.W.), 77
Nicholls, R.A., 76
Nietzsche, Friedrich W., 51, 119
Niland, D'Arcy, 100, 101
Nobel Prize (literature), 2, 112, 114, 122
Nolan, Sidney, 124
Norfolk Island, 55
North America, 1, 4, 76, 79, 111, 126
Northern Territory (A.), 34, 53
Novel (as genre: decline of), 87; (relation to modern life), 113. *See also* English novel
Nullarbor Plain, 70

Oakley, Barry, 103, 106–107, 109
"Ockers" (social class), 111
O'Donnell, G.C., 72
O'Dowd, Bernard, 26
O'Ferrall, Ernest, 42
O'Grady, John Patrick: Nino Cullota, 33, 41
Oliver, H.J., 33
Ollif, Lorna, 19
O'Reilly, John Boyle, 4
Ovid, 85

Palmer, Nettie, 18, 25, 34
Palmer, Vance, 34–36, 39, 42, 56, 61, 117, 126
Papua New Guinea, 60, 71–72, 86
Paris, 90
Park, Ruth, 49, 101
Parker, Catherine Langloh, 42
Paterson, A.B. ("Banjo"), 15, 19, 25, 26
Patrick, John, 69

Pearl, Cyril, 103
Penn-Smith, Frank, 42
Penton, Brian, 50–51
Perth, 4, 70
Phelan, Nancy, 72
Philippines, 60
Phillips, A.A., 18, 28, 32, 63
Pinney, Peter, 72
Pocohontas, 91
Polynesia, 19, 42, 72, 76
Popular fiction, 50, 94, 100–103
Porter, Hal, 7, 37, 57, 88–90, 126
Praed, Rosa, 23–24, 26, 36, 42, 126
Prichard, Katharine S., 33, 43, 46–48, 49, 53, 54, 61, 126
Proust, Marcel, 105
Psychology (and fiction), 88
Publishing (in A.), 34

Queensland, 23, 34, 35, 50, 67, 71, 76, 84, 93

Rabelais, François, 30, 106
Radcliffe, Anne, 1
Ramson, W.S., 7
Reade, Charles, 9
Reidy, Dan, 104
Richardson, Henry Handel. *See* Robertson, Mrs. Ethel F.
Richardson, Samuel, 1
Richler, Mordecai, 106
Riverina, 30
Robertson, Mrs. Ethel F.: Henry Handel Richardson, 23, 28, 43, 44–46, 48, 49, 50, 88, 94, 95, 116, 117, 126
Robinson, Roland, 65
Roderick, Colin, 50
Rölvaag, O.E., 76
Rolleston, Juliet, 107
Rome, 55
Ronan, Tom, 67
Rorabacher, Louise E., 42, 49, 73

Rose, Lyndon, 69
Rowcroft, Charles, 4, 6
Rowlands, Lesley, 44, 94
Roy, Thomas A., 71
Rudd, Steele. *See* Davis, A.H.
Ruhen, Olaf, 100
Russia, 82
Rustaveli, Shota, 82

Sade, Marquis de, 110
Salter, Elizabeth, 124
Salverson, Laura, 76
Sandoz, Mari, 76
Saroyan, William, 76
Satire, 19, 72, 93, 100, 103, 110
Savery, Henry, 3, 4
Scanlan, Nell M., 51
Schlunke, E.O., 43, 74
Schopenhauer, Arthur, 119
Scott, Sir Walter, 1, 2, 100
Semmler, Clement, 91, 121
Serle, Geoffrey, 2, 34, 49, 87, 100
Settlement (fiction about), 6–7
Shakespeare, William, 119
Short story (in A.), 41–43, 60–62
Shute, Nevil, 73
Sidney, Samuel, 9
Simons, Kosti, 2
Simpson, Helen, 49, 50
Singapore, 104
Sinnett, Frederick, 22, 127
Skinner, M.L., 36
Smith (W.H.) Prize, 118
Smollett, Tobias, 1
Socialism, 20, 32, 76–78, 90, 105
South America, 82
South Australia, 50, 65, 70, 74
Southey, Robert, 26
Spence, Catherine Helen, 21–22, 26, 126
Spinoza, Baruch, 104
Sri Lanka, 82
Stead, Christina, 33, 49, 90–92, 93, 95, 117, 126

Stein, Gertrude, 115
Steinbeck, John, 39
Stephens, A.G., 13, 15, 26, 30, 42
Sterne, Laurence, 1
Stevenson, Robert Louis, 19
Stewart, Douglas, 43, 61, 62
Stivens, Dal, 59, 61, 126
Stone, Louis, 32–33, 126
Stow, Randolph, 41, 54, 57, 66, 94, 95, 97–99, 126
Stuart, Donald, 68–69, 126
Sweden, 120
Swift, Jonathan, 106, 120
Sydney, 2, 32, 34, 36, 49, 52, 59, 77, 83, 84, 90, 92, 95, 101, 109, 121
Sydney *Bulletin*. *See Bulletin*
Szymanski, Lesek, 72

Tasma. *See* Couvrer, Jessie
Tasmania, 3, 5, 6, 89–90
Tennant, Kylie, 41, 49, 83–85, 126
Thiele, Colin, 50, 74
Thomas, Dylan, 111
Thoreau, Henry D., 104
Timms, E.V., 50
Tolstoy, Leo, 104
Townsend, Christine, 71
Trist, Margaret, 61
Trollope, Anthony, 9, 11–12
Tucker, James, 4
Turgenev, Ivan S., 60
Twain, Mark, 12, 30, 32, 60, 100, 107, 112

United Nations, 83
United States, 1, 4, 22, 29, 73, 109, 113, 118
Upfield, Arthur, 70, 126

Venice, 89
Vickers, F.B., 67–68

Victoria (queen), 1
Victoria (A. colony and state), 8, 9, 22, 34, 46, 73, 90, 111
Vidal, Mary Theresa (Johnson), 6
Vienna, 78

Walker, Joe, 65
Wallace-Crabbe, Chris, 126
Walsh, William, 119, 121–22
Warung, Price. *See* Astley, William
Washington, D.C., 90
Waten, Judah, 74–75
West, Morris, 100, 126
West Australia, 4, 34, 46, 66, 74, 81, 97
West Irian, 71
White, Patrick, 4, 7, 31, 37, 57, 73, 82, 94, 95, 105, 112–25, 126
White Australia policy, 64, 106
Whitelock, Derek, 71
Whitman, Walt, 53
Wilding, Michael, 15, 104, 110, 111

Wilkes, G.A., 35
Willbanks, Ray, 99
Williams, Masyln, 72
Wilson, Erle, 39
Wolfe, Dusty, 94
Women writers (of A. fiction), 5, 21–24, 26–29, 44–52, 75, 77–79, 83–86, 90–92, 94, 101–102, 126
Woolf, Virginia, 113
Woollomooloo, 90
World War I, 2, 55, 57–59, 84, 96
World War II, 25, 44, 54, 55, 57, 60, 63, 67, 71, 77, 81, 82, 95, 96
Wright, Judith, 61–62, 63, 64
Wyatt, Geoff, 111

Yugoslavia, 75, 96

Zen Buddhism, 112
Zulus, 125